HEY, BACK OFF!

HEY, BACK OFF!

Tips for Stopping
Teen Harassment

Jennie Withers with Phyllis Hendrickson, M. Ed.

New Horizon Press
Far Hills, NJ

New Horizon Press
P.O. Box 669
Far Hills, NJ 07931

Withers, Jennie and Hendrickson, Phyllis
Hey, Back Off!: Tips for Stopping Teen Harassment

Cover design: Robert Aulicino
Interior design: Charley Nasta

Library of Congress Control Number: 2011923244

ISBN 13: 978-0-88282-365-2
New Horizon Press

Manufactured in the U.S.A.

15   14   13   12   11   1   2   3   4   5

AUTHORS' NOTE

This book is based on the authors' research, personal experiences, clients' real life experiences and information from school administrators, school resource officers, teachers, high school students and parents. In order to protect privacy, names have been changed and identifying characteristics have been altered except for contributing experts.

For purposes of simplifying usage, the pronouns he/she and him/her are sometimes used interchangeably. The information contained herein is not meant to be a substitute for professional evaluation and therapy with mental health professionals.

Contents

Introduction

An Overview for Teen Readers

Jennie's daughter's first bullies were some children who rode on her kindergarten school bus. In junior and senior high, bullies are called harassers and they do more than just refuse to let a little girl sit by them on the bus. Harassers become more varied in their attacks, are slyer and are more hurtful. *Hey, Back Off!* gives teens tips, strategies and explanations about what harassment is, how behavior originates from personality types and how to deal with harassers.

Each section contains activities. They will help you handle difficult situations as well as provide you with strategies to deal with harassment. We suggest using a separate notebook or computer word processing program as a journal. Use your journal to write your thoughts and feelings as you read or for whatever you wish. You can put your thoughts down, continue activities or questions from a chapter or doodle. It is entirely up to you.

 Throughout the book you will see stop signs followed by instructions to complete an activity located at the end of the section. If a parent is reading with you, he or she will have assignments too.

The stories and activities enhance the information in *Hey, Back Off!* It is our hope that together they will teach you how to prevent harassment.

Your parents also need to learn the facts and gain the tools to help you handle teen harassment. There is information just for them at the end of each chapter. The purpose is to help your parents realize how tough today's bullying and harassment problems can be for you as a teenager.

An Overview for Parent Readers

Being a parent of a teen today is not an easy task, particularly if your teen is a target for harassers. You want to help your teen, to protect him or her, but teens also need to be empowered to deal with situations on their own. How can you tell if your teen is suffering if he or she won't talk to you? How do you know when you should help your teen and when you should let him or her handle it? How can you help your teen stop harassment? It is our sincerest hope that *Hey, Back Off!* and the parent information provided within will help you answer these tough questions.

There is information specifically for parents at the end of each chapter, but parents should read the entire book. The teen sections provide needed information, resources, ideas and topics to discuss with your teen. In the teen sections you will also see examples we gathered working with the parents of teenagers. The parent sections in this book are included to offer direction to parents who want information on how to support their teens in harassment situations. Many of the suggestions apply generally to positive parenting, but we should point out that *Hey, Back Off!* is not a complete guide to parenting adolescents. If you feel you need more support and information on how to become an assertive person and parent, then books, DVDs, classes and counseling professionals can provide you with comprehensive parenting advice.

Hey, Back Off! focuses more on the victims of harassers than it does on the harassers. For those of you who have teens who are bullies, however, there is still valuable information, such as the effects on the victims, the consequences harassers can expect and how to recognize and change aggressive behavior.

 Throughout the book you will see stop signs followed by instructions to complete an activity located at the end of the section. Your teen will have assignments too. These activities should prompt discussion between you and your teen.

Please know that your teen wants your help and support. The main purpose of *Hey, Back Off!* is to empower teens to prevent harassment, but part of that empowerment is teens and parents knowing when an adult needs to intervene. The best advocates for teens are their parents. Parents are also an important part of the harassment prevention equation which includes schools, law enforcement, teens and you.

Chapter One

Understanding the Meaning of Harassment

Emma and Dillon, a True Story of Harassment

Emma's story illustrates the effects bullying can have on victims. When Emma starts avoiding activities she loves, Emma's mother becomes troubled. With support from her mom and a good friend, Emma is able to address the issues of harassment.

"Hey, Emma, are you sure you're a chick? You sure don't look or act like one."

Emma's superior size was evident as she towered over her attacker. But Dillon knew what everyone in the hallway knew: Emma was too nice to beat up short, scrawny Dillon. If only they were in hockey uniforms it would be a different story. Emma was a powerhouse hockey player.

"So what are you?"

Emma turned crimson. She glanced around at the students gathered in the hall. Some of them were supposed to be her friends, but nobody looked her in the eye.

Blaine stood at Dillon's side as he always did. He said, "I know—she's a fag."

Dillon flashed Blaine a look to shut him up. When it worked, Dillon turned his attention back to Emma. He made the shape of a woman's body with his hands. "Yeah, you want some of that, don't you?"

Two girls, Ashley and Heather, giggled. They would follow Dillon no matter where he was leading them.

The bell rang and the uncomfortable students watching, except Dillon's crew of three and one other, fled the scene. A girl shoved her way through Dillon's crew to get to Dillon. She was smaller than Dillon, but she grabbed him and flipped him around anyway. She looped her thumbs through the straps on her backpack and thrust her chin out, giving her the appearance of a turtle. "Dillon, leave her alone."

"Aw, Emma's lover Bailey came to rescue her."

"Come on, Emma," said Bailey. She turned away, expecting Emma to follow her.

Emma stared at the floor, careful not to look at Dillon as she retreated on Bailey's heels. Emma knocked into Dillon. She said, "Sorry."

Dillon regained his balance and his tough guy stance. He yelled down the hall, "Look at that big dyke go!"

"When are you going to do something about him?" Bailey didn't wait for an answer. "I mean, he's been picking on you since I've known you, which is like, what—since the fifth grade?"

"He hasn't picked on me the whole time. He takes breaks. Besides, what do you expect me to do? I've killed him with kindness like my mom told me to, but that didn't work. And I've tried to avoid him, but that is obviously not working. This is the third time this week he's cornered me in the hall like that. I wish I weren't so easy to find."

"You shouldn't have to hide, Emma. He's getting worse, especially lately. He used to knock books out of your hands, bump into you. Then in seventh grade he caught and threw a bee at you, which stung you on the arm. That was pretty bad, but now…"

"Good thing I'm not allergic."

"That doesn't make it okay. But anyway, what he's doing now is worse; it's personal. You've tried to tell him to leave you alone and you've tried to ignore him. It's time to do something."

"You want me to beat him up?"

"Honestly, I would love to see you pummel that poisonous, white-livered, canker-blossom!"

"What?"

"Never mind, it's Shakespeare. What I meant was beating up that twit is tempting, but it's not a good solution. Not only would it get you into trouble, but also you would sink to that vile worm's level. Your only solution is to go tell the counselor what's going on."

"Maybe I…"

"Maybe nothing. Dillon won't stop, Em, and I'm not always around to help you. I gotta get to class. Think about it. I'll go with you if you want. Talk to you later."

Emma leaned against the wall outside her first period classroom. She was thinking. The tardy bell and the feeling that Bailey was absolutely right about the poisonous, white-livered, canker-blossom helped make her decision. She might as well go see the counselor and avoid another tardy.

Dillon snatched the familiar green call slip out of his teacher's hand. He wondered briefly what the vice principal, Mr. Leslie, was busting him for this time. He'd already visited the main office for knocking books out of people's hands, pushing students into lockers, mouthing off in class and cheating.

Dillon strutted through the open door of the vice principal's office. He stopped short when he noticed his dad sitting in the chair that was usually his when he visited Mr. Leslie. Mr. Leslie usually called his dad on the phone, but Dillon's dad had never come to the school before.

Dillon quickly tried to hide his shock and flopped into the chair next to his dad. Dillon was careful to ignore him. He asked Mr. Leslie, "What did I do now?"

Mr. Leslie removed his glasses and laid them on the desk in front of him. "We've talked before about how egotistical you have to be to think that you can harass people and they're going to take it from you. Don't you think at some point your victims will say, 'Enough'?"

"Huh? What do you mean?"

"You know what I mean."

"We were just playing around. Emma thinks it's funny. You weren't there. You don't know."

"She doesn't think it's funny and her parents certainly don't either. It happened, didn't it?"

"Who told?"

"It doesn't matter," Dillon's dad said. "You've been suspended, Dillon. Go get your stuff."

"And Dillon," Mr. Leslie said as he stood, "you don't talk to Emma, don't touch her, don't even look at her. Do you understand?"

"He'd better understand." Dillon's dad stood and tugged at his son's shirt.

"Whatever. Get your hands off me."

Mr. Leslie only said *Dillon* couldn't harass Emma. At least that was what Dillon heard. Mr. Leslie didn't say anything about calling in recruits. Heather and Ashley would help him out. And they happened to ride Emma's bus. He could instant message them after school. Dillon knew he could count on Blaine too and sent him a text message. Not only would Dillon be staying away from Emma like Mr. Leslie said, but also he could move on to other targets. He would have to find some who weren't tattletales.

Emma dreaded school and this time it wasn't because of Dillon. He'd been leaving Emma alone, but his friends were relentless and vile.

Ashley and Heather sat close to Emma on their bus. They grabbed at parts of Emma's body. "You like it when a girl touches you, don't you? You're really not one of us. You're not a girl. Dillon was right. You are a freak, a hockey-playing freak."

Emma sat, her large frame hunched in a ball to escape grabbing hands and provide a shield from sharp words. Her face burned with anger and hurt, but she didn't want Ashley and Heather to see. Her twenty-minute bus ride seemed like hours.

Emma got no reprieve when she arrived at school, because that was when Blaine took over. Emma had one class with Blaine and his locker was next to hers. She couldn't avoid him. As often as he could without being noticed by a teacher, Blaine quietly taunted her, saying the things Dillon used to as well as adding some of his own crude comments. "Hey, Emma, I'm man enough to make you straight." Blaine grabbed his crotch. "Come and get some of this, big girl."

Emma wished she'd never gone to the counselor. It had only made things worse.

Emma didn't know what else to do except get "sick." Staying home from school with a fake illness allowed Emma to escape the harassment, but it also meant she couldn't play hockey. Emma weighed the two options and decided that she would rather miss blocking shots and running over forwards who dared come near her net than go through abuse at school every day.

It didn't take long for Emma's friends and family to figure out what a perfectly healthy Emma was doing. Emma listened from the hallway as her mother called Mr. Leslie on the phone. "Mr. Leslie, my daughter wants me to drive her to school and if I can't, she wants to transfer out of your school. I can't drive her, because I work, and I'm not going to let her transfer. Nor am I okay with her pretending to be sick so she doesn't have to go to school. I want you to stop what's happening to her. If it's all right with you, Emma and I will be in to talk with you tomorrow morning at seven thirty. I should have done this when you called a week ago."

Dillon strutted to Mr. Leslie's office. After all, he couldn't be in trouble. He wasn't doing any harassing. He was about to enter when he heard his dad's voice. Dillon flattened himself against the wall next to Mr. Leslie's partially opened door so he could hear what his dad was saying without being seen.

"I don't know what to do with Dillon. I can't leave work to come down here all the time. We've been going to counseling, but it isn't working. Do you think I should send him to boot camp or something, Mr. Leslie?"

"I'm not in a position to say. What does your counselor say about Dillon?" Mr. Leslie asked.

"That Dillon acts out, because he's angry his mom left," Dillon's dad replied.

Dillon was so angry he could hardly breathe, but he was sure his anger had nothing to do with his mom and everything to do with his dad's big mouth. Dillon stepped away from the wall and hit the door solidly with the palms of his hands. He felt some vindication when he heard the solid wood door make contact with his dad. Dillon stepped into the office. "Sit down, Dad." Dillon's dad obeyed.

"That was uncalled for, Dillon. I suggest you sit down too. Now." Mr. Leslie removed his glasses and rubbed his eyes.

Dillon sat. "Lay it on me. Why am I here this time?"

"Do you think getting your friends to harass Emma isn't going to get you in trouble? It's still a form of retaliation, which I warned you against."

"Uh uh, wasn't me. I have no idea what you're talking about."

"I'm sure you don't," Mr. Leslie said sarcastically.

"How can I? I wasn't even there."

Dillon's dad stood. He looked at the floor as he asked, "How long is he suspended for?"

"Four days."

"Will there be legal charges?"

"That's for Emma's parents and our school resource officer to decide."

TEEN CONNECTIONS

- Why was Dillon's and his friends' behaviors considered harassment?
- Was their harassment quid pro quo or hostile environment?
- What types of harassment did they participate in?

PARENT CONNECTIONS

- Dillon and his dad have an unhealthy relationship. What can we assume may be the cause?
- What behaviors did Emma exhibit that were hints to her parents about what was happening to her?
- What questions did Emma's parents ask or should have asked to help their daughter open up about what was happening at school?

Teen Section 1

What's Harassment?

Victims, parents of victims, school administrators and police officers won't care if you weren't aware your behavior was harassment. Their focus is going to be on making the harassment stop and then punishing the harasser. This section is all about teaching you the best way to avoid harassing others and to know when you're a victim of harassment.

Harassment is a term that is commonly used, but so are words like bullying, sexual harassment, hazing, stalking and cyberbullying. These are all types of harassment. Let's talk about the types of harassment as well as discuss the difference between a *quid pro quo* and a *hostile environment* in relation to harassment.

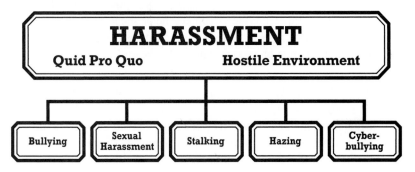

Harassment

Harassment is a term that covers a wide array of behaviors that are offensive, disturbing, upsetting or threatening. Harassment can be verbal, physical, psychological, visual and sexual. When you are the victim, harassment can make you feel unsafe and insecure and prevent you from participating in or benefiting from a program or activity.

Quid Pro Quo and Hostile Environment

The two possible goals of a harasser are quid pro quo and a hostile environment. *Quid pro quo* in Latin means "this for that." It could mean the harasser promises you something if you do things for him or her. "If you help me cheat on the test, you can hang out with me." It could also mean the harasser threatens to treat you worse if you don't do what he or she wants.

"If you don't steal the test answer key for me, I'll tell everyone that you…"
It is a deal that is being made and the harasser always gets the best end of
the bargain. The harasser's price is always high and because he or she is a
coward, he or she risks nothing. Natalie's story is an example of a quid pro
quo problem.

> Natalie wanted nothing more than to be popular. So she was
> absolutely thrilled when Abby, the queen of the cool clique, invited
> her to the mall. Natalie thought she'd finally made it. In the jewelry
> section of a trendy store, Abby picked up a pair of gold earrings. She
> handed them to Natalie. "If you really want to be my friend and hang
> out with me, you will steal these earrings for me." When Natalie was
> arrested for shoplifting, Abby was nowhere to be found.

A *hostile environment* creates an uncomfortable and/or unsafe setting
for the victim. When a victim feels he or she is in a hostile environment it
can interfere with school, work, extracurricular activities or social life. The
harasser steals security from the victim and he or she may no longer excel
at, enjoy or even participate in the things he or she normally would. Hector's
story is a good example of harassing through a hostile environment.

> Hector was a well-known gang member who blatantly practiced
> harassment outside of school. In school, however, his methods had to
> be more subtle. He always wore his gang's colors and flashed gang
> signs when authorities weren't watching. Hector often showed up late
> to his classes so he could make an entrance. Upon that entrance,
> his classmates' behavior changed. They no longer participated in
> class. Despite the subtlety of Hector's harassment, his teachers knew
> what was happening. They went to the administration and Hector was
> expelled for interrupting the educational process.

Harassment can be any repeated behavior that makes another person
feel offended, disturbed, intimidated or threatened. Even with the
categories of *quid pro quo* and *hostile environment,* the definition of
harassment is too broad. Narrowing the definition through the use of other
terms avoids confusion and makes the creation of laws and educational
programs possible.

Bullying

Bullying is defined as a repeated act of aggression for the purpose of
harming someone physically or psychologically. Bullying is the broadest
of the harassment classifications and therefore overlaps with many of

them. Anyone who participates in harassing behaviors is known as a bully. Think of bullying as the word that makes sure all obnoxious behaviors are covered.

Bullying

Example Behaviors

- Name calling
- Obscene gestures
- Pushing or shoving
- Threats
- Vandalism
- Spreading rumors, gossip
- Taunting
- Hate speech
- Teasing
- Hitting
- Spitting at someone
- Theft
- Graffiti
- Excluding others
- Intimidation
- Leers and stares
- Words used in a derogatory manner, e.g., "That's so gay."
- Derogatory displays, e.g., racist cartoons
- Threatening clothing, e.g., color, logo, slogan
- Obnoxious behaviors, e.g., knocking books out of someone's hands, pushing and shoving in a hallway
- Assault or battery

We have probably all participated in bullying and have been victims too. The key to staying out of trouble, however, is stopping when someone asks us to.

- **MYTH:** Bullies/harassers are physically big.
- **TRUTH:** Bullies come in all sizes. They can be male or female and are not specific to any race, social or economic class. Being a bully has to do with personality, as we'll discuss in chapter 5. It's all about what's inside.

USING THE PAGE PROVIDED AT THE END OF THIS SECTION, LIST THE BULLYING BEHAVIORS YOU HAVE EXPERIENCED IN THE "FELT IT" COLUMN. LIST THE BULLYING BEHAVIORS IN WHICH YOU HAVE PARTICIPATED IN THE "DID IT" COLUMN.

Sexual Harassment

Sexual harassment is distinct from general harassment and bullying, because it is sexual in nature. Sexual harassment can be quid pro quo, such as "If you don't go out with me, I'll ruin your reputation," but most often it is hostile environment. Sexual harassers embarrass, intimidate, scare and confuse their victims, which interferes with their abilities to participate in normal life.

Sexual Harassment

Example Behaviors

- Commenting about a person's body
- Spreading sexual rumors
- Touching inappropriately, e.g., grabbing, rubbing, massaging
- Voicing sexual remarks or accusations
- Sharing dirty jokes or stories
- Displaying or sending naked pictures or pornography
- Making obscene gestures, e.g., licking your lips suggestively
- Asking someone out repeatedly when he or she has said no
- Flirting that is one-sided, where one person feels uncomfortable
- Calling someone "gay", "fag", "lesbian", etc.
- Snapping bra straps or underwear elastic, de-pantsing
- Flashing, mooning or touching oneself sexually
- Assaulting sexually or attempting sexual assault
- Displaying affection in public
- Wearing obscene t-shirts, hats, pins, etc.
- Wearing clothing that shows a lot of skin or underwear

Sexual harassment is not just things done by a stereotypical pervert. It can also be a shirt you're wearing, a word you use or a joke you share that has a sexual connotation. It can even be a look that creates an uneasy feeling. Kara's story illustrates a sexual harassment situation.

> Kara was in the school-to-work program at her school. After an orientation in which the school counselor discussed sexual harassment, Kara began interning at a daycare center. Kara liked the work, but the man who was co-owner gave her the creeps. He looked her up and down and licked his lips. And he seemed to try and put himself in situations where he could touch her. Kara went to her counselor and described his behaviors and the way he made her feel. The counselor immediately found a better situation for Kara.

Sexual harassment is common. One of the reasons it is prevalent is because it is subjective, meaning that it's up to individual interpretation and opinion. If someone tells you he or she is uncomfortable or that your behavior is sexual harassment, don't argue with the person. If your behavior is offensive to him or her, then it is against the law. Saying "I was just joking" or "He or she is just too sensitive" won't get you out of trouble.

- **MYTH:** Only men sexually harass women.
- **TRUTH:** In addition to men sexually harassing women, women can sexually harass men, men can sexually harass men and women can sexually harass women. Harassers are not specific to gender, age or a particular economic or social group either.

 USING THE PAGE PROVIDED AT THE END OF THIS SECTION, LIST THE SEXUAL HARASSMENT BEHAVIORS YOU HAVE EXPERIENCED IN THE "FELT IT" COLUMN. LIST THE SEXUAL HARASSMENT BEHAVIORS IN WHICH YOU HAVE PARTICIPATED IN THE "DID IT" COLUMN.

Stalking

Harassment is unwanted attention, but stalking takes things a step further. The victim is unable to ever be away from the harasser. The victim is followed or put under surveillance. It violates the victim's right to privacy. When people's privacy is taken away they fear for their safety. Stalking is illegal in all fifty states. It is taken very seriously, because if it is not stopped it may lead to a serious crime against the victim.

Example Behaviors

- Following
- Watching the victim's house or other places he or she frequents
- Making unwanted telephone calls
- Sending unwanted e-mails, text messages or notes

It is an incredibly frightening thing for the victim to know someone is watching. Because of this, stalking creates a hostile environment. Heather's story describes stalking behavior that made her feel uncomfortable and unsafe.

> Heather was a smart, friendly and beautiful fourteen-year-old girl. She was excited to start high school. Unfortunately, within the first week of school, one of her teachers, Mr. Samm, asked her for her cell phone number. She was uncomfortable giving it to him, but she did, because he was a teacher.
>
> Mr. Samm's first text messages to Heather complimented her on assignments she'd done in his class. Heather didn't answer any of the texts, hoping Mr. Samm would stop. He didn't stop and his texts became more sinister.
>
> Mr. Samm texted how beautiful and graceful he thought Heather was at basketball practice and how much he liked to see her laugh with friends at lunch. To make it worse, Heather was almost positive she saw Mr. Samm drive by her house.
>
> Heather found herself looking over her shoulder wherever she was and dreaded checking her cell phone messages. Heather decided it was time to tell her parents because the stress was too much.

Psychologists split stalkers into three different categories:

- **Love Obsession:** The stalker has a fixation on a person even though there is not, nor ever has been, a personal relationship with the victim.

- **Erotomania:** This stalker harasses someone with whom he or she has no relationship. The difference between the Love Obsession stalker and the Erotomania stalker is that the Erotomania stalker believes or wants to believe the victim loves him or her. The target is often a well-known person. This could be the popular girl or boy at school or a famous actor or actress.

- **Simple Obsession:** This is probably the single most common form of stalking and is triggered by rejection. The stalker has a previous relationship with the victim, like a marriage, boyfriend/girlfriend relationship, friendship, etc. When the person is rejected, he or she attempts to "get back at them" through stalking.

Like other forms of harassment, the victim decides if he or she is being stalked. If the victim feels that his or her privacy is being violated and therefore he or she is unsafe, then it is stalking. If someone ever tells you that he or she feels you are following him or her, contacting him or her too often, giving too much attention to him or her and/or writing or saying things that make him or her uncomfortable, listen to the person's objections and BACK OFF!

- **MYTH:** Stalkers are mostly harmless.
- **TRUTH:** While not all stalking incidents turn violent, some of them do. Even if the stalker never gets violent, there is an invasion of privacy as the victim constantly fears being watched. Any time that someone is made to feel uncomfortable by another person's behavior toward him or her, it's not harmless.

 USING THE PAGE PROVIDED AT THE END OF THIS SECTION, LIST THE STALKING BEHAVIORS YOU HAVE EXPERIENCED IN THE "FELT IT" COLUMN. LIST THE STALKING BEHAVIORS IN WHICH YOU HAVE PARTICIPATED IN THE "DID IT" COLUMN.

Hazing

Hazing is harassment used by groups to maintain a pecking order. New members, the low men on the totem pole, are hazed into a group or a gang by proving their worthiness to join the group. It is the ultimate quid pro quo harassment. The victims may be willing, but that doesn't make this form of harassment any less physically or psychologically damaging.

Hazing is the most deliberate and planned form of harassment. The activities are called traditions, because the victims have the attitude to do unto others as was done to them—only worse. After a victim is hazed into a group, he or she gets to be the perpetrator, the doer. Many times, however, the perpetrator wants to leave his or her mark on the tradition, so he or she thinks of something far worse than what he or she went through. That's why hazing traditions have the possibility of spiraling out of control. For instance, in an upper middle class high school outside of Chicago, initiation for junior girls entering their senior year had been happening since the 1970s. The school banned the hazing ritual, but the students continued the tradition on their own. In 2003, the initiation became violent. The junior girls showed up expecting a football game and light hazing, such as having food smeared into their hair. What they got was punched, kicked, slapped, hit with buckets, pig intestines wrapped around their necks, urine, feces and fish guts thrown at them and at least one girl said she was forced to eat mud. The boys who came to watch joined in the "fun" and someone videotaped the event. When it was done, five junior girls were taken to the hospital and an undisclosed number of senior girls were taken to court.[1]

There is no high school, college or government institution that supports hazing. Besides, tradition is a pretty thin excuse for carrying on harassment. Traditions are easily broken: don't participate in them once and then no more tradition. Nothing, not even tradition, justifies harassment.

Hazing

Example Behaviors

- Public nudity
- Compelled ingestion, e.g., alcohol, drugs, food
- Wearing something obscene in public
- Being physically burdened
- Participating in physical contests
- Physical or sexual assault, e.g., being beaten or raped
- Abandonment or confinement
- Sleep deprivation
- Pranks or crimes

As you can see from the list of example hazing behaviors, the required activities are humiliating, intimidating, dangerous and exhausting. It can be hard to believe anyone would agree to be hazed, but it happens. And too many times hazing comes with dire consequences, including death. You shouldn't have to sacrifice your well-being, physical or psychological, to be a part of a group.

Be very cautious of any membership that comes with an initiation of any kind. Be confident enough in yourself to see that you don't have to sacrifice your dignity to be accepted. Those groups that ask this of you cannot be worthwhile. Also, know that enduring hazing is not a courageous act. Real courage is demonstrated when you stand up and refuse to participate in hazing. Look for groups that know how to build cohesion and character without hazing.

- **MYTH:** Hazing just a little is okay.
- **TRUTH:** There is no such thing as "just a little." Low-level hazing crosses the line and is still not acceptable. Things get out of hand too easily and people are impacted negatively even if it is unintended. Hazing others even a little will get you into trouble, because you are still a harasser and it is still hazing.

 USING THE PAGE PROVIDED AT THE END OF THIS SECTION, LIST THE HAZING BEHAVIORS YOU HAVE EXPERIENCED IN THE "FELT IT" COLUMN. LIST THE HAZING BEHAVIORS IN WHICH YOU HAVE PARTICI-PATED IN THE "DID IT" COLUMN.

Cyberbullying

Cyberbullying is the use of cell phones, the Internet or other digital devices to send messages or images that are intended to embarrass, slander or harm another person. The harassing behaviors take place in cyberspace.

Cyberbullying is a recent phenomenon. Therefore, the federal and state governments are clamoring to catch up with legislation and education. Many states have already passed laws requiring schools to develop policies to prevent, detect and punish cyberbullies. There have been disastrous cases of cyberbullying. Some of them have even led to the victims' suicides. These cases tend to get the attention of the country and its lawmakers. We will discuss the federal and state laws that are in place and those that may be coming in chapter 2.

Cyberbullying is fast becoming an epidemic, because it's harassment made easy. Many teens will do things on the Internet or a cell phone that they would never do in person. The reason may be that the bully is not in the physical vicinity of the victim. The harasser doesn't see the victim's reaction, therefore any feeling of remorse or guilt is far removed. Cyberbullies also don't experience immediate consequences as they may in school. Nobody is there to haul them to the principal's office, arrest them or even provide a good lecture. Because it's easy, cyberbullying is the ultimate act of cowardice.

Cyberbullying

Example Behaviors

- Repeated e-mails, text messages, instant messages or postings to a person's Web page/social networking page after the person has told you to stop

- Posting lies to humiliate a victim

- Hate speech aimed at a race, religion or sexual orientation

- Ridiculing someone in public forums

- Giving out a victim's personal information

- Posting comments in the victim's name

- Posing as the victim or someone else in cyberspace

- Using digital means to recruit others against a victim

- Using digital means to spread rumors or gossip

- Sexting (sending pornographic material through e-mail or cell phone)

The National Crime Prevention Council surveyed American teens and found that cyberbullying affected almost half of teens. Of the 50 percent who are being cyberbullied, only 15 percent are getting help.[1] This indicates that victims need to know that what is happening to them is harassment and that their harassers can be punished. Cyberbullying can be recognized in the story of Kyle and Andrea.

Kyle really liked Andrea. He thought she liked him too. In reality, Kyle made Andrea nervous. He was extremely possessive and often jealous. Andrea tried to explain to Kyle that she wanted to be friends. Andrea found out how hard Kyle took rejection when she started dating Travis.

Kyle posted threats on Andrea's and Travis's Facebook pages. Kyle called Andrea a slut and lied about sexual things she'd done. He threatened to make her "pay for being such a whore." Kyle also threatened to kill Travis for stealing his girlfriend.

When Travis and Andrea blocked Kyle from their Facebook pages, he planned to make good on his promises. Kyle brought a knife to school. Luckily, a school official caught him with the knife before he was able to do any harm.

Sexting

One type of cyberbullying is sexting. Sexting is sending or receiving sexual messages or photos of yourself or others using computers, cell phones or other electronic devices. Olivia's story shows how sexting can make you feel uncomfortable.

Zoe was Olivia's friend and teammate on the basketball team. While Olivia showered one night after a game, Zoe jerked back the curtain and took a cell phone photo of Olivia. Olivia was upset so Zoe made a show of supposedly deleting the picture and promised that no one would see it.

The following Monday Olivia was walking down the hall before first period. A younger boy Olivia didn't know said as he passed, "Your boobs are bigger than they look."

Olivia's friend Rob, whom she hoped would soon be her boy-friend, was looking at his phone as she approached her locker. When he noticed Olivia, Rob slammed the phone shut. "Hey, Olivia, I just remembered I have to…talk to…gotta go."

Soon Olivia learned that Zoe had sent the picture of her in the shower to another teammate. Olivia was mortified. She had no idea how many people had seen the picture. And she was hurt that Zoe, her friend and teammate, would humiliate her like that.

Olivia found Zoe in the hallway. "How could you? I can't talk to Rob anymore. How many saw? What did I ever do to you?"

"It was just a joke," Zoe shrugged. "Besides, you look good."

Think before you type, text or photograph and definitely before you hit the *send* button. The legal consequences for cyberbullying are harsh, perhaps stiffer than other kinds of harassment, because it is so cowardly. But there are social consequences as well. You will no longer be trusted, you could lose friends and you may be ridiculed by peers for doing something so low.

Remember that anything you put out electronically is really out there. It can be seen or read by an infinite number of people. Just because you sent a message or picture to only one person doesn't mean that person can't forward it. Electronic information isn't private and it never goes away. It can circulate forever, which means that when you go to apply to a college, get a job, even get a date, your cyberspace trail can be found easily.

- **MYTH:** Cyberbullying shouldn't be a big deal, because it's not like the victim is being physically abused.
- **TRUTH:** There are serious consequences for the victim. Victims usually develop low self-esteem, increased suicidal tendencies, frustration, fright, anger and depression. As with any type of harassment, victims of cyberbullying begin to avoid friends and activities they normally enjoy. Words and pictures can be hurtful.

 USING THE PAGE PROVIDED AT THE END OF THIS SECTION, LIST THE CYBERBULLYING BEHAVIORS YOU HAVE EXPERIENCED IN THE "FELT IT" COLUMN. LIST THE CYBERBULLYING BEHAVIORS IN WHICH YOU HAVE PARTICIPATED IN THE "DID IT" COLUMN.

Now you've learned what harassment is and about all its ugly forms. What you do with this knowledge and the rest of the information in this book is entirely up to you. We would like to assert that our homes, schools, communities, states, countries and world would be much better places if everyone worked to make harassment obsolete.

TEEN CONNECTIONS

- Why was Dillon's and his friends' behavior considered harassment?

    Dillon's and his friend's behaviors were offensive, disturbing, upsetting and threatening to Emma.

- Was their harassment quid pro quo or hostile environment?

    Their harassment created a hostile environment, because Emma was uncomfortable in places like the school bus and school where it was her right to feel safe and secure. Ultimately, the hostile environment prompted Emma to skip school and give up hockey, her favorite sport.

- What types of harassment did they participate in?

The shorter answer would be the types in which they didn't participate. This story is a perfect example of how behavior can qualify as several different types of harassment.

Dillon, Blaine, Ashley and Heather exhibited bullying behaviors like teasing, obscene gestures, spreading rumors, taunting, hate speech, intimidation, assault and generally obnoxious behaviors. Their sexual harassment violations came in the form of spreading sexual rumors, commenting about Emma's body, inappropriate touching, making obscene sexual gestures, calling someone gay and touching oneself sexually.

Dillon's requesting his friends attack Emma on the bus and at school could also be considered stalking. His recruiting also took place on the Internet, which is cyberbullying. Hazing is the only form of harassment Dillon and his friends did not use.

Bullying

List the bullying behaviors you have experienced in the "Felt It" column. List the bullying behaviors in which you have participated in the "Did It" column.

FELT IT	DID IT

Sexual Harassment

List the sexual harassment behaviors you have experienced in the "Felt It" column. List the sexual harassment behaviors in which you have participated in the "Did It" column.

FELT IT	DID IT

Stalking

List the stalking behaviors you have experienced in the "Felt It" column. List the stalking behaviors in which you have participated in the "Did It" column.

FELT IT	DID IT

Hazing

List the hazing behaviors you have experienced in the "Felt It" column. List the hazing behaviors in which you have participated in the "Did It" column.

FELT IT	DID IT

Cyberbullying

List the cyberbullying behaviors you have experienced in the "Felt It" column. List the cyberbullying behaviors in which you have participated in the "Did It" column.

FELT IT	DID IT

Parent Section 1

Harassment Vocabulary

No matter how detailed the definition, harassment is arbitrary. If the victim feels that he or she is being harassed, then it is harassment. This is a difficult concept for teens, because interpreting emotions and making rational decisions is something that happens in parts of the brain that are still developing. Their unfinished brains, coupled with their social desire to assert their independence, may be clues as to why harassment reaches its peak in the early teen years.

The organization ACT for Youth: Upstate Center of Excellence states that according to new research from the National Institute of Mental Health, "the greatest changes to the parts of the brain that are responsible for functions such as self-control, judgment, emotions, and organization occur between puberty and young adulthood. This may help explain certain teenage behavior that adults can find mystifying, such as poor decision making, recklessness, and emotional outbursts."[1]

Teen Brain Development[2]

- **Frontal Lobe** – self-control, judgment, emotional regulation; restructured in teen years
- **Corpus Callosum** – intelligence, consciousness and self awareness; reaches full maturity in twenties
- **Parietal Lobes** – integrate auditory, visual, and tactile signals; immature until age sixteen
- **Temporal Lobes** – emotional maturity; still developing after age sixteen

---

Despite the biological and psychological obstacles, you can help your teen understand what harassment is and why he or she needs to know what constitutes harassment in addition to furthering your teen's understanding of his or her role as victim or perpetrator. Discussing harassment with your teen may sound like a daunting task, but you will find that it really isn't.

Beginning the Discussion

Starting with definitions and examples of harassment is a safe way for teens to begin thinking about the topic and hopefully prompt them to analyze their experiences. In the teaching world, it is called background knowledge. Familiarity with vocabulary is one kind of background knowledge; personal experience is another. After reading chapter 1, you and your teen will have some shared background knowledge. However, the ability to discuss harassment with our adolescents hinges on the realization that our generation's experience with harassment is different from theirs.

Things have changed since today's parents were children. No longer is harassment and bullying considered harmless, nor is it considered a rite of passage that is a part of growing up. It's become far too dangerous for that. There are now categories and sub-categories of harassment that didn't exist before. There are even new kinds of harassment; the most recent phenomenon is cyberbullying. Today's parents never had to deal with this insidious form of harassment while growing up. What all this means is that today's parents have to be willing to look at this problem with the eyes and hearts of modern teens.

How Do You Know Your Teen Needs You?

According to *Merriam-Webster's Collegiate Dictionary, empathy* is "the action of understanding, being aware of, being sensitive to, and vicariously experiencing the feelings, thoughts, and experience of another."[3]

Your teen is probably not going to march up to you and tell you he or she is experiencing harassment even if he or she does know harassment's vocabulary. Most teens expect their parents to figure out exactly what is happening with them. In their minds, information is something that is guarded and protected, especially from adults. That is why picking your battles is important. In order to choose wisely, you must employ your instincts and your powers of observation.

Trust Your Instincts

As a parent, you know your teen better than anybody else. Your teen may tell you, even scream at you, that you don't know him or her. Don't listen to this. You most likely have been with your teen his or her entire life. Not knowing your teen is impossible. Therefore, trust your gut instinct. It may sound simple and it's definitely not scientific, but it's accurate. If you feel like there's something wrong with your child, then there is.

Pay Attention

In order to have instincts, you must be paying attention. If your teen is experiencing harassment, there will be clues. Most of them have to do with changes and since you know your child best, there is nobody better to figure out your enigmatic teen.

Pay Attention!

- **Routines:** Is your teen doing or not doing something he or she usually does?

- **Appearance:** Has what your teen wears or how he or she wears it changed? How about hair? What about posture?

- **Behavior:** Is your teen acting out or getting into trouble? Does he or she act depressed? Angry?

- **Verbally:** Does he or she drop hints? Make odd comments? Yell? Whisper?

- **Socially:** Have his or her friends changed? His or her hangouts? How about social activities?

As human beings, we are creatures of habit. We don't change quickly and we certainly don't change dramatically unless we feel forced. Your teen is no different. If you observe that your teen has gone from wearing pastel polo shirts one day to a black trench coat the next, your instincts should be telling you something is going on. In chapter 1 we discussed how harassment makes its victims feel unsafe and insecure and prevents them from participating in or benefitting from programs and activities. If you pay attention, you will notice these things manifesting themselves in your teen's behavior. In Sissy's case, her mom saw behavioral changes and asked what was going on.

Sissy washed and dried her shoulder-length hair every morning, then curled her bangs just right. Her mom didn't think it was a strange request when Sissy asked if she could grow her bangs out. Sissy told her that was the latest style. As time went on, however, Sissy's mom came to suspect there was something going on with Sissy.

Sissy grew her bangs out, but she didn't do anything with them.

She let them hang over her eyes. It seemed to Sissy's mom that Sissy was hiding from the world behind her hair.

Instead of attacking Sissy about how awful her hair looked, Sissy's mom began making general observations about her hair and other changes, asking about her days at school, whom she was hanging out with and what they were doing. Before long, Sissy shared with her mom that she was being harassed.

Teens have a difficult time understanding why they do some of the things they do. But they too have instincts. Chapter 1 attempts to give them some words to use to describe that something isn't right. When it comes to connecting harassment and changes they've made, however, some teens are mature enough to see the connection but others are not. Therefore it is important that their parents help them make those connections.

Taking Action

If your instincts are telling you something is wrong with your teen and you've observed that things are changing, what comes next? You have to get your teen to talk about what's going on. Please realize that your teen may not be able to express how he or she feels. That is something that comes with maturity. Therefore, facilitating conversations, particularly about a sensitive, arbitrary subject like harassment, is going to be different with a teen than it would be with an adult. When speaking with your teen, don't focus on feelings, but ask open-ended questions, be a good listener and be open and honest with him or her.

Not the Feelings

Teens may not be able to express how they feel when faced with a problem. They will only be aware that there is a problem. If you start a conversation by concentrating on the how and why of a teen's feelings, you won't get very far. Focus on *what happened* or *what is happening*. Teens will be much more comfortable working through situations than they will be with describing feelings. Once you know what happened, then you can tie it to a specific type of harassment that you learned in chapter 1. This serves two purposes: you have started a conversation with your teen that he or she is comfortable with and you have validated what he or she is going through by giving it a name.

It is true with anyone that if a person feels validated he or she will feel comfortable in saying more and delving deeper into any subject. Chances are, if you focus on the concrete subject of what happened and then define it, your teen may be more comfortable and trusting when investigating the feelings created by the situation.

Ask Open-Ended Questions

Many times we are frustrated when talking to teens, because the responses we get from them are simply yes or no or perhaps not words at all, like a grunt or an eye roll. This may actually be our fault. If you are not asking open-ended questions then you are talking *at* a teen, not *to* him or her. Open-ended questions are those that cannot be answered with one word or a non-verbal signal. They are the questions that bring teens into a conversation.

Examples of Open-Ended Questions

- Why did your school counselor call and ask to meet with me?
- Why hasn't Mary been over lately?
- You seemed excited about ski club and now you want to quit. What has changed?
- What happened at Tina's party?
- Why is your friend Greg worried about you?
- I'm concerned about your headaches. What's causing them?
- What does that have to do with what happened last week?
- What did you do or say after that happened?
- Why do you think that was harassment?

Just because you ask an open-ended question doesn't mean your teen will answer it. He or she may choose to say nothing or respond with "I don't know" or a shoulder shrug. Don't let him or her off easily. Keep asking open-ended questions that are focused on the situation and give your teen time to respond. It's not a bad idea to share something from your own experiences if you're sure it relates. Just make certain that you are giving your teen room to talk and you're not telling your teen what happened to him or her, assuming what he or she thinks or feels about it or forcing words of wisdom upon him or her.

Genuine Listening

We know when someone isn't really listening. Teenagers are no different. If you want your teen to talk to you then you have to listen. Often parents think they are listening, but they're not. Teens won't speak to you if you are giving them unrequested advice or lecturing them instead of hearing what they have to say. Your teen is going to learn some information on listening in chapter 5, but parents need to have it now, because if you're not listening to your teen, he or she is not going to talk to you. If your teen won't talk, you can't help him or her. Here are some tips to become a better listener:

- **Stop talking.** Don't interrupt and don't finish your teen's thoughts. You know your teen very well and can probably guess what he or she is going to say, but if you interrupt or finish a teen's thoughts, you will lose him or her in the discussion. Don't give advice or lecture. This may be very difficult, because parents often feel they know best. Part of being a teen, however, is learning how to handle situations independently. If you want your teen to be empowered, you can't tell him or her what to do. Chances are, if you try, your teen will do the teen rebellion thing and stop talking to you at all. Chapter 7 discusses in more detail what you can say, but in general, you need to wait until your teen asks for advice.

- **Watch body language.** Body language is the majority of human beings' communication. If you're missing your teen's body language, you may be missing the full meaning of what he or she is saying. A teen may say, "I don't need your help", but if his or her voice is soft and his or her eyes are pleading, the words don't mean much.

- **Pay attention to your body language.** There are the common things like making frequent eye contact and not folding your arms, but there are other aspects to consider. If your teen needs to talk about a serious situation like harassment, that has to be your sole focus. Have a discussion with just your teen. Don't try to talk while you're doing something else or while siblings are around. Teens will feel like victims all over again if they feel as if they're not important enough to deserve your undivided attention.

Teens dealing with harassment have to feel that they are being heard. Parents should be the people they can count on to hear them.

Be Open and Honest

Teens naturally have a sense when it comes to discerning whether an adult is being honest with them. If you are not honest or you are hiding something, your teen will know. It is naïve to think that because our children are under eighteen we can hide things from them or lie to them. It's like parents spelling words they don't want a child to understand when that child can already read. Teens can read their parents. You have to be open and honest with your teen or he or she will shut down. In Sean's case, his father spoke to him from his heart about his love and hopes for Sean.

> When Sean's parents divorced at the beginning of his senior year and his father moved away to begin a new life with a new partner, Sean's grades tanked and he started to do things, including harassing behaviors, to get into trouble. He never thought his dad would call the school and set up a meeting with Sean and his counselor, Mr. Lang.
>
> Sean was very defensive at the beginning of the meeting and resented that his dad was now choosing to pretend to be a father.
>
> Sean's dad picked up on his son's mood. "Excuse me, can I say something?" He turned to his son. The emotion was evident in his eyes. "Sean, I got into a lot of trouble when I was your age; so much trouble I had to drop out of high school. Your mom and I were on the same bad track. We married when we were too young. I know I was a terrible husband and an even worse father. I came here today, because I want better for you and I want to do everything I can to make that happen, because I love you."
>
> Mr. Lang handed both father and son tissues. Then they discussed how Sean was going to improve his behavior and his grades and set goals for his future.

The next activity is for you to do and share with your teen. It may test your ability to be open and honest. You are going to talk about the bad and the ugly when it comes to your personal experience with harassment. Your teen is going to do the same activity, but you should expect to show yours first. Your teen needs to know that you've experienced harassment or have been the harasser. Some of your experiences may be tough to talk about, but please know that your teen needs to hear what happened and how you felt about it. Talking about your feelings honestly will help your teen get to a place where he or she can talk about his or her feelings and experiences.

Every conversation must begin somewhere. Reading this book with your teen is an excellent start. Talk to your teen about what you are learning, the end-of-section activities and your experiences. Create an atmosphere of empathy, openness and trust. If your teen is struggling with harassment, he or she needs you.

- **MYTH:** Teens these days need to toughen up.
- **TRUTH:** Society's treatment of harassment needed to change. Even if you came through adolescence unscathed, there were those who didn't. Besides, if harassment had been taken more seriously in the past, perhaps it wouldn't have escalated into the dangerous behaviors we're dealing with in the present.

 USING THE PAGES PROVIDED AT THE END OF THIS SECTION, LIST THE PAST AND PRESENT HARASSING BEHAVIORS YOU HAVE EXPERIENCED IN THE "FELT IT" COLUMNS. LIST THE PAST AND PRESENT HARASSING BEHAVIORS IN WHICH YOU HAVE PARTICIPATED IN THE "DID IT" COLUMNS. REMEMBER, BE HONEST AND DEMONSTRATE YOUR WILLINGNESS TO BE OPEN WHILE DISCUSSING YOUR RESPONSES WITH YOUR TEEN.

PARENT CONNECTIONS

- Dillon and his dad have an unhealthy relationship. What can we assume may be the cause?

  Dillon's dad was passive with Dillon and let his son abuse and harass him. He expected others to set boundaries and rules for Dillon. He forfeited his parenting to the schools and even wanted to send Dillon to a boot camp for wayward adolescents, probably because he'd given up as a parent.

- What behaviors did Emma exhibit that were hints to her parents about what was happening to her?

  The big tip-offs, of course, were that she didn't want to ride the bus, pretended to be sick so she could stay home from school, lost interest in hockey and wanted to switch schools. Other things a parent may have noticed were changes in posture and social inter-actions with friends.

- What questions did Emma's parents ask or should have asked to help their daughter open up about what was happening at school?

    Some situational questions could have been: Why did the vice principal call me today and want to set up a meeting? What's going on at school that would make you want to transfer? Hockey is your passion; why aren't you interested in playing anymore? What happened on the bus?

Bullying

List the bullying behaviors you have experienced in the "Felt It" column. List the bullying behaviors in which you have participated in the "Did It" column.

FELT IT	DID IT

Sexual Harassment

List the sexual harassment behaviors you have experienced in the "Felt It" column. List the sexual harassment behaviors in which you have participated in the "Did It" column.

FELT IT	DID IT

Stalking

List the stalking behaviors you have experienced in the "Felt It" column. List the stalking behaviors in which you have participated in the "Did It" column.

FELT IT	DID IT

Hazing

List the hazing behaviors you have experienced in the "Felt It" column. List the hazing behaviors in which you have participated in the "Did It" column.

FELT IT	DID IT

Cyberbullying

List the cyberbullying behaviors you have experienced in the "Felt It" column. List the cyberbullying behaviors in which you have participated in the "Did It" column.

FELT IT	DID IT

Chapter Two

Learning about the Law and Support Resources

Lisa and Dillon, a True Story of Harassment

Dillon amplified his harassing behaviors, this time victimizing Lisa. In Lisa's case, a concerned teacher stepped in and tried to get Lisa's parents involved. The story describes some of the legal procedures regarding both harassers and victims. (The legal and school policies referenced in the story are from the state of Idaho.) Dillon had known Lisa since the third grade. Back then she was someone he stole lunch money from and called names, but now they were in the ninth grade and Lisa was no longer a skinny, knobby-kneed girl with crooked teeth and glasses. She was petite and quiet and her pleading blue eyes advertised vulnerability.

It was a combination that excited Dillon. He couldn't harass Emma anymore and he couldn't get his friends to do it either. He knew a third suspension would mean an expulsion hearing. Dillon had to move on, so he decided simply to focus on making Lisa go out with him.

Dillon had plenty of opportunity to pay attention to Lisa. He was in Art and Technical Reading with Lisa and her locker was close to his. Blaine was in the Technical Reading class too, so he could run interference. Dillon had to be careful with the Technical Reading teacher, Mrs. Paterson, because she was observant enough to catch him cheating a few weeks back.

As always, Lisa was in her seat when Dillon and Blaine entered Mrs. Paterson's classroom. Dillon's seat in class was conveniently close to Lisa's, so it wasn't suspicious that he was in that part of the room. He only needed to make sure that Mrs. Paterson couldn't see. Dillon nodded to Blaine, who knew what he was supposed to do. Blaine placed himself between Dillon and Mrs. Paterson, in her line of sight.

Dillon stood next to Lisa. Although she didn't look at Dillon, he knew Lisa was aware of him, because she started to pick at her fingernails. Dillon laid his hand on top of Lisa's head and let it run down her long blonde hair to her ear where he gently tucked it behind. Lisa shuddered in response, which only inspired Dillon to go further. Dillon bent and his lips brushed Lisa's ear as he whispered, "Lisa, you know you want me. I want you too."

Dillon knew he should sit down before the tardy bell rang. Mrs. Paterson seemed busy, but Dillon needed to act quickly. Not only was the bell about to ring, but his lookout had become distracted.

Dillon reached forward with his palm facing Lisa's body. He grazed her shoulder and then briefly cupped Lisa's breast before grabbing a pencil on the table. "Oops. I just wanted to see your pencil." The bell rang.

"Dillon and Blaine, please sit down so I can take roll call."

"Whatever you say." Dillon tossed Lisa's pencil back on the desktop. "Thanks for the feel," he said to her. "Talk to you later."

After class Mrs. Paterson approached Lisa. "Lisa, can I see you for a minute?" She led Lisa into an empty classroom and pointed to a desk. Mrs. Paterson sat across the aisle.

"I e-mailed your mom yesterday about your grade. It's been on a downhill slide." Mrs. Paterson paused long enough for Lisa to reply if she wished, but she didn't. "I received a message from your mom this morning. She said the reason for your lack of effort was due in part to a couple of boys bothering you in class. Is this true?"

Lisa stared at her fidgeting hands.

"I have to admit I was surprised Dillon was harassing a student right under my nose. Sometimes it's hard to make the distinction between goofing off and harassment. But I apologize, because Dillon is a student I try to keep an eye on. What I think I saw today was not normal messing around. Did Dillon touch you inappropriately?"

Lisa glanced briefly at Mrs. Paterson before answering. "Yes."

"Is Blaine involved too?" Mrs. Paterson leaned in so she could hear Lisa speak.

Lisa nodded. "It's mostly Dillon. I was going to ask if you could move me."

"I can move you, but that won't solve the problem. Dillon will seek you out no matter where you sit. Is it only in my class he and Blaine are harassing you?"

"No, I have eighth period Art with him and he does it in the hall sometimes." Lisa started picking at the polish on her chewed-up fingernails. "He's done stuff to me since third grade."

"He's been harassing you since the third grade?"

"Not all the time; sort of off and on. He stopped, but I guess he decided to…" The polish came off in large flakes and fell to the floor.

Mrs. Paterson touched Lisa's hand. She stopped picking. "Lisa, will you think about something for me?"

"Okay."

"Write a statement against him. Include everything he's ever done to you."

"I don't think so."

"Lisa…" Mrs. Paterson's tone prompted Lisa to make eye contact. "Dillon won't stop. In fact, he will continue to escalate this, because he thinks he can get away with it. I will report it to Mr. Leslie, but it really needs to come from you."

"Would Dillon know I wrote the statement?"

"Yes, but it's for your protection. Don't you think when Dillon gets into trouble he would know who told on him anyway? We can threaten him with further action if he retaliates. Writing a complaint is the safest way to stop him. He's getting worse, isn't he?"

"Yes."

"Look, this is up to you, but I think if you wrote a statement it would not only protect you from him, but also be very empowering for you. Do you know what that means?"

"I would feel better about myself."

"Exactly. Will you think about it?"

"Yes."

"Would it be all right if I called and talked to your mom about what I said to you today? Writing the statement should be a family decision."

"Okay. Can I go now?"

After school, Mrs. Paterson spoke to Lisa's mom. She related the conversation she'd had with Lisa. "Mrs. Hinterland, I saw Dillon touch Lisa's breast today. After reporting Dillon to Mr. Leslie, I know he's been suspended twice for harassment already. Suspending him from school hasn't been working. He's just moving on to other victims and with each victim his behavior escalates. We need your permission to let Lisa write a statement. Mr. Leslie will be contacting you about that."

Lisa's mom replied, "Dillon has always given Lisa a hard time, but he's never touched her sexually. That worries me. I work in human resources so I've dealt with this sort of thing quite a bit. At least we can fire harassers and then that's the end of it. We'll talk about it when Lisa's dad gets home tonight."

When Mrs. Paterson got off the phone she felt sure Lisa would write a statement. After all, Lisa's mom was a concerned parent with a background in human resources. Mrs. Paterson gave Mr. Leslie the good news.

Mr. Leslie replied, "If we can get Lisa and her parents involved, then Dillon can be charged with a misdemeanor. In the meantime, because Dillon's behavior is severe, persistent and pervasive, I'll give it to the school resource officer (SRO). I'm sure he'll write a citation that will cost Dillon some money and he'll have to go before a judge. So, with or without Lisa's written statement, Dillon's file is going to Officer Strictor tomorrow. And, of course, I will suspend him again."

"Maybe it's time to expel Dillon. We can do that without a misdemeanor, right?"

"This will be his third suspension, so I'm starting the paperwork. Dillon will get a citation, which is just an infraction, but on top of that he has a list of minor discipline violations and he's been suspended twice for major violations."

"What about Blaine?"

"He'll be suspended. I wish he'd figure out that following Dillon is never going to take him anywhere good."

The next day Mr. Leslie went to Mrs. Paterson's room to talk to her about his meeting with Lisa's parents. "Lisa's not going to write a statement," he told her.

"What? How could...? After talking to her mom I was so sure they were going to. Do they realize what they're doing to Lisa? Do they think she's going to magically stop being a target? It would've given her a huge self-esteem boost to finally stand up to Dillon. Do you know he's been after her since the third grade? I can't believe it."

"I know, but Lisa's dad won't let her. He said that Dillon would retaliate. I tried to tell him she would be safer writing a statement than not writing one, but he wouldn't budge. That excuse aside, I think he's kind of one of those 'boys will be boys' types. He thinks Dillon will suddenly grow up and leave Lisa alone. In addition, he accused us of harassment, because we were trying to get Lisa to write a statement. He said neither you nor anybody else is to talk to Lisa about Dillon anymore."

"Is Lisa's dad a bully? He must be, because last night Lisa's mom was in agreement."

"It seems to me Lisa's dad makes rash decisions based on whether it's good for him. He says, 'This is the way I want it right now, do it, done.' I don't think he has Lisa's best interests at heart. But I have your report and I have Dillon's file. Officer Strictor is going to write up the infraction and then we'll file for expulsion."

"At least we'll have Dillon away from our students."

"There is that, but it bothers me that we haven't been able to do anything to change his behavior. Maybe expulsion will do that. Something needs to turn him around. Otherwise he may be headed to prison."

TEEN CONNECTIONS

- How were Lisa's rights being violated?
- Why does Dillon's behavior fall under the terms *persistent* and *pervasive*?
- Why did Lisa's parents have to be involved?

PARENT CONNECTIONS

- What could Lisa's parents have done prior to the harassment becoming persistent and pervasive?
- When the teacher contacted Lisa's parents, what should have been the next step for the parents?
- Did Lisa's parents put her in more danger by not allowing her to make a statement?

Teen Section 2

Because It's the Law

This chapter outlines the harassment laws and policies in place in the United States, your state and your school. You may wonder why you need to know this. The answer is because you should know that you have rights, what those rights are and what consequences can be expected when your rights are violated through harassment.

There is one thing that you will find different in the treatment of harassment cases for your age group. You and your peers are minors; therefore, the parents or guardians of any minors who are involved in a harassment case (harassers and victims) will be involved in making sure individual rights are protected. However, you can expect that your due process rights (cases need to have documented evidence) will be protected just like every other citizen of this country.

Harassment and the Constitution

Laws against harassment have roots in the United States Constitution. The Constitution contains what is referred to as the Rights of Personhood. One of those rights is "not to be injured or abused." We have many rights living in this great country, but the Harassment Law chart on the following page lists only those that harassment violates.

The Constitution provides guidance for federal lawmakers to write bills. Once a bill is passed by Congress, it becomes an act or an amendment to an act and is then federal law. The most influential act relating to outlawing harassment is the Civil Rights Act of 1964, which made discrimination illegal. The Title IX Education Act Amendment and the Americans with Disabilities Act were also used to create harassment laws.

Once a bill is passed and becomes an act, it's up to states to create laws and punishments based on those acts. If someone gets involved with the justice system it's because he or she has broken state law. Offenders under the age of eighteen go through a state's juvenile justice system.

When the state has laws in place, school districts then write district and school policy based on state law. School policy is where the rules for individual school districts come from. In many cases, when a student breaks school rules, he or she is also breaking the law. This is particularly true with harassment. Therefore, schools can request police involvement.

HARASSMENT LAW[1]

The Constitution of the United States
The Rights of Personhood

Personal Security:
- Not to be killed
- Not to be injured or abused

Personal Liberty:
- To move freely
- To express or publish one's opinions or those of others
- To practice one's religion
- To be secure in one's person, house, papers, vehicle and effects against unreasonable searches and seizures
- To enjoy privacy in all matters in which the rights of others are not violated

Civil Rights Act of 1964

An Act to enforce the constitutional right to vote, to confer jurisdiction upon the district courts of the United States of America to provide relief against discrimination in public accommodations, to authorize the Attorney General to institute suits to protect constitutional rights in public facilities and public education, to extend the Commission on Civil Rights, to prevent discrimination in federally assisted programs, to establish a Commission on Equal Employment Opportunity and for other purposes.

Title IX of the Education Amendments of 1972

No person in the United States shall, on the basis of sex, be excluded from participation in, be denied the benefits of, or be subjected to discrimination under any education program or activity receiving Federal financial assistance.

Americans with Disabilities Act

Prohibits, under certain circumstances, discrimination based on disability.

State Laws

The laws of each U.S. state are passed by the state legislature and signed into law by the governor. These laws parallel United States federal law.

School District Policies

Guidelines stating how a district will create and support a positive educational environment.

As you can see, harassment isn't tolerated on a national, state or school level. Even though there are fifty states and thousands of school districts, state law and school harassment policies are similar because they are based on federal law.

- **MYTH:** I can say whatever I want, because according to the Bill of Rights I have free speech.
- **TRUTH:** Everyone has rights, including the person who is being harassed verbally. The victim's right not to be abused is every bit as important as your right to free speech. Say what you want as long as you're not violating anyone else's rights.

Student Handbook

Schools are required to give students handbooks that summarize the districts' policies. You are probably familiar with your school's handbook. If not, please read it thoroughly. Many schools review the student handbook during class time, so a student can't say, "I didn't know that was against the rules." Every handbook in every district includes a harassment policy. If you are being harassed or think your behavior might be harassment, your student handbook is a good place to start looking for definitions, violations and consequences.

School District Policy

The handbook is given to students and parents, but there is a much longer document known as district policy. Harassment and bullying most often begin at school or students are affected while at school. Therefore, schools are the first line of defense. Every school's goal is to provide a safe learning environment for all the students. Policies are written in order to maintain a setting where education can occur. That means harassers who disrupt the educational process will be punished and if the harasser continues, he or she will move into the state juvenile justice system and will likely be removed from school.

School policies against harassment have been around a long time, but after the 1999 school shooting tragedy at Columbine High School, schools have paid a lot more attention to them. Here are some procedures that have changed because of Columbine:

- Awareness of student dress and development of dress codes.
- More awareness of comments, writing, art projects, graffiti, etc., which may indicate student intent.

- Monitoring student computer use, tracking Web sites visited and requiring audio/visual use contracts.
- New district policies regarding weapons and anything that can be used as a weapon.
- Harassment policies that can lead to expulsion.
- Security measures that include local police, fire departments, etc.
- Emergency plans that include lockdown, evacuation, codes, bomb squads and dogs.
- Visitor passes and badges for teachers, awareness of any unauthorized people in the building or on campus.
- Camera systems and metal detectors to screen students and visitors.
- Policies concerning backpacks and lockers.
- Serious consideration of all reports and comments of harassment.

There were schools that had some of the policies listed above before Columbine. The high school where Jennie taught incorporated some of these initiatives. Prior to the tragedy, none of us imagined such a horrible occurrence. But, like virtually all school districts in the United States, we followed the procedures on this list after Columbine. Each school district must have a detailed harassment policy and those policies must include some basic items such as an objective statement, the complaint process and policies on confidentiality, discipline, location and prevention.

Objective Statement

This statement describes what the school district hopes to accomplish through its harassment policy. It includes a statement about creating an environment that is safe for learning. For example, the objective statement of the Spaulding Union High School harassment policy reads:

> The Spaulding Union High School District is committed to providing a safe and supportive school environment in which all students are treated with respect.[2]

Complaint Process

Here is information on how to make a complaint and to whom to deliver it. A complaint or grievance can be given either verbally or in written form. Give it to any adult you trust at the school. This trusted adult will pass the complaint to school administration or a person whose job is to deal with school reports of harassment.

Teachers and other district employees at a school have to pass any incidents of harassment on to their administrators, primarily for reasons of liability. If they don't, they can be held accountable for the harasser's actions. As employees of the school, staff members are responsible for the well-being of the students. Therefore, they have to report harassment to the administration in order to protect students. Besides, teachers and other staff should not have to handle something as serious as harassment on their own.

Confidentiality

District policies promise privacy, meaning administrators won't tell anyone who doesn't need to know, but they can't promise anonymity if you want them to take action. Here's an example from the Elk Grove Unified School District policy:

> Each complaint of sexual harassment shall be promptly investigated in a way that respects the privacy of all parties concerned.[3]

When you give an anonymous tip, the school administrators are very limited in what they can do, because harassers (and criminals in general) have the right to know what they're accused of and who their accusers are. This is termed *due process* and everyone has due process rights. Administrators must have concrete information in order to begin the disciplinary process, just as the police do. High school administrator Joseph Hendrickson shares vital information on this subject:

> Concrete information needs an observation, documentation or a complaint from the victim. Generally, without the victim coming forward at some time in the process, discipline falls short or cannot be accomplished. As in a court of law, the accused has the right to due process and should be able to confront the victim, which usually requires more than an anonymous report or a third party accusation. Documentation and information in writing from all parties is important in the accusation and disciplinary process.[4]

When an administrator gets an anonymous tip, he or she can meet with the harasser and go over the harassment policy, observe the accused harasser's reactions and begin to document the harasser's behavior. This may work, but if it doesn't and the harassment continues, you will probably have to give your name. And really, it is safer to stand by your complaint.

Discipline

District policy covers disciplinary actions for harassment, retaliation and false accusations. Harassing behavior in a school creates a hostile environment. It must be stopped so that all students can learn and school staff like teachers can do their jobs. Disciplinary action for harassment is clearly described in district policy. Also, district policy will detail when harassment is considered severe, persistent or pervasive. Policy against retaliation is one of the reasons you should give your name when filing a complaint. If your name is known, the administration and the law can protect you and punish the harasser. False accusations are when someone accuses an innocent person of harassment. In some cases, these false accusations are treated as harshly as harassment. Take Anthony's story, for example, where his false accusation ended in serious consequences for him. Anthony learned not only his school disciplinary policy, but also how the law deals with liars.

> Anthony earned an F in math for the semester. That was bad enough, but because of the failing grade, he wasn't allowed to play on the basketball team. Basketball was Anthony's passion. Anthony blamed his problems on Ms. Byron, his math teacher. He was so angry that when he heard a news story about a female teacher having an affair with a student, it gave him an idea.
>
> To get back at his math teacher, Anthony filed a complaint against Ms. Byron for sexual harassment. He made up a convincing story about her supposed misconduct. Anthony's parents, the school administration and law enforcement officials got involved. Ms. Byron was put on leave while the case was investigated.
>
> As lies often do, Anthony's story fell apart and Ms. Byron was cleared. For his false accusation, Anthony was expelled from the school district and charged with a misdemeanor. Ms. Byron filed a lawsuit against Anthony and his parents.

Accusing a person of something that he or she didn't do is never a good idea.

School district policies are designed to anticipate problems and make the punishment fit the crime. Therefore, there are steps to be followed. If the crime is severe, normal policy steps may be skipped. Dillon's harassment of Emma and Lisa is an example of how steps in a disciplinary policy commonly work:

- Administrators met with Dillon and he received detention for minor discipline violations like cheating, knocking books out of peoples' hands and shoving others into lockers.

- Dillon was suspended for a major disciplinary violation: harassing Emma.

- Dillon was suspended for a major disciplinary violation: recruiting others for the purpose of retaliation against Emma.

- Dillon was suspended for a major disciplinary violation: harassing Lisa.

- The school resource officer became involved for the issue of an infraction. If Lisa's parents had agreed to allow Lisa to make a statement, it would have been a misdemeanor.

- The administration scheduled an expulsion hearing before the school board.

It probably sounds like district disciplinary policies are aimed only at students, but they're not. A harasser can be a student, a visitor to the district or an employee of the district. In the next case, a parent got out of line and the district had to decide what to do.

> Mrs. Carver's son, Bradon, was on the varsity basketball team. Mrs. Carver was an avid supporter of her son but seemed to work to find fault with Bradon's coach. During games, Mrs. Carver screamed things like, "Come on, Coach, call a play for somebody who can actually shoot the ball!" or "Even junior high teams know how to press!"
>
> Administrators talked to Mrs. Carver about her behavior, but she didn't stop. After throwing a pen at the coach's head during a time-out, Mrs. Carver was escorted from the gym by a police officer. Bradon's coach was given the option of pressing charges for assault and battery against Mrs. Carver and the district banned her from all future school functions, including when the team traveled to other sites.

The disciplinary policy of the Boise School District states:

Discipline shall be appropriate to the offense, age and status of the individual. The Superintendent or designee shall submit the case to the appropriate law enforcement agency when the charges warrant such action.[5]

Location

Harassment that takes place on school property, in school vehicles or at school-sponsored activities is punishable by the school administration. In policy, there is usually a clause about a situation affecting students "at school." Affecting students at school means that even if the harassment takes place off school grounds it still can be punishable by the school district if it is making it difficult for any student to learn or participate while in the classroom or at school functions. This is particularly important in instances of cyberbullying, which rarely happen on school grounds but can affect a victim's ability to perform at school.

The description of harassment location by the Clark County School District reads:

> On District premises or at any District sponsored activity, regardless of location: shall include, but not be limited to buildings, facilities, and grounds on District campus, school busses, District parking areas; and the location of any District sponsored activity. This includes instances in which the conduct occurs off District premises but impacts a District related activity.[6]

Just because the harassment doesn't happen at school doesn't mean the harasser won't get in trouble, as we see in Miranda's story.

> Two of Miranda's classmates, Lani and Sierra, posted several threatening messages on Miranda's Facebook page. "We're going to make you bleed" and "You are dead" were common messages. Miranda was understandably afraid to go to school. When Miranda was caught skipping school, the administration and her parents discovered the reason for her truancy.
>
> Lani and Sierra were surprised when they and their parents were called in to see the administrator for cyberbullying. They believed that because they didn't bully Miranda at school, they couldn't get into trouble. It was explained to them that because their behavior affected Miranda's participation in school, they could indeed be punished. The two girls were suspended.

Although cyberbullying commonly happens off school grounds, there are laws for cyberbullying, including sexting, being implemented today. Information on harassment laws regarding all types of harassment in your state may be viewed at:
http://www.cyberbullying.us/cyberbullying_state_laws.php.

Prevention

This policy section states what a school district is doing in order to prevent harassment. There are basic prevention techniques all districts use: making policies public, posting policies in schools, training teachers and reviewing handbooks with students and parents.

These are the areas covered in every district policy. Your district may include more than these items or they may use different headings, but the information we cover here will be there. However your district policy is written, know that a school always has the right to punish a harasser if his or her behavior is affecting the educational environment. If the school administrators are not able to control the situation through their internal disciplinary steps or the harassment is severe, persistent or pervasive, the police will be alerted and criminal charges will be filed.

- **MYTH:** I can't get into trouble if I fight off school property.
- **TRUTH:** School district policies are far reaching. If the fighting is disrupting the educational process in any way, then the school administrators may take action. The police are usually informed as well.

When Do the Police Come?

Police may get involved in a harassment case when a civil or criminal law is broken. Some of those laws govern unwanted physical violence, verbal threats of physical harm, intimidation, theft, vandalism, disorderly conduct and disruption of the educational process. This list pretty much covers a typical harasser's actions, but school administrators try to stop the behavior within their systems first.

Law enforcement will be notified when the harasser's actions are severe, persistent and pervasive or a victim's parents want the police involved. When police are engaged in a harassment case, they determine the severity of the harassment and decide whether to charge the student with an infraction, a misdemeanor or a felony.

Severe

In severe cases of harassment, not only will law enforcement be involved, but also schools can skip steps in their disciplinary policies. Severe harassment is a serious threat to the well-being of others and will be taken care of quickly. Some specific examples are: physical violence, threats of physical violence (either spoken or written) and over-the-top verbal assault. If a harasser recruits others to do these things, that could be considered severe as well. In Yanella's situation, she took her issue into her own hands.

Yanella was a student who was not only new to the school, but also new to the country. She had no friends and didn't speak English. When a group of girls started harassing her, she had no idea what she was supposed to do. Yanella thought her only option to make the girls stop taunting her and shoving her around was bringing a knife to school.

A staff member at Yanella's school discovered the knife and brought it to the school resource officer. Yanella was arrested and expelled from school, because her actions were severe.

Persistent and Pervasive

Police are asked to get involved when the harassment is persistent. When the school has already punished a bully and the individual continues bullying, the police are going to get involved.

Pervasive means that the harassment is spreading. If the harasser is recruiting others to harass and/or the number of those affected by the harasser's actions is becoming greater, this is pervasive. For example, gang members try to recruit additional people, because it gives them more power.

Parental Request

A victim's parent or guardian can request police involvement. One way parents can do this, as you know from Dillon's story, is to encourage their child to write a statement.

Parents or guardians also have the option to sue the harasser's parents. This is called a civil suit. If the harasser loses a civil case it can mean large monetary payouts, hopefully leaving the harasser wondering if his or her behavior was worth it. Civil suits are one reason why schools have very clear policies. If schools do not, then they leave themselves open to costly lawsuits.

Infraction

An infraction is a minor violation of the law that is usually punished with a fine or penalty. This is law enforcement's first step with a harasser. In cases where the parents of the victim refuse to let their child make a statement, it is law enforcement's only option.

Misdemeanor

A misdemeanor is a minor crime that can mean an appearance before a judge, a trial, time in juvenile detention, community service, probation and/or restitution (money) to the victim. In order to charge a student with a misdemeanor, officers need a victim willing to make a statement. Students under the age of eighteen can't be considered a victim without their parents' consent.

Felony

A felony is a serious crime and thus comes with serious punishments. Juveniles charged with felonies can be charged as adults, which means adult punishments, including prison. Any harassment in the extreme, such as murder, rape and hate crimes, can be considered for felony charges.

We hope you won't need to use this information on the laws and policies that protect you, but if you do, we hope it's helpful. Schools and police officers want to stop harassers as early as they can. They know that young bullies become harassers and harassers become serious abusers. If they can break that cycle early, they may save a young person from becoming the kind of adult who is a repetitive part of this country's criminal justice system.

- **MYTH:** A cop can't arrest me without my parent/guardian there.
- **TRUTH:** Yes, they can. If you've committed a crime that warrants your arrest, police officers can arrest you without a parent present. Officers sign a form at the school stating that they are taking custody of you. Your parents will be notified shortly after the arrest.

 COMPLETE THE QUESTIONNAIRE AT THE END OF THIS SECTION TO DETERMINE WHETHER HARASSMENT IS AN ISSUE AT YOUR SCHOOL.

TEEN CONNECTIONS

- How were Lisa's rights being violated?

    Lisa has the right not to be abused, she has the right to be secure and she has the right to enjoy privacy in all matters. What Dillon said and did to her was abusive; it made her feel insecure. Also, touching her inappropriately violated her personal privacy.

- Why does Dillon's behavior fall under the terms *persistent* and *pervasive*?

    Dillon was repeatedly harassing others even after he received punishment; this is persistent. In addition, because he had multiple victims and he was recruiting others to help him in his harassment, it would be considered pervasive.

• Why did Lisa's parents have to be involved?

Because she is not an adult. Therefore, the law won't recognize her as a victim without her parents' consent.

Does Harassment Happen at Your School?

Now let's determine whether you or someone you know is being harassed at the school you attend. If this is occurring, the proper methods need to be utilized in order to stop the menacing and/or inappropriate behavior and to make the students at the school feel safe.

1. At your school, do you hear other students being taunted, teased or called names?

       A. often   B. sometimes   C. never

2. Does physical harassment such as tripping, shoving, hitting or kicking happen?

       A. often   B. sometimes   C. never

3. Have you observed inappropriate touching, grabbing or groping?

       A. often   B. sometimes   C. never

4. Are there students whose possessions are frequently taken or hidden?

       A. often   B. sometimes   C. never

5. Are there students who are excluded or rejected because of looks, height or weight?

       A. often   B. sometimes   C. never

6. Are there students who are excluded or rejected because of race or religion?

       A. often   B. sometimes   C. never

7. Are there students who are excluded or rejected because of their lack of self-confidence or social skills?

       A. often   B. sometimes   C. never

8. Are there students who are excluded or rejected because of academic ability, high or low?

       A. often   B. sometimes   C. never

9. Are there students who are excluded or rejected because of disabilities?
   A. often   B. sometimes   C. never

10. How often have you been harassed at school during the past year?
    A. often   B. sometimes   C. never

11. How often have you harassed anyone at school during the past year?
    A. often   B. sometimes   C. never

12. If you saw someone being harassed at school, how often did you ignore it?
    A. often   B. sometimes   C. never

13. How often are there no adults in the hallways or gathering places monitoring the students?
    A. often   B. sometimes   C. never

14. How often are you unaware of the rules and consequences of harassment at your school?
    A. often   B. sometimes   C. never

15. Do you feel that the rules against harassment are blown off at your school?
    A. often   B. sometimes   C. never

In a perfect world, all the answers would be *never*. However, we don't live in a perfect world and our schools can't possibly be perfect either. But if you had a lot of *A* and *B* answers, this is cause for concern. If you are reading this book with a parent or guardian, share your answers to this quiz with him or her.

As schools are not perfect, neither are the students. Your school has a responsibility to create a learning environment that is free of harassment, but you, as a student, have an equal responsibility in helping to prevent harassment. Schools cannot possibly create that environment on their own. Think about your answers. Are you being a harasser? Are you not stepping forward when you see others harassed? Are you the victim who is frightened and doesn't stand up against a harasser?

Remember, an effective, positive, safe and fun school environment is everyone's responsibility!

Parent Section 2

Finding Support

As a parent, learning your state laws that address harassment is a good idea. Knowing your school district policy is essential. Schools are the first line of defense against harassment involving teens. This is due to the fact that the vast majority of harassment starts at school, is perpetrated at school or affects students while at school. Schools have a responsibility to keep their institutions safe and secure so the students can learn. Parents have the responsibility to work with the schools and advocate for their children's safety and education. You cannot be effective in this role if you do not know the policies.

As we discussed in teen section 2, many school districts are paying close attention to possible harassing behaviors. If schools are focusing on these in order to protect their students, then it would follow that parents should be taking the same precautions at home in order to prevent harassment. If harassment is going to stop, it will take legislators, law enforcement, schools, parents and students working together to make it happen.

Working with Your School

With few exceptions (the interview you will read in chapter 7 is one example of an exception), schools attempt to prevent and resolve harassment issues. Solutions are expedited when the parents are involved and working with the educational institution. Schools have a legal liability to end harassment, but more than that, people who choose education as a career like children and teenagers and they want to help them succeed. Teens cannot succeed if they are being harassed or if they are harassing others. The information in this section will help you approach the school administration, use the district policy to help you check on your child's behavior at home and, if needed, take your issue to law enforcement.

Approaching the School

Students are issued a student handbook at the beginning of every school year. It is reviewed in class or in an assembly and often students are assigned to bring it home for parents to examine. You should be familiar with all the rules your teen is expected to follow. If a problem with harassment arises, however, you may need more detailed information than what is in the student handbook. You will find that information in the district policy.

Teen section 2 outlines the things that are common to most school district policies, but there are rules and procedures that may be different from district to district, so it is beneficial to look at your district's policy specifically. You can usually find your district policy online, but if it isn't there, it is a public record and you can request a copy from the district office. Reading through the district policy will give you an idea of how situations are handled and what you can expect from your school's process. You will be a better advocate for your teen if you know what you can expect from your school district.

If harassment has become severe, persistent or pervasive and your teen has tried and failed to handle it on his or her own, your first step is to meet with school officials. They may call a meeting or you have the right to ask for a meeting at any time. Not only is it important that you go into this meeting educated about policy, but it is also crucial that you go in with the right attitude. You will get a lot further and help your teen a lot more if your position is that you are going to work together with school officials to resolve the issue. You should be assertive (a detailed explanation of assertive behavior is in chapter 6).

Policy as Parenting Help

Teen section 2 outlines the situations and behaviors to which school districts are paying attention. These are issues that require your vigilance as well. One of the benefits of reading through a district harassment policy is that its focus can help you know what you should be looking for in your teen's behavior and appearance.

- **Student dress:** Pay attention to what your teen wears to school and outside of school. Is what your teen wears going to make others uncomfortable, because it's revealing, related to a gang, sexually suggestive or violent? Is what your teen wears going to make your son or daughter a target for bullies, because it's out of style, overdressed (wearing a coat all the time, for example), unkempt, unclean, revealing, an attempt to hide (hair in the face, for example) or displays inappropriate slogans or style choice? Sometimes appearance can make teens a target or brand them as harassers.

- **Assignments, writing, art projects, graffiti:** Many times teens act out in subtle ways when dealing with harassment. These subtleties may include a change in your child's behaviors, as we discussed in parent section 1, and/or troubles may manifest themselves in a teen's writing, drawing or the way in which a teen decorates his or her spaces. Take an interest in your teen's schoolwork. Ask your teen what he or she is learning and doing in classes; ask to see assignments. Offer to help your teen with homework and check up on his or her grades. Wander into his or her bedroom on occasion. You don't have to invade your teen's space or be a tyrant to let your teen know you're an interested party in his or her life.

Teens who know they're being monitored are less likely to get into trouble and they are less likely to ignore negative things that happen to them at school. If a teacher communicates concern over something that your teen did or said in class, take it seriously. Teen victims and harassers alike often find outlets for their feelings in their schoolwork, their writings (on paper as well as on a computer) or their personal spaces. Watch for hints of obsession with violence, death (of others or their own) or weapons. Teens aren't good secret keepers, so if you're paying attention the clues will be there. You need to search for these clues diligently.

- **Computer use:** Checking your teen's Facebook page, other social networking site pages, personal Web site or blog is a good way to see what's going on in your teen's life. Also, use the browser's history feature to check where your teen has been online. There are also blocking controls parents can set through Internet providers, but computer-savvy teens may be able to get around these. Keeping an eye on a teen's cell phone use is also important. This is being a parent, not a snoop, and you are not violating your child's rights. Talk to your teen about the importance of keeping his or her private life private. Keep reiterating that whatever he or she or someone else puts into cyberspace is out there for anyone and everyone to see forever.

The toughest thing about cyberbullying is that so much of it happens in secret. In the interest of protecting your teen, you need to make the computer(s) in your home public. In other words, don't let your teen keep a computer in his or her bedroom. Explain to your teen that while you don't want to invade his or her privacy, you are interested in his or her safety. Tell your teen about the stories you see and hear about cyberbullying from other parents, television, newspapers and magazines. The reason you monitor your child is because you care about him or her, not because you don't trust him or her.

Cyberbullying Facts[1]

- 30 percent of middle school students were victims of cyberbullying two or more times in the past thirty days

- 22 percent of middle school students admitted to engaging in cyberbullying two or more times in the past thirty days

- Cyberbullying victims and offenders reported significantly lower self-esteem than youths who hadn't experienced cyberbullying

- **Know what constitutes harassment:** Refer to chapter 1 for explanations of types of harassment. Not only will knowing the definitions validate your teen, but also it will be an indicator as to when you need to step in and talk with your teen and/or help him or her.

- **Backpacks:** District policies state that backpacks should be checked only if there's probable cause. Parents should adhere to the same rule. If you're worried about something your teen has in his or her backpack (or doesn't have in there), that's probable cause.

- **Know friends:** Most districts monitor visitors who come into their schools. For parents, this means monitoring the visitors in your teen's home life. Do you know who your teen's friends are? Have you met their parents? Do you know where your teen is and what he or she is doing? If you want to keep your child safe and secure, you should know with whom he or she is hanging out and what the group is doing.

- **An emergency plan:** Most schools in our nation have an emergency plan and these schools use drills in order to prepare. You and your teen should have an emergency plan as well. In chapter 7, you and your teen will create a My Safety Plan. Both you and your teen will feel safer and more secure if there is a plan in place.

- **Take all reports and comments seriously:** Schools are generally required to treat all reports and suspicions seriously when it comes to harassment. They are also required to act on them even if that action means they find out it's nothing. Parents should do the same.

District policies aren't just roadmaps for parents to work with their schools to solve harassment issues; they are also helpful parent guides. Keep in mind that these policies are developed from the experiences of school districts all over the country, so they are based on the knowledge of what works. Use that information to your advantage.

Going Beyond Your School District

You have the right to file a complaint with law enforcement about harassment issues at any time. If you determine that you and your teen need to proceed into the justice system, the best way is to work with your school district. Schools either have school resource officers or they are assigned a police officer to help them with legal issues regarding students.

States depend on school districts to be the first line of defense against harassment, so the proper channels to go through regarding a harassment issue with your teen begin with school officials. School personnel are trained to handle these situations and they can help you sort out legalities, make referrals and guide your decisions on when and how to contact law enforcement. You can bypass the school district if you prefer, but law enforcement officials will ask you about your experience within the school process.

Going beyond your school district means you will be utilizing state laws. There are harassment laws in place in most states, but if there aren't, keep in mind there are federal laws that protect your teen's right not to be abused. If you are curious to see whether your state has harassment laws in place or if they are being proposed, go to **http://www.cyberbullying. us/cyberbullying_state_laws.php**. If you don't like what you see, perhaps you should get involved and contact your representatives.

If your child is the harasser, as his or her parent you can be held liable for his or her behavior. This can mean anything from court-mandated parenting classes to civil suits for monetary compensation. It is in your best interest to get to know the material in this book, your school district's policy and your state's laws so you can change your teen's behavior before it costs you.

- **MYTH:** It's an invasion of my teen's privacy if I monitor his or her computer, schoolwork or bedroom.
- **TRUTH:** The law doesn't see teens as adults with adult rights and neither should you. They are still children and therefore need to be protected, sometimes from themselves. There is a balance between

monitoring and disciplining, however. Don't make looking at your teen's things a disciplinary action; make it a simple checkup for your teen's safety and success. Explain to your teen what you're doing and why you're doing it. Your child may not like it, but he or she will understand your actions.

 REVIEW WITH YOUR TEEN THE QUESTIONNAIRE HE OR SHE COMPLETED AT THE END OF TEEN SECTION 2 AND FIND OUT HOW YOUR TEEN THINKS HIS OR HER SCHOOL IS DOING REGARDING HARASSMENT. KEEP IN MIND THAT NO SCHOOL IS PERFECT. IF THE RESULTS AREN'T WHAT YOU WOULD LIKE, BECOME A POSITIVE PART OF THE SOLUTION.

The parents at a junior high were concerned about students' behavior and developed a solution to work with and aid the school's administration.

The junior high was having a problem on early release days for holidays and on the last day of school. There were harassing behaviors of all types happening as the excited students made their ways through the halls and out to their buses. Students threw papers and books out of lockers onto the floors, grabbed, hit and pushed one another and pulled fire alarms. There wasn't enough school staff to observe every student in every part of the school.

The school administration then went to the Parent Teacher Organization (PTO) with the issue. The PTO came up with a very good solution. On early release days and the last day of school, thirty to forty parent volunteers came into the school a few minutes before the last bell was scheduled to ring. They were stationed throughout the school in all the stairwells, by the bathrooms, next to banks of lockers, throughout the hallways and near the buses. When watchful eyes monitored the students in every nook and cranny of their school, the students corrected their behavior.

PARENT CONNECTIONS

- What could Lisa's parents have done prior to the harassment becoming persistent and pervasive?

Lisa's parents may have tried to help her deal with Dillon in the beginning, but it wasn't working. It was time to let Lisa stand up for herself, with the support of school officials and her parents, to stop Dillon. The school officials met their obligation by notifying the parents of incidents that they knew about and by punishing Dillon. However, until a victim stands up to a harasser in some way, he or she will continue to be a target.

- When the teacher contacted Lisa's parents, what should have been the next step for the parents?

  They actually got the next step right, which was to set up a meeting with school officials. The results of that meeting were not satisfactory for anyone involved except perhaps Lisa's dad. Schools cannot force parents into advocating for their children. In a best case scenario, Lisa's parents would have consented to letting her make a statement and then they and the school could have worked together to deal with Dillon and his harassment. More important than punishing Dillon, however, was that they would have empowered their daughter.

- Did Lisa's parents put her in more danger by not allowing her to make a statement?

  When a student is participating in harassing behaviors, the school has a legal liability to act. Dillon or any other harasser is going to know why they're being punished. When a student's parents don't allow their child to make a statement, the school and law enforcement do not legally have a victim. Therefore, they are limited in the protections they can offer to the person who was harmed and in what they can do to punish the harasser.

Chapter Three

Taking the Personality Quiz

Teen Section 3

Who Am I?

The personality quiz in this section will reveal whether you are assertive, aggressive or passive. It may seem as if we are switching topics, but trust us when we assure you that knowledge of passive, aggressive and assertive personality types is key to harassment prevention.

This quiz is all about you and how you would respond to different situations. Understand, however, that it is not about personality in the sense of asking what you like, dislike or think is funny. The quiz focuses on the part of your personality you are in charge of, the part that you can change. Learning about passive, aggressive and assertive personality types will help you know whether you are working to make your life successful or if you are making life difficult through the decisions you make.

Before you take the personality quiz, let's briefly discuss what we tell our own students: This is a short and easy personality quiz so it's not going to tell you everything about whether you have a passive, aggressive or assertive personality, but it will give you some ideas regarding your personality type and what you need to explore.

Passive, Aggressive and Assertive
Personality Quiz for Teens

Choose the letter of the answer that describes how you would react in each situation. Do not over-think your answers. Choose the one that is your gut reaction to the question, because that is usually the most truthful. Remember, the results will be accurate only if you answer the questions honestly.

1. You see a popular jock and some of his friends stuffing an underclass-man into a garbage can. You:
    A. walk the other way and pretend you didn't see anything.
    B. find the adult on hall duty and tell him or her what is happening.
    C. join the crowd of onlookers and cheer them on.

2. Your family has planned a vacation and you need to find someone to make your newspaper deliveries while you are gone. You:
    A. give up your job, because you are sure no one would want to deliver your papers.
    B. know that some of your friends could use the extra money so you ask one of them.
    C. tell one of your friends he is going to make the deliveries, because he owes you.

3. Your friend teases you about your hand-me-down bike. You:
    A. don't say anything and act like it doesn't bother you.
    B. tell him the bike has sentimental value and you like it.
    C. say something sarcastic to your friend that you know will embarrass him.

4. You and your friend disagree on what movie to see, so you:
    A. go along with your friend despite the fact you don't like the choice.
    B. suggest you find a movie you would both like.
    C. insist that you go to your movie choice.

5. There is an interesting debate taking place in one of your classes. You:
    A. hope you're not called on to express an opinion.
    B. listen carefully to what others have to say and add your opinion too.
    C. get frustrated when others don't agree with you.

6. Your friend asked to borrow your favorite hoodie and you let her. She's had it for two weeks, so you:
   - A. try not to think about it.
   - B. ask her to bring it back and if she doesn't, give her a day and time you will be over to pick it up.
   - C. demand it back "right now or else!"

7. You always do well on math tests. Your friend asks you to position your answer sheet so she can copy your test. You:
   - A. don't want to lose your friend so you agree to cheat.
   - B. tell your friend you don't want to be dishonest nor risk getting both of you in trouble.
   - C. tell her you'll do it, but only if she lets you copy her history homework for a month.

8. When you get your report card you have a much lower grade in science than you expected. You:
   - A. decide to work harder next grading period, because you can't talk to a teacher.
   - B. make an appointment with the teacher to ask about the grade.
   - C. confront the teacher about the mistake he or she made on your grade.

9. You and your friends are shopping for clothes. You:
   - A. buy what your friends like even though it is not your favorite.
   - B. listen to your friends' opinions but choose what you like.
   - C. make fun of what they try on.

10. Your parents are encouraging you to choose a college. You:
   - A. find out where your friends are going.
   - B. talk with your parents, teachers and counselors and make plans to attend college fairs.
   - C. buy a car and ditch the college plan.

11. Your waitress is horrible and she's very rude. She has to be reminded several times to bring your fork. You:
   - A. give her a generous tip anyway.
   - B. leave her a tip you think she actually earned and fill out a comment card.
   - C. make a mess of your table to let her know how bad she was.

12. Your friends are making fun of a handicapped student. You:
    A. smile and say nothing.
    B. ask them to stop and tell them you admire the student's courage.
    C. join in by coming up with some jokes of your own.

13. One of the local service clubs is recruiting students to help with an after-school program. You:
    A. would like to volunteer but are sure there's nothing helpful you could do.
    B. ask what help is needed.
    C. wouldn't waste your time doing work for free.

14. You are scrambling to finish an important assignment. A friend asks you to help him with his. Your friend hasn't even started the project. You:
    A. agree to help him but wonder how you are going to finish your project.
    B. explain that you are trying to finish too but will help if you have the time.
    C. refuse outright to help someone who is so lazy.

15. You were late getting up and quickly grabbed an orange for your lunch. Later at lunch, your friend wants you to share. You:
    A. give him the orange.
    B. explain that this is all the lunch you have.
    C. tell him no and take one of his sandwiches.

16. Your friend comes from a wealthy family and always has money to spend. You:
    A. are uncomfortable going places with her, because you have to watch your spending.
    B. pay your way but suggest inexpensive activities for you to do together.
    C. let her pay for everything.

17. The clerk in the shoe store is rude when you ask to try on a third pair of shoes. You:
    A. say you are sorry and buy the last pair you tried on even though you don't love them.
    B. tell the clerk you didn't like the first two pairs of shoes and leave the store.
    C. tell the clerk you think he's a jerk and his shoes stink and then storm out of the store.

18. Your friend is being abused by her boyfriend. You:
    A. worry about your friend but say nothing because it's none of your business.
    B. help your friend come up with ways to stay safe and get help.
    C. badmouth the boyfriend and tell your friend she's stupid for letting him do that to her.

19. You hear a vicious rumor about Vicki, whom you don't like. You:
    A. go along and continue spreading the rumor to those you know don't like Vicki.
    B. don't spread the rumor, because you don't know if it's true.
    C. embellish the rumor, tell everyone you can and tease Vicki.

20. Your friend is angry with you and you have no idea why. You:
    A. apologize even though you don't know what you did.
    B. find out what's wrong and then decide if an apology is necessary.
    C. tell your friend he's being stupid and you're not his friend anymore.

21. You need a ride to the Department of Motor Vehicles to take your driver's test. That driver's license is really important to you. You:
    A. drop hints about what you need and hope someone offers.
    B. explain how important this is to you and respectfully ask for a ride.
    C. demand a ride, because it is important to you.

22. You are interviewing for a job. You:
   A. find that making eye contact with the interviewer makes you uncomfortable so you look somewhere else.
   B. find it easy to make eye contact with the interviewer.
   C. stare at the interviewer so he knows how much you want the job.

23. When standing from a seated position (you could try it right now), you:
   A. make yourself small—your feet together, arms close to your body, head down and slouched.
   B. are comfortable—your feet are shoulder width apart, arms are hanging at your side, head is up and your posture is good.
   C. make yourself big—your feet are far apart, arms folded tightly or on your hips, your posture is stiff or rigid.

24. You have a funny story about your weekend to tell your friends. While telling them, you:
   A. don't use hand gestures often, but when you do they are very small.
   B. use hand gestures that illustrate your story, but do not invade others' space.
   C. use big hand gestures and often touch others while you tell the story.

25. When it comes to respect, you:
   A. believe that you are not respected.
   B. are satisfied with the level of respect you give and receive.
   C. have little respect for most others.

Number of *A* answers _____

Number of *B* answers _____

Number of *C* answers _____

A **Answers**

A answers represent passive behaviors. Passive is not something you want to be, because in general it means you have a low self-esteem, have a difficult time standing up for yourself and are therefore a victim. It is passive personalities who have the most problems with bullies.

The number of passive answers indicates how serious your passive behavior is. If you have ten or more passive answers, your passive issues are quite serious. If you have only a few passive answers, you will want to work on the situations described in those questions. Being a victim or passive is never healthy.

We will describe in depth what it means to be passive, why people are passive and how passive behavior can be changed in teen section 4, *The Doormat Kid.* Before continuing, fill out the form so you realize the situations where you are passive.

Question #	SITUATION

B **Answers**

B answers represent assertive behaviors. Assertive is what you want to be, so the more assertive answers you have the better off you are. Assertive people are those who have confidence in themselves, know their rights and are not afraid to stand up for those rights. They also know how to get what they want without hurting others. This means assertive people are not harassers, nor are they victims.

The number of assertive answers indicates how assertive you are. If you have fifteen or more assertive answers, you are on the right track. However, unless all of your answers are *B* then you have things to work on. We don't know anyone, teen or adult, who will have a perfect score, because as humans we aren't perfect, particularly when it comes to how we treat ourselves and others.

We will describe what it means to be assertive, why it's great to be assertive and how assertive behavior can be maintained in depth in teen section 6, *How to be a Winner.* Before continuing, fill out the form. You will see what you're doing right.

Question #	SITUATION

C **Answers**

C answers represent aggressive behaviors. Aggressive personalities are insecure (even though they come across as egotistical), controlling and angry. Aggressive personalities desire to control situations and people, not to mention that their anger drives them to be harassers. Aggressive personalities don't realize that controlling situations and people won't lead to confidence, success or happiness. Without aggressive personalities, there would be no need for this book.

The number of aggressive answers indicates how serious your aggressive behavior is. If you have ten or more aggressive answers, your aggressive issues are quite serious. If you have only a few aggressive answers, you will want to work on them, because those are situations when you are being a bully.

We will describe what it means to be aggressive, why people are aggressive and how aggressive behavior can be changed in depth in teen section 5, *The Bully*. Fill out the form before you continue so you are aware of specific situations where you behave aggressively.

Question #	SITUATION

As you continue reading and hopefully discussing the issues brought up in this book, think of other ways that you are acting passively, aggressively or assertively. After completing the quiz you will have gained some knowledge about personalities which will be helpful to you. You have to be willing to admit you are not perfect and you have to think about the information and how it applies to you. Becoming the kind of person everyone likes to be around and who is confident, respected and successful means taking the challenge to become that person.

If you are reading with a parent or guardian, share your quiz results with him or her so he or she can help and support you with harassment prevention. Parents will also be given a quiz and you should request to see the results.

Now you can see how passive, aggressive and assertive personalities tie into the topic of harassment. If you can change your passive ways, you will not be a target for harassers and will therefore not be a victim. If you can change your aggressive ways, the world could become a harassment-free place where nobody fears being bullied. Now let's look at ways you can become more assertive and gain the respect you deserve.

Parent Section 3

Who Am I as a Person and as a Parent?

Just like the teen quiz your son or daughter took, the parent quiz will reveal whether you are assertive, aggressive or passive. Your quiz may tell you something about your teen as well. If parents are exhibiting passive or aggressive behaviors then chances are their teens will too. They would probably never admit it, but your children watch you, listen to you and learn from you.

It may not be easy to learn some of these things about yourself, but please keep in mind the point of this quiz isn't to make you feel guilty or think you are a bad parent. The point is to change some of your negative behaviors so you can help your teen overcome harassment. Not only can you solve your teen's problem with peers but you can also become an improved parent through utilizing this information.

This is a short quiz so it will not tell you everything about your assertive, passive or aggressive personality traits or whether you exhibit passive, aggressive or assertive parenting styles. Nor will the teen quiz tell teens everything they need to know. However, we hope that you will gain insight into how to strengthen your personality, which in turn will strengthen your teen's. Be open and honest with your teen about the results on your quiz. Help each other to set SMART goals and make some positive life changes.

Passive, Aggressive and Assertive
Personality Quiz for Parents

Choose the letter of the answer that describes how you would react in each situation. Do not over-think your answer. Choose the one that is your gut reaction to the question, because that is usually the most truthful. Remember, the results will be accurate only if you answer the questions honestly.

1. Your friend asks you to go to a political meeting with her. You really don't want to go. You:
    A. agree to go with her even though you find the group's views offensive.
    B. tell her that you don't agree with the group's views but would like to do something with her another time.
    C. tell her how stupid this group is and you absolutely do not want to go to the meeting.

2. When you leave the office for lunch one of your coworkers often asks you to bring him something back. He never offers to pay for it until you ask for the money. You:
    A. just let it go thinking it's not worth the hassle.
    B. tell him you will be glad to pick something up for him but need the money before you leave.
    C. tell him to get his own lunch. You're not the lunch wagon.

3. The coach of your daughter's team seldom plays her despite the fact that she never misses practice and tries to do everything she is asked. You:
    A. feel bad for your daughter but know there's nothing you can do.
    B. talk with the coach about how you can help your daughter improve her skills.
    C. confront the coach about playing favorites and not teaching the girls anything.

4. You have been standing in the checkout line for a very long time. The clerk has spent more time answering the phone than waiting on customers. You:
    A. patiently wait while the clerk takes another call.
    B. ask the clerk to please help you before answering the phone.
    C. tell the clerk if she touches the phone you are going straight to the manager.

5. One of your coworkers sends you e-mail messages that are sexually explicit. You:
   A. are too embarrassed to do anything about it.
   B. explain in person that you find the e-mails offensive and if the person does not stop, you will report the coworker for harassment.
   C. print the e-mails out, put the coworker's name on them in large letters and post them in the break room.

6. Your teen is diabetic. He is starting high school. You:
   A. hope he will be careful about what he eats and will take his medication.
   B. make an appointment for you and your son to inform school personnel about his medical needs.
   C. take a list of all his medications and food restrictions to the school and insist they monitor him.

7. You suspect your teen is being harassed at school. You:
   A. talk with him about how important it is to be nice and make friends with others.
   B. call his counselor and ask to talk with him about what you suspect.
   C. call the suspected harasser on the phone and threaten her.

8. Everyone in your family has assigned chores. One of your children refuses to do her share. You:
   A. tell her that if she does her chores, you will help her.
   B. remind her of the consequence if she doesn't do her chores and tell her it's her choice.
   C. yell at her and send her to her room.

9. Your preteen has an aversion to showering. You:
   A. know he would be embarrassed if you brought it up so you just hope he will outgrow it.
   B. find a private moment to have a frank talk with him about the importance of good hygiene.
   C. tell him you're going to lock him in the bathroom until he takes a shower.

10. Your sister calls you every day and talks on and on. You:
   A. just listen, because it is rude to interrupt.
   B. mention you have a prior commitment and tell her goodbye.
   C. hang up on her.

11. A friend calls and asks if you will take care of his pet iguana while he is on vacation. You:
   A. don't want to do it but finally say you will.
   B. admit that you have no idea how to care for an iguana and that you don't want to be responsible for it.
   C. tell him iguanas disgust you and wish him good luck finding someone to take his repulsive pet.

12. An elderly neighbor tells you that your son and some of his friends stole some fruit off her trees. You:
   A. apologize profusely and offer to replace the fruit.
   B. confront your son about the fruit and go with him while he apologizes to the neighbor and arranges to do some chores to repay her for the fruit.
   C. chalk it up to "boys will be boys."

13. Your teen's grades are falling. You:
   A. hire a tutor.
   B. have a discussion about why the grades are falling and what she is going to do about it.
   C. blame her teachers.

14. You have been offered a promotion, but it entails moving to another state. You:
   A. turn down the promotion, because you know your family would not like moving.
   B. tell your family about the promotion and the move. Ask for family members' input on the decision.
   C. tell your family members to pack their bags.

15. A teacher at your teen's school contacts you and says that your son confided in him about being harassed. You:
   A. feel hurt and inadequate that your son didn't come to you.
   B. thank the teacher and ask who to call to set up an appointment with the school official who handles harassment cases.
   C. tell the teacher to mind his own business.

Number of *A* answers _____

Number of *B* answers _____

Number of *C* answers _____

A **Answers**

A answers represent passive behaviors. Passive people are quite often victims. If your teen is a harassment victim, he or she has passive personality traits. If you possess passive personality traits, your teen could be emulating your passive behavior.

The number of passive answers indicates how serious your passive behavior is. If you have only a few passive answers, you will want to work on the types of situations described in the questions, because those are instances when you are being passive. Being a victim or passive is never healthy for you or your teen.

We will describe what it means to be passive, why people are passive and how passive behavior can be changed in depth in teen section 4, *The Doormat Kid.* The information will apply to both you and your teen. Then in the subsequent section for parents, we will discuss what passive parents' behavior means for teens.

B **Answers**

B answers represent assertive behaviors. Assertive answers are the answers you want to strive for. The more assertive you are and the more assertive your teen is the better. Assertive people are not harassers, nor are they victims. For parents, an assertive personality translates to strong parenting skills and therefore teens who are likely to be well adjusted and successful.

Unless all of your answers are *B* then you have things to work on. We don't know anyone, teen or adult, who will have a perfect score, because as human beings we aren't perfect.

Assertive personalities are described in teen section 6, *How to be a Winner.* This information will apply to both you and your teen. Then, in the subsequent parent section, we will describe how and why assertive parents foster assertive teens.

C **Answers**

C answers represent aggressive behaviors. Aggressive personalities desire to control situations and people, not to mention that their anger drives them to be harassers and abusers. Aggressive personalities become abusive parents. The aggressive parent usually creates a teen who emulates his or her parent's behavior by becoming a harasser or becomes passive after being victimized by an aggressive parent.

Even if you have only a few aggressive answers, you will want to work on them, because your personality can have a profound effect on how your teen treats others or is treated by them. Aggressive personalities will be explained in teen section 5, *The Bully.* The information will apply to both you and your teen. Then in the subsequent parent chapter, we will discuss the effects aggressive parents' behavior may have on their teens.

As you continue reading and discussing the issues of bullying and harassment with your teenage son or daughter, we are sure you will think of other ways you are passive, aggressive or assertive and how your teen exhibits these personality traits as well. Therefore, the parent quiz serves many purposes. You need to think about this information both as an individual and as a parent who wants to be a positive influence on your teen. Share the good, the bad and the ugly of your results with your teen. Own up to the things you do well and the things you need to change. Look at your teen's quiz and discuss the results. Is there a correlation between your quiz and your teen's? Keep the results in mind as you read the chapters on passive, assertive and aggressive personalities.

Just as there are no perfect people, there are no perfect parents. The key to being effective is a willingness to learn, to monitor and to adjust when needed. Hopefully the insights about your teen and yourself revealed in *Hey, Back Off!* will provide guidance and strategies to navigate through the issues of bullying and harassment which arise during your son's or daughter's tumultuous teenage years.

Chapter Four

Doormat Kids
and Passive Parents

Digital Media Player as Change Agent, Part 1

Rachel, a bully, sees an opportunity to take advantage of Amar. With help from his proactive friend Kaylee, Amar's experience with harassment causes him to change his passive ways, create effective goals and achieve positive results.

Gunfire, explosions and his mother's frightened sobs were some of Amar's first memories. They were running from the bad men in the middle of the night. He didn't know it then, but they were going to the United States.

That night they fled their country by foot, by car and finally by plane. Amar and his family landed in their new home with nothing, but they adapted to life in the United States and although they weren't rich they were happy.

To help his family financially, Amar got a job bussing tables at a local restaurant. He used his money to buy the things he needed in the way of clothes and school supplies, but he also managed to save a little here and there for the really important things like his new digital media player (DMP). Amar's family chipped in some cash for his birthday so he could pay for song downloads. It added up to be the most expensive thing Amar had ever owned.

The morning after his birthday, Amar sat with a group of friends in the hall before school. Amar was showing them his DMP when Rachel plopped down next to him. "What ya got?" She grabbed the DMP from Kaylee. "This is awesome. Whose is it?"

"It's Amar's."

"No kidding. Where did you get the money for this, Amar? Did you steal it? I mean you can't even afford decent clothes, much less a DMP."

Kaylee snatched the DMP. "He got it for his birthday and there's nothing wrong with his clothes." Kaylee handed the DMP back to Amar.

"Sorry! Wow, wake up on the wrong side of the bed? Amar knows I was just kidding. Don't you, Amar? Right, Amar? Just say *jess* or however you say it!"

Amar nodded. He didn't like Rachel, but she was popular. Besides, Amar considered himself lucky that Rachel liked him. She was absolutely nasty to those she hated.

Amar unzipped the front pocket of his backpack and placed the DMP inside. As he was about to zip it closed, Rachel grabbed his sandwich in its plastic container. "Can I have this? I'm starving!"

Kaylee answered for Amar. "No, you can't have it. It's his lunch."

"Amar can speak, can't you Amar? Just say *jess!*" Amar reached for his sandwich, but Rachel flipped it to Corbin across the circle.

When Amar reached for the sandwich, Corbin tossed it to someone else. Amar couldn't believe he was sixteen years old and having to be "it" in a game of keep-away with his lunch. Kaylee intercepted the sandwich for Amar as the bell rang.

At morning break, Amar went straight to his locker to get his DMP. Panic filled his chest to the point of explosion when he realized the brand new, coolest, most expensive thing he ever owned wasn't there. He dug frantically through his bag and then his locker, but the DMP was gone.

"What are you doing, Amar?" Kaylee asked.

"I can't find it! I can't find it!"

"What?"

"My DMP!" Amar wrung his hands and stepped aside to let Kaylee look. "It was in my backpack."

Kaylee looked for a minute before she said, "I'm sorry, Amar. It's just not here. Are you sure it was in your bag?"

"Yes." Amar slid to the floor. "I put it back after I showed it to everyone."

"I remember. It was right before Rachel stole your sandwich."

"Yes, but what has that got…"

"I'll see ya later, Amar."

Amar could think of little else besides his DMP during the rest of his morning classes. How could he tell his parents he lost it? It made his stomach hurt so much he couldn't eat his lunch. Instead of going to the cafeteria, Amar checked the lost and found, then retraced his steps looking for his DMP. Back at his locker, Amar tore everything out of it and emptied his backpack. He turned up nothing.

"Where have you been?" Kaylee asked. "I've been looking all over the place for you."

"I was trying to find my DMP."

"I know where it is."

Amar snapped to attention. "Where? Give it to me."

"I don't have it, Amar."

"Then who does?"

"Rachel."

"What?"

"You know how Rachel started a game of keep-away with your sandwich this morning?" Kaylee began explaining.

"Yeah, it was totally stupid."

"Well, while we were paying attention to that little game she stole your DMP."

"How do you know? Did you see her?"

"Well, no, but I did just see her with your DMP on the basketball courts at break."

"Are you sure?" Amar asked.

"Yep, pretty sure."

"What should I do?"

"Come on, let's go talk to her. Maybe we'll catch her with it and she'll just give it back to you."

Amar followed Kaylee but not willingly. He didn't want to confront Rachel, because he knew she was like a badger when cornered. She tore a person to shreds if she felt threatened. Accusing her of stealing was bound to make her feel threatened. But Amar's optimistic side hoped that Rachel had the DMP and that she would hand it over and then make a joke about how she tricked him. It would be funny. Wouldn't it?

Kaylee marched over to Rachel. Amar stayed a few steps back, but he could see Rachel didn't have the DMP. "Rachel, do you have Amar's DMP?"

"No," Rachel stepped toward Kaylee. "Why would I?"

"I saw you with it, Rachel."

"No you didn't. I didn't steal it."

"Nobody said anything about stealing except you. All I'm saying is I saw you with it."

"I don't care what you think you saw. Listen very carefully to me, because I'm only saying this one more time. I...don't...have...it." Rachel stepped around Kaylee. "Amar, do you believe her?"

Amar watched in amazement as Rachel seemed to flip a switch. She blinked hard and then started crying. When the first large tear spilled onto her cheek, Rachel said, "Why would I steal from you? I wouldn't do that. You are my freaky foreign friend. I love you."

Kaylee rolled her eyes. "Really?"

Rachel wiped her eyes and sniffled. "I can't believe this. Kaylee, what did I do to you? I thought you were my friend."

"I'm sorry, Rachel," said Amar. He turned and started to walk away.

Kaylee was immediately on his heels. "Ugh! Amar, you can't believe her! I saw her with your DMP! I know I did."

"Maybe she has one like it."

"Amar, she doesn't. Even if she did, don't you think she would have said so? She took yours. I know it."

"I don't know. I think I need more proof."

"Fine. Somebody else is bound to see her. Check your e-mail tonight."

"Okay." Amar didn't want to admit that he too thought Rachel stole his DMP and he was afraid of turning her in. He didn't want to be badgered until his reputation was in ruins. What if Kaylee kept her word and got proof? Then what would he do?

After returning home that night from bussing tables, Amar quickly grabbed a snack and went to his room. He turned on his computer and logged into his e-mail account. He saw there were five e-mails from various friends as well as one from Kaylee.

Amar opened the first:

Amar, I saw Rachel with your DMP in the locker room before our game. I asked her where she got it and she told me she bought it yesterday. Good luck! – Anna

The other e-mails were similar and they were all from reliable people. He opened Kaylee's e-mail last:

Amar, I hope everyone sent their e-mails to you. There's your proof. If you want your DMP back, you have to turn her in! Print out the e-mails and bring them to school and I'll help you. See you tomorrow. – Kaylee

Amar felt like a little boy again in the backseat of the car as his father drove wildly through abandoned streets without the headlights on while escaping their country. Why should he feel that way? He was in no danger. The very fact that he felt that way made him angry.

Amar sprang up from his seat and began pacing. He mumbled to himself, "Who am I? Why am I scared? I'm not the one who did something wrong. Why should I be afraid of Rachel? What kind of man am I? I have to stand up like my parents did! If they hadn't, we would have nothing, including our lives."

Amar's rants were interrupted by a pounding on his door. "Amar! What are you doing? Is your homework finished?" his father called.

"Yes. I mean no."

"Then get it done. Maybe you should put that new gadget away so you can concentrate."

"Yeah, I'll do that."

Amar sat at his computer and started a new document. He typed *My Goals* at the top. He thought for a minute about how to set SMART goals like his careers teacher had taught him. The first goal he wrote: *Ask Kaylee out.* His second: *Turn Rachel in for stealing my DMP.* Amar typed a plan for completing the two goals and continued on. He was on a roll and didn't want to stop.

Amar stayed up well into the night setting goals. Some of them he could and would do right away while others were long-term and needed a lot of work, but together his goals would create a strong, confident Amar.

The next morning Kaylee was waiting for Amar. "You look terrible," she said. "Who do you want to go to: Mr. Leslie or Officer Strictor?"

"Mr. Leslie, I guess."

"Do you want me to go in with you?"

"I do," Amar said, "but I think I better go by myself. It's my DMP. I would like to ask you about something at break, though."

By the end of the school day, Amar had his DMP back and a date with Kaylee for the upcoming weekend. But most importantly, Amar had his self-respect.

TEEN CONNECTIONS

- In what ways does Amar fit the definition of a passive personality?
- Why do you think Amar is passive?
- How does Amar change his passive behaviors?

PARENT CONNECTIONS

- Why didn't Amar's parents need to get involved in this situation?
- Why is it important to empower your teen to deal with peers?
- What about this situation made it safe for Amar to handle it on his own?

Teen Section 4

The Doormat Kid

Passive behavior is indicated by letter *A* answers on your quiz. If these make up ten or more of your answers, we have one thing to say to you: STOP BEING A VICTIM! Passive personalities make perfect targets for harassers. A passive person's worst enemy, however, is not a bully. It's him or herself. How can that be? Passive people have a lose-win attitude. They see themselves as life's losers while everyone else is a winner. They act out of that belief. Passive people won't stand up for themselves, because in their minds they're going to lose anyway. Bullies pick on those who won't stand up for themselves and their rights. If passive people want to stop being victims, they have to become assertive.

Some of you may be thinking that you didn't have very many passive answers, but if you had *any A* answers you have things to work on. We are sure that while reading this section you will come across things that make you say, "Hey, I do that sometimes." That means you have some passive tendencies that you need to fix. As you read you may also find yourself thinking, "Hey, I let someone else be passive." If you let someone be passive, you aren't doing him or her any favors. You are helping that person maintain a losing attitude.

Whether you are passive, have a few passive things to work on or don't mind having a few passive friends, this section will reveal to you what it means to be passive, why people are passive and how passive people can become assertive.

What Does Being Passive Mean?

We've seen how passive people are victims. Now, as you read through the characteristics of a passive person, ask yourself if you do those things or if you allow someone else to do them. You don't have to fit all of the definitions in order to be passive and there are varying degrees of passiveness. Think about situations and people that may prompt you to act passively. Look back on your list of *A* answers in teen section 3. Remember, nobody is perfect. Here are some traits passive people portray.

Letting Others Make Decisions for Them

Passive people don't make decisions. They depend on others to tell them what to do and what to think. This becomes dangerous when the people giving orders are aggressive. Passive people need to realize that those they let make decisions for them may not care about their well-being.

Just because you are a teen and adults sometimes tell you what to do, this does not mean that anybody can tell you what to think. If you are assertive you don't let your peers tell you what to think or do. It's like that old saying, "If your friends jumped off a cliff, would you?" Passive people wouldn't think twice about jumping.

Believing Their Thoughts or Feelings Don't Count

Passive people don't make their own decisions, so they are not going to feel that anything going on inside their heads or hearts means anything. Why would they? Passive people believe if they express how they feel or what they think then others won't like them. It's more comfortable for the passive person to take on the thoughts and feelings of someone else. In fact, they pretty much want to be someone else. In the example, the conversation among the girls shows how easily a passive person will sway.

> Mrs. Thompson was monitoring her hallway at school early one afternoon and overheard this conversation:
> Tina, a popular girl, stated, "I really like tacos. I think we should go to the taco stand today."
> Bethany replied, "I like tacos too. That sounds good to me."
> This was when Laura, the ultimate in popularity, joined in the conversation. "I hate tacos and the taco stand is just gross anyway. Let's go somewhere else."
> "Yeah, I don't really like tacos either. I was just kidding," Bethany said.
> This conversation may seem trivial, but the more Mrs. Thompson thought about it, the more she worried about Bethany. If she would give in so easily on tacos and where to get them, what else would she give way to in order to fit in?

Putting Themselves Last

Passive people believe that putting everyone else first is their most positive characteristic. After all, what can be better than taking care of others? It is a great thing to think about friends and family, but when you're always putting yourself last, *you* are always last. That is not a good feeling. Keeping yourself in mind doesn't mean that you don't care about other people. It just means that you value yourself as well as your relationships. Melissa's determination to put her family members' concerns before her own put her in a dangerous situation.

Melissa was sexually molested by her uncle. She didn't tell anyone about the abuse. Melissa decided to put her aunt, her cousins, her grandma and her parents first. She didn't want to ruin her aunt's marriage, take away her cousins' father or admit to her grandmother she wasn't strong. She also felt she needed to protect her parents, who would believe the abuse was somehow their fault.

The abuse went on until Melissa couldn't take it anymore. She realized that she couldn't protect everyone any longer. Melissa's secrets were eating at her from the inside and affecting her ability to function. She had to stop protecting her family and take care of herself if she hoped to experience security and happiness.

Striving to Please Others

Passive people use an amazing amount of energy trying to be a part of the popular clique or being perfect for their parents or teachers. They live to please others. Unfortunately, aggressive people find them and use that need to please to their advantage. Passive people have to understand that taking care of themselves and doing what feels right to them has to happen in order to reach independence and a positive sense of self. When they can do that, they will no longer be targets for aggressive people.

If you are not the classic passive case, there are probably people or situations that make you want to be passive. The key is to know when you're feeling this way and make an effort not to be passive.

- **MYTH:** If I don't fit into all the definitions, then I must not be passive.
- **TRUTH:** Any passive behaviors will hurt your chances at confidence and success. Harassers sense and exploit any passive weaknesses.

Why Be Passive?

Even though being passive can be incredibly self-destructive, there are still people who regularly behave passively. So why do they do it? Because it's a habit and there are rewards for being passive.

Not all of the things we will discuss apply to all passive people. For example, some passive people seek attention while others become loners. Please keep in mind that we're not giving you this information to you to make you feel bad. We're giving it to you in the hope of prompting some change. Here are several reasons people become passive.

They Fear the Loss of Approval

Passive people are people pleasers. They fold under peer pressure and generally are followers. They believe nobody will like them if they stand up for themselves. They can only see themselves through others' eyes. What they fail to realize is that in their desire to gain approval, they get used by others, especially harassers. Being used is not the same as being liked. In fact, passive people are never really a part of any group, because people don't respect those who won't stand up for themselves. Strong relationships are based on respect.

They Become Loners

There are those passive people whose motto is, "I don't care" and that is the way they live. They don't care to talk, to make friends, to have relationships, to do schoolwork, to get a job, to really live. The more they retreat from life, however, the more harassers seek them out. The student Layne portrays many of these passive attitudes:

> Layne walked through the noisy cafeteria on his way to the table in the back where he always sat alone to eat. He held his tray, with a piece of pizza balanced on top, close to his body as he shuffled past the *cool* table. Layne was almost clear of the noisy hum of popularity when a hand reached out and took the pizza off his tray.
>
> Layne kept walking. It wasn't the first time he wouldn't get to eat his lunch.

They Hate Conflict

Passive people not only dislike and avoid conflict but also have a distorted view of what conflict is. A healthy debate is instead viewed as an argument. Standing up for themselves might be considered to be fighting or mean. Passive people let others tell them what to think. Bullies believe that passive people will never tell on them, because passive people avoid conflict at all costs.

They View Passiveness as Feminine

Statistically there are more females who are passive than males. Historically, women in most cultures were taught to be subservient. Even today, some are told that being passive is a feminine characteristic. How wrong that is.

We're sure you can think of extreme examples such as a woman who stays in an abusive relationship or one who lets a guy boss her around, but there are more subtle examples as well. One of our pet peeves is a girl who is very intelligent, but when she hangs out with guys she becomes the world's biggest airhead. A young woman who acts like this believes appearing smart isn't feminine and men won't be attracted to her. In actuality, the guys she will attract are those who are aggressive. It is not feminine to be a victim.

They Fear Responsibility

If you never think for yourself or make your own decisions, then you never have to take responsibility for anything! Passive people lose their independence when they refuse to be responsible. Everything, including their very happiness, is handed over to someone else. Unfortunately, it's usually a bully who is willing to take over.

If confidence, happiness, healthy relationships, independence and success are important to you, then you have to be assertive. You will never gain those things by being passive. Fearing responsibility is like saying you fear those things we just mentioned. When you look at it that way, it just doesn't make much sense to be passive, does it?

It's What They Know

Passive behavior is often learned. If you don't know how to be anything else but passive, it is hard to admit that you are indeed passive. The first step is admitting you have a problem and you need to unlearn some things.

Where do you learn passive behavior? In an abusive relationship, a passive person often pairs with an aggressive person. When these two people happen to be your parents or someone else you're around a lot, it's hard to be assertive. Children from these types of homes usually choose either the passive person or the aggressive person to copy. That's why abuse is a cycle, because it's passed from one generation to the next. We do what we know and we know how those we are close to behave. This doesn't mean that if you come from a dysfunctional family you can't become assertive. It won't be easy, because you have to unlearn and create new habits, but it is possible and it will be worth it. In Brock's instance, the passive behavior of his grandmother greatly affected his own actions.

> Brock was very close to his grandmother. He grew up wanting to be just like her. Brock's grandfather called his grandma fat and stupid all the time. Brock's aunt stole money from his grandma's purse to buy drugs. Brock's grandma never said or did anything about any of it. Brock naturally believed that a relationship meant that those you loved had the right to treat you like dirt.

When Brock was in high school, he had a girlfriend who treated him poorly, called him names and on occasion hit him. But Brock was like his role model, his grandma, so he worked hard trying to make his girlfriend happy so she would love him.

They Like the Rewards for Being the Victim

This is the hardest thing for passive people to hear. Therefore, it is also the one that passive people deny the most. Being a victim is what passive people know. It's how they get attention. That attention is their reward and passive people thrive on it.

Here's a common example and a situation that most of us have encountered. There's a girl in the hall, maybe she's a friend, but she looks sad or angry. You ask, "What's the matter?"

She replies, "Nothing."

You know the game; you know you're supposed to ask again and again until she finally tells why she's upset. Why do you have to ask so many times? Why is there always something wrong? Because passive people are addicted to the attention they get when there's drama in their lives. Assertive people wouldn't want that kind of attention, but passive people do.

Sadly, there are often very tragic and dramatic things going on in a passive person's life. Many times, after we get through the "nothing" answers, there is indeed a real reason for them to be sad or angry. What the passive person needs to realize is that there will always be tragedy in their lives if they continue to let things happen *to* them. Who's doing those things to them? It's the aggressive personalities, the harassers of our society. When you don't stand up for yourself or your rights, you take no responsibility and you let others make your decisions, life is going to be hard, dramatic and often tragic.

Now we've looked into the whys of passiveness. However, that doesn't mean you're off the hook for your passive behaviors. Your actions or lack of actions are your responsibility. It is also your responsibility to make the changes to become an independent person who is no longer harassed.

- **MYTH:** Passive people deserve to be bullied.
- **TRUTH:** *Nobody* deserves to be bullied! However, there are situations where a passive person is so addicted to being a victim that he or she will attempt to provoke a bully. In these cases, both the passive person and the aggressive person should be held accountable. We will cover this type of behavior (called passive/aggressive) in chapter 7 *Dealing with Harassment Issues*.

Changing the Passive to Assertive

Until passive people decide to stand up and be assertive, which means taking control of their lives, they will always be victims. Some of our passive readers may be saying, "I don't care," because that is what passive people say a lot. You may say it, but we don't believe you. Really, you don't care if you get picked on, walked over, ignored and left out? You don't care that you get little positive attention, you live in fear and your life is a constant, stressful drama? We don't think so.

We're not going to tell you it's easy to change, because it's not. The things in our lives that are the most important are usually not easy. But now is the time to change. It will only get harder as you get older.

Many times passive students believe they can wait before becoming assertive, because they won't be in school forever. It's the "everything will go away when I graduate" theory. The truth is a passive personality will not magically go away when you leave school. There are plenty of adult bullies waiting for passive people in relationships and in the workplace. And there will be far fewer people who want or have the time to help you than there are right now. So become assertive now.

Habits are hard to break, particularly bad ones. Because it is difficult, know that you can't do it all at once. You need to be SMART when it comes to setting goals.

SMART Goals[1]

S = Specific. What are you going to do? How are you going to do it? Why is it important to do it?

M = Measurable. How are you going to measure it? When will you know the goal is accomplished?

A = Attainable. Is the goal challenging but reachable? Does it require a commitment but won't stretch you too thin?

R = Realistic. Do you have a reasonable plan to reach the goal? Will the achievement be satisfying?

T = Timely. When are you going to start working on your goal? Do you have a time frame for completing this goal?

Using the SMART method of goal setting will help you decide on goals that are right for you. Next are things that passive people need to work on. Be SMART and don't try to do all of them at once. Choose one or two and start small.

Change the Way You Look

How do you change the way you look and what does that have to do with being passive? Well, passive people show outward signs that they are passive. It's like a poker player who smirks when he has a good hand. Everyone at the table knows to fold. This is called a *tell*. If you can change your passive tells, you can bluff others into believing you're assertive. It's the "fake it 'til you make it" principle. You will be amazed how differently others will treat you just because of your assertive appearance.

To get some ideas for changing the "victim look," observe assertive people. You know who they are, but if you're not sure, look at chapter 6. Copy what assertive people do: facial expressions, posture, tone of voice, eye contact and the way they carry themselves. Practice in front of a mirror, speak into a recorder or videotape yourself to gain some confidence before trying these things out in real situations. If you have someone you trust, someone you know is assertive and will give you honest feedback, practice with that person.

- **Eye contact:** When you speak to someone, do you look the person in the eye or do you prefer the floor, the ceiling, anywhere but the eyes? When there is no eye contact, the person you are speaking to is left wondering if you are lying, if he or she is too hideous to look at or if you're listening at all. The lack of eye contact is very common to passive personalities.

- **Voice:** Is your voice soft or whiny? Do you sound like you are about to cry? Do you never talk at all? Confident, assertive people talk with ease at a normal volume level and tone.

- **Posture:** Do you try to make yourself as small and unnoticeable as possible? Passive people believe if they sink low enough in a chair then no one will see them there, teachers won't ask them questions and nobody will pick on them. It won't work, so you might as well concentrate on being comfortable in your own skin. Stand or sit against a wall with your back, shoulders and head touching it. This is what good posture feels like; practice it. Stacey made the decision to change her body language and spent time working on her assertive mannerisms.

Stacey knew she should change her passive ways, but it was overwhelming. She decided she would start with trying not to appear passive. Stacey told her friend, "I'm not going to look like such a weenie anymore. If I can change what's going on with the outside, nobody will know how scared I am about everything on the inside."

After working on eye contact, voice and posture, Stacey said, "It's amazing, because when I stopped looking like a passive person, people stopped treating me like one. I know I have a lot more work to do, but I feel more confident than I ever have."

Make a Decision

If you are a seriously passive person, start making small decisions or pick one situation where you can take charge. Maybe it's where to eat, what to read or what to wear. Once you get used to making decisions on little things, it will be easier to make them on bigger issues. Remember to ask yourself these two questions: "How do *I* feel about this?" and "What do *I* want?"

Express a Thought or a Feeling

If expressing your thoughts or feelings is something you never do, begin by making small changes, because they will be uncomfortable at first. You may even feel like you're picking a fight, because mistaking assertiveness for aggressiveness is part of being passive. Pick a class where you feel safest and add to the discussion or tell a friend about something you like or dislike and don't change your viewpoint if another person disagrees.

Using "I" statements may make expressing yourself easier. "I" statements are simply those that begin with "I". These are good to practice in front of a mirror or with someone you trust for some extra confidence. Here are some examples, but you need to fill in the rest of the sentences.

"I" Statements

- I want...
- I need...
- I like/love...
- I dislike...
- I don't like it when you...
- I feel like...
- I'm not going to...
- I agree/disagree because...
- I can/can't...

If you didn't notice, making "I" statements makes you put yourself first, which is something passive people don't do. It feels great to think of yourself first and say what you feel.

Put Yourself First

It is not selfish to set aside time for yourself to take care of your needs and wants. If you have never done this, start with an hour. For one hour a day, you are going to do nothing but what you want to do. That may be going for a walk, watching a favorite TV program, using the computer—whatever sounds good to you. If you do this for one hour, you will get used to doing the things you want to do and it will become an important part of your life.

Part of putting yourself first is getting out of "people pleaser" mode. How do you do that? Learn to say no to the things that you don't want to do and the things that are not good for you. Of course, you are a teenager, so we don't suggest practicing this skill on adults who have your best interest at heart.

When you are being asked or told to do something by a peer, ask yourself these questions: Is this something I want? Is this something that is healthy for me? If the answer to either or both of these questions is "no", then decline your peer's request. Use your "I" statements or use an excuse if you need to: "No, I can't go, because my mom expects me home." David took some time to work up the courage to say no to doing something he didn't want to do.

David knew he needed to learn to say no. He decided that he should start by expressing his disagreement to his best friend Chad. Chad had started going to wild parties, smoking and drinking to excess. Chad wanted David to do these things with him. At first, David couldn't say no to his friend so he went along and participated. They had not been caught yet, but David knew it was only a matter of time. David worried about his ability to make the baseball team and also didn't like the way partying made him feel physically.

David dreaded the next weekend, because he knew Chad would ask him to go to a party. When that happened, David said, "I can't."

"Why not?"

"I want to make the baseball team and that's more important to me than going to some party. I don't want to lose you as a friend, but I don't want to go where you're going."

It's probably not a good idea to start working on the new, assertive you with your harasser or the person who frightens you the most. You may find, however, that as you become more assertive the bullying will take care of itself. Assertive people scare harassers, because they have the confidence vibe that says they can deal with pretty much anybody or any situation that comes their way. With some courage and determination, that can be you!

- **MYTH:** Becoming violent will solve my passive problems.
- **TRUTH:** No, it won't. If you beat up a bully or do something worse, it will only get you into trouble. Then you are no better than the bully. In the story of Emma and Dillon we discussed previously, Emma could have beaten up Dillon, but she chose the higher road. It may not have been easier, but it was better. In a fight, the law or your school isn't going to take your need to stand up for yourself into account. The best and healthiest way to stop bullying is to be assertive. If you feel like you want to be violent, please find a trusted adult and tell him or her what's going on.

FILL OUT AT LEAST ONE GOAL SETTING SHEET AT THE END OF THIS SECTION. STICK TO YOUR GOAL. USE THE OTHER SHEETS FOR GUIDANCE UNTIL YOU GET USED TO SETTING AND ACHIEVING GOALS. DON'T FORGET TO BE SMART!

TEEN CONNECTIONS

- In what ways does Amar fit the definition of a passive personality?

  Amar allowed others to make decisions for him. He let Rachel decide he didn't need a DMP and he let Kaylee decide he shouldn't let Rachel get away with it. He put himself last, because it wasn't about his rights, it was about not getting Rachel into trouble or not disappointing Kaylee. This was also a part of being a people pleaser. Amar tried to please Rachel, because she was popular, Kaylee, because he liked her, and his parents, because he didn't want to disappoint them.

- Why do you think Amar is passive?

  We can only guess about the why, but to us there are only two reasons why Amar was passive: he was a people pleaser and hated conflict. He wasn't a loner, he didn't fear responsibility and his behavior was not learned. However, we think he feared the loss of approval. Amar wanted to make everyone happy. In this situation, like many, this was impossible. Amar also hated conflict. If he didn't, he would have had no problem asking Rachel for his DMP or turning her in.

- How does Amar change his passive behaviors?

  Amar did the right thing by setting goals and creating a plan and a timeline for completing them. He was very SMART. The specific things about which he set goals were making decisions, expressing a thought or a feeling and putting himself first. If he had not done this, Amar would have lost his DMP for good and never asked Kaylee out.

Now we have looked at some ways you can change your passive speech and behavior, ways to stop doing things you don't like and ways to prevent things you don't want to happen. Remember, start with small changes and gradually you'll become the person you want to be.

SMART Goal:

Today's date: Completion date:

Why do I need to reach this goal?	How and when will I work toward this goal?	# of times (per day, week, month)	Status (how's it going)

Possible Difficulties:

SMART Goal:

Today's date: Completion date:

Why do I need to reach this goal?	How and when will I work toward this goal?	# of times (per day, week, month)	Status (how's it going)

Possible Difficulties:

SMART Goal:

Today's date: Completion date:

Why do I need to reach this goal?	How and when will I work toward this goal?	# of times (per day, week, month)	Status (how's it going)

Possible Difficulties:

SMART Goal:

Today's date: Completion date:

Why do I need to reach this goal?	How and when will I work toward this goal?	# of times (per day, week, month)	Status (how's it going)

Possible Difficulties:

Parent Section 4

The Passive Parent

Passive behavior is indicated by letter *A* answers on the quiz you completed. The parent quiz involves questions about individual behaviors as well as parenting behaviors. In teen section 4 you learned what it means to have a passive personality, why people are passive and how to become assertive. The information in teen section 4 applies to all individuals, not just teens. Like your teen, if you have any passive answers you have things to work on, particularly because if you have passive personality traits you will parent passively. Through becoming assertive you are not only bettering yourself but also helping your teen.

This parent section focuses on the passive parenting skills that may be contributing to your teen's victimization or to your teen's aggression. Keep in mind that the reason you picked up this book is to help your teen become someone who is not a victim or an abuser. Honestly analyzing your parenting skills is important in building an assertive teen. There is no such thing as a perfect parent and nobody has all the right answers, but this section can provide insight by defining a passive parent and giving you examples of passive thought processes that may contribute to your teens' issues with harassment.

What Is a Passive Parent?

Parents have a great deal of influence on their children. A teen may be struggling with passivity because of learned behavior. Conversely, a teen may be exhibiting aggressive behaviors, because passive parents give complete control to him or her and the teen takes advantage of that power. If you want your teen to become an assertive person who is not a victim or an aggressor, you have to stop parenting passively.

We care for our children and want them to be successful. Keep that desire in mind as you read what it means for your teen when you are a passive parent. Here are some traits passive parents portray.

Letting Others Make Decisions for Them

Passive people don't make decisions. Neither do passive parents. Passive parents don't have boundaries or rules for their teens or if they do, they don't follow through with consequences or rewards. All of those things require decisions. Passive parents yield to schools, church leaders, law enforcement, relatives or spouses to make decisions regarding their teens. The product of this lack of decision making by parents is teens who passively allow others to run their lives when they should be beginning to make some decisions on their own in order to gain independence. Unfortunately, those who are willing to make decisions for your teen are harassers.

Lack of decision making on the part of parents may also create teens who are harassers. These teens take complete charge of decision making in their lives when their maturity level or brain development is not actually ready to handle it. The result is teens who make negative decisions and then are completely surprised when they suffer uncomfortable consequences for those choices.

Passive parents avoid decision making; thus, they don't model the decision making process for their teens, nor do they guide their teens through the practice of making decisions for themselves. Passive parents need to make decisions and take responsibility for those decisions. Then they can teach their children to do the same. Teens who know how to make decisions for themselves are far less likely to be victims or harassers, because they have the self-confidence that comes with being responsible and in control of their lives.

Believing Their Thoughts or Feelings Don't Count

Parents who have the passive belief that their thoughts and feelings don't count may foster teenage sons and daughters who behave and speak in ways that are not respected by their peers, because they are emulating their parents' behavior. Passive parents don't believe the thoughts and feelings of their teens count for much either. Therefore, passive parents don't listen to their teens. If teens aren't being validated at home, what would make them think that the other teenagers at school or in any social group would care about what they think or feel about anything?

Peer respect is a huge concern for teens. Many teens equate respect with popularity. It is true that some of the so-called popular teens are harassers, but it is also true that those kings and queens of the junior and senior high school halls are not afraid to stand up for themselves. Teens who don't express—much less stand up for—their thoughts and feelings will never gain respect from their peers. Neither will teens who aggressively force their points of view on everyone. Parents have the responsibility to model and teach their children how to express themselves effectively yet kindly.

Adolescents need to know what their parents stand for. They are watching and listening to you. If you've done your job right, they won't always agree with you. The decisions we make are based on what we think and how we feel about things. Therefore, the lack of expression, decision making and responsibility as well as a disregard for personal rights contribute to the victimization of passive parents' teens.

Putting Themselves Last

If you ask passive people about their best qualities they will probably say they take care of everyone else before themselves. The passive parent says the same. However, always putting yourself last comes not only at a great personal cost, but also at a cost for your teen. If you put yourself last, your teen may believe that is what it means to be a good person. In actuality, it will make him or her a target for harassers. It's a sad fact that the teens who put themselves last are the ones who have low self-esteem, get taken advantage of and are harassed.

Passive parents who put themselves last may also have teens who take advantage of them emotionally, physically and financially. Making sure your teen gets whatever he or she wants at any cost will not gain you respect or admiration. It will only alert your aggressive teenage son or daughter to the fact that he or she can walk all over you and still get whatever he or she wants. It will not stop until you put your needs and desires first.

You cannot truly take care of someone else if your own needs aren't satisfied. Assertive parents model and guide their teens to the realization that taking care of others requires balance. It requires equality between the individual's needs and the needs of the people he or she cares about. When balance is achieved, so is respect.

Striving to Please Their Teens

When passive parents aim to please, their teens may become people pleasers themselves. These teens make easy targets for harassers. They won't tell on bullies, because they don't want to get anyone in trouble. They try to convince themselves and others that a harasser's behavior is okay, maybe even funny. Perhaps most importantly, when a victim confides in a passive parent, the advice he or she receives is not at all helpful, because the passive parent doesn't want to cause any problems. Thus, people pleasing can become dangerous, because the teen's safety and security takes a backseat to pleasing others.

Passive parents may also end up with aggressive teenagers, because they hand all the power to their teens. Teens are not mature enough to receive that kind of control. Passive parents aim to be their teens' friends.

Boundaries for a parent figure are different from those for a friend, because parents should set rules, consequences and rewards. Assertive parents are not always liked by their teens, but they are respected. Assertive parents guide their teens to success, independence and assertiveness. Teens already have friends; they need their parents to be parents. In Gina's instance, her passive parenting resulted in her son Max bullying her and not achieving his potential.

> "Mom, I need your cell phone. I can't find mine."
> "Sorry, Max, but I have an important call for work I have to make." Immediately Gina regretted turning her son down.
> "I said I need your phone and I need it now."
> Gina didn't understand how her son had gotten this way. After all, he shouldn't have been at home; he should have been at school working on a high school diploma. At the very least, he should have been at one of the countless jobs Gina and her husband Dan had used their personal connections to get him. Gina whispered, "No."
> "Stupid bitch!" Max grabbed Gina by the shoulders and drove her into an open closet. He slammed it shut and jammed a chair under the knob.
> Gina listened to Max dig through her purse, finding the cell phone and whatever cash she had. As she tried not to listen to Max using her phone to arrange purchasing drugs, she thought about how she'd ended up in a closet. She and Dan had given Max anything he wanted and whenever he got into trouble they bailed him out using any means necessary. They were his friends.

Trying to please others, including your teen, is a dangerous game. If you try to appease everyone, you are in essence giving control over to someone else. Unfortunately, those who are willing to take that control from you won't care about your teen's rights or your rights either. Parenting is not about pleasing anyone; it's about ensuring that your child is safe and secure and has a genuine chance at happiness.

Fearing Taking Responsibility for Their Teens

It is the parents' job to take care of their children's physical and emotional needs and raise them to become lifelong learners and contributors to society. In order to become assertive parents, passive parents have to quit letting others be responsible for their children. Teens like to think they are old enough to take care of themselves, but there is biological and psychological evidence to the contrary. You are the best choice to raise an assertive teen, not a school, church or law enforcement agency.

If you want to be an assertive parent, step up and take responsibility for your teenage son or daughter. If your teen is currently a victim, you need to ask yourself these questions:

- Is my passive parenting style contributing to the victimization of my teen?
- What personality changes do I need to make in order to model assertive behavior?
- What are my teen's passive behaviors that may be making him or her a target?
- Does my teen need me to back off and let him or her handle something on his or her own?

Taking responsibility means owning up to some things that may not be pretty. There are reasons why your teens are victims. It's your responsibility to discover those reasons and what you need to do to help them, even if it means letting them be independent.

Passive parenting skills may also induce your teen to become aggressive. If your teen is a harasser, you need to ask yourself these questions:

- Is my passive parenting style contributing to the aggression of my teen?
- What personality changes do I need to make in order to model assertive behavior?
- Do I need to stand up for myself with my teen?
- Does my teen need me to back off and let him or her experience negative consequences for his or her behavior?

Again, taking responsibility for the child you have raised is not always easy, particularly if you have a teen who is hurting. If you are honest in your answers to these questions, you are well on your way to taking responsibility. The next step is to honestly discuss how to obtain and maintain a harassment-free future with your teen. Your teen has to know that you are stepping up to take responsibility. An excellent way to begin talking is by sharing with them the SMART goals you will create at the end of this section.

Assertive parents, unlike passive or aggressive parents, excel at taking responsibility for their teenagers. They also teach their children how to be responsible for themselves through modeling and acting as guides regarding decision making, including rewards when those decisions are good ones and consequences when their choices are not so good. When you are responsible and you teach your child responsibility, parenting becomes a much easier and less stressful proposition.

Adolescents need parents to be responsible, make decisions and stand up for their rights and beliefs. Change is possible; helping your teen is possible. It will take some work, but don't give up on yourself or your child. When you give up, you allow your teen the option of giving up too. In a possibly hostile environment, surrendering can have dire consequences.

Passive versus Assertive Thought Processes

Now you know what being a passive person and a passive parent means as well as how to become an assertive individual and therefore an assertive parent. Here are some examples of the thought processes of a passive parent versus an assertive one. If you recognize any of these passive thought patterns as being similar to your own, you have work to do to become an assertive parent.

Passive Parent Thinking	Assertive Parent Knowing
It's not my fault my teen is a victim/harasser.	I am responsible for my teen. I have a part in what he or she is doing and what is happening to him or her. My teen's behaviors may be learned from me so I need to look objectively at my actions and my decisions.
I want to be my teen's friend and I don't understand why he or she doesn't respect me.	Teens need parents, not friends. Good parents have boundaries, rules, consequences and rewards for their teens. I will also stand up for my rights and express my thoughts and feelings to my teen. I will earn respect if I am a parent.

Passive Parent Thinking	Assertive Parent Knowing
My teen is too young to make his or her own decisions or stand up for him or herself, particularly when it comes to something like harassment. It is my job to do that.	My teen is at a stage in his or her life when I need to back off and let him or her handle some things on his or her own. I have done my job, in that I have modeled good decision making and how to assert personal rights. I will act as a guide and offer advice when it is asked for. Unless the harassment is severe, persistent or pervasive, I will help my teen handle it on his or her own.
My teen is old enough to take care of him or herself.	I know my teen is at a stage of life when he or she needs a parent to guide him or her, create boundaries and teach how to learn from personal mistakes. My teen may not always like me and may try to convince me I'm not needed, but I know better, because I am the parent.
My teen is the victim of harassment and therefore has no responsibility in the situation.	Because I am a responsible parent, I teach my teen responsibility. If harassment is happening, we will discuss how to make it stop, which will include how my teen may be making him or herself a target for harassers.
My teen's school administration will take care of any problems with harassment he or she is having.	It is not a school administrator's responsibility to solve my teen's problems. Nor is it a counselor's, law enforcement's or anyone else's. It is mine. I know that there are many school officials and others who will be good resources for me and offer me helpful services, but I have to be an advocate for my teen.

Passive Parent Thinking	Assertive Parent Knowing
My teen is perfectly behaved. I don't understand why he or she is a victim at school.	Normal teens make mistakes, take reasonable risks, rebel, talk back and test boundaries with adults. So-called "perfect" teens are people pleasers and therefore likely targets for harassers.
I believe teens will be teens. I don't want to get anyone in trouble.	Harassment is a serious behavior at any age. If my teen feels like he or she is being harassed, then he or she is. I will try to help my teen prevent being harassed, but if the harassment is severe, persistent or pervasive, I am not afraid to get someone in trouble in the interest of keeping my teen safe and secure.
When dealing with a harasser, my teen only needs to "kill him with kindness" and try really hard to become his or her friend.	Helping my teen become assertive will stop the harassment. If I tell my teen to make friends with a harasser when this person doesn't have any respect for him or her, it will only cause the harassment to escalate.
I don't know why I deserve to be humiliated or physically abused by my teen.	I won't let anyone abuse me, especially my teen. I respect myself and therefore earn respect from my teen. I set boundaries with my teen and therefore he or she will not humiliate or abuse me. I know that no one deserves to be harassed.

It is never too late to become an assertive parent. Become an assertive person first and the assertive parenting will follow. Once you are assertive, you can model assertiveness and be a guide for your teen as he or she works to become an independent member of society. It is the best thing you can do to ensure your child does not become a lifetime victim or abuser. Teens are watching and hearing their parents even when parents think they are not. If you're not a victim in your own life, it will go a long way toward ensuring your teen is not a victim either.

- **MYTH:** Teens who are nice to everyone will always be treated well by others.
- **TRUTH:** Being nice is great, but niceness without self-esteem makes teens targets, because bullies know the "too nice" teens will not stand up for themselves. Teens need to observe their parents' behavior as well as learn from them that being nice doesn't equal being respected.

 USING THE GOAL SETTING SHEETS AT THE END OF THIS SECTION, FILL OUT AT LEAST ONE FOR A PASSIVE BEHAVIOR YOU HAVE AND ONE FOR A PASSIVE PARENTING SKILL YOU HAVE. USE THE OTHER SHEETS FOR GUIDANCE UNTIL YOU GET USED TO SETTING AND ACHIEVING GOALS. DON'T FORGET TO BE A SMART PARENT!

PARENT CONNECTIONS

- Why didn't Amar's parents need to get involved in this situation?

  Amar's safety wasn't compromised. Even if his parents were made aware of the situation, it would have been a wise decision for them to back off and let Amar handle Rachel's behavior. When parents let teens handle harassment that is not severe, persistent or pervasive on their own, they empower their teens. With empowerment comes self-respect and independence.

- Why is it important to empower your teen to deal with peers?

  If parents dictate their teens' decisions when dealing with harassing situations rather than acting as guides for them, they will create adults who are powerless and don't know how to be independent. Amar's parents obviously modeled and taught him how to be independent, because he knew he had to deal with the theft of his DMP or he would lose his self-respect.

- What about this situation made it safe for Amar to handle it on his own?

> The key word is safe. He wasn't in any physical danger and the emotional danger was losing self-respect if he let Rachel get away with stealing his most prized possession. If the harassment is not severe, persistent or pervasive, parents should let teens make their own decisions about what to do.

Becoming an assertive parent doesn't mean you won't pay attention to your teenager's opinions and desires. In fact, you'll listen and watch more closely, but you'll respond not as a companion but as a parent, teaching your growing child to be responsible and independent.

SMART Goal:

Today's date: Completion date:

Why do I need to reach this goal?	How and when will I work toward this goal?	# of times (per day, week, month)	Status (how's it going)

Possible Difficulties:

SMART Goal:

Today's date: Completion date:

Why do I need to reach this goal?	How and when will I work toward this goal?	# of times (per day, week, month)	Status (how's it going)

Possible Difficulties:

SMART Goal:

Today's date: Completion date:

Why do I need to reach this goal?	How and when will I work toward this goal?	# of times (per day, week, month)	Status (how's it going)

Possible Difficulties:

SMART Goal:

Today's date: Completion date:

Why do I need to reach this goal?	How and when will I work toward this goal?	# of times (per day, week, month)	Status (how's it going)

Possible Difficulties:

Chapter Five

Bullies and Aggressive Parents

Digital Media Player as Change Agent, Part 2

A closer look at Rachel, the bully who stole Amar's DMP, reveals the effects parents can have on their children and the behaviors their children learn. In Rachel's case, her mother's aggressive personality leads Rachel to act aggressively toward others. Serious legal consequences help Rachel realize she must change her ways in order to embark on the career path she desires.

Nothing happened during first period, during second period, not even during break. Rachel sauntered into English class feeling satisfied, because she was going to get away with it. Rachel was the proud owner of a brand new DMP, which she easily took from Amar. She told herself that if taking it was that easy, Amar didn't deserve to have it.

Rachel slid into her desk sideways and stretched her legs out in front of her. She smugly remembered the events of the previous day. It had actually started out as a horrible day. She woke up with the remnants of a hangover from Saturday night's party. She hoped the headache was the only thing she picked up at the party. She couldn't remember much, but there was some guy.

The headache wasn't made any better when Rachel stepped onto the bus and realized her usual seat was taken. Rachel couldn't do anything about it, because she almost got kicked off the bus last week for harassing some chick. Rachel tried to tell her mom it

113

wasn't her fault, that she was just joking and the bus driver didn't like her anyway, but her mom didn't buy it. She'd been punished with a beating and a screaming lecture for the bus incident. It was hard for Rachel to figure out when her mom was going to be on her side and when she wasn't, but when she wasn't Rachel paid a heavy price.

Rachel's next thought was just to get off the bus and stay home, but she knew she'd get screamed at or worse. She remembered grumpily that she couldn't miss any more days in the semester or she'd lose credit. "I just can't wait to get out of this prison," Rachel mumbled as she plopped onto an empty seat at the front of the bus.

Rachel believed things were only going to get worse when she saw Kaylee's group sitting next to her locker. She hated that girl. Kaylee thought she was so much better than everyone else. Rachel remembered thinking she would love the chance to show Kaylee who was in charge.

Rachel decided to sit with the group, because there were a few people, including Amar, whom Rachel liked. Besides, Rachel noticed the DMP. Rachel wanted one, but she knew the only way she was going to get a DMP was by stealing one. A DMP was much too cool for somebody like Amar. He probably had some weird foreign music on it anyway.

Rachel couldn't pass up the opportunity to steal Amar's DMP. The whole scheme flashed into her mind in just a few seconds and it worked perfectly. People were such idiots, so easy to distract. Rachel quickly realized that Kaylee was the only one she needed to keep an eye on, but even Kaylee wasn't paying attention, because she was focused on helping Amar get his lunch back. Playing keep-away with the sandwich was so simple it was brilliant. Rachel swiftly transferred the DMP from Amar's backpack to her purse.

Rachel smiled as she remembered what had happened. The students entering the classroom noticed the wicked smile on Rachel's face, but they knew better than to say anything to her about it.

Rachel was barely aware of students coming into the room and finding their seats until someone tripped over her feet. "Sorry," the girl who tripped said as she righted herself.

"That's right, you retard! Watch where you're going!" The girl practically ran to her desk, leaving Rachel with a few more seconds to reflect before the bell rang.

Rachel wanted to laugh at how easily she'd made Amar back down when he asked about the DMP. All it took was a few tears. Not even Kaylee could get Amar past those. It was because of Kaylee that Rachel decided to leave the DMP home the next day. That witch couldn't do anything if there was no evidence. Rachel wished she had the option of skipping just one day of school until things cooled off, but she didn't.

The bell rang and Mr. Hernandez took roll call before he stood in front of the class. "Today we're starting an American classic, *To Kill a Mockingbird.*"

"A book about bird hunting? Sounds stupid!" Rachel got a few snickers from the room.

Mr. Hernandez gave Rachel a nasty teacher look. "Rachel, how about if you sit up and turn to face the front?"

Rachel turned in her seat but wasn't about to sit up. She wasn't in the mood to take crap from a teacher who called her mom every other day. Rachel knew she could count on her mom to be on her side with teachers. Rachel's mom always said, "You've got to fight for yourself and not be wishy-washy." Her mom didn't do anything about the phone calls, but it was annoying anyway. Rachel actually wanted to go to college and become a teacher, but she was going to be a better one than Mr. Hernandez. She would be cool.

If Rachel had sat up, maybe she would have seen Mr. Leslie and Officer Strictor enter the room. "Mr. Hernandez, can we interrupt for a second?"

Officer Strictor didn't wait for an answer but headed toward Rachel's desk.

When he reached her, Rachel blurted, "What did I do?"

"Let's talk in the hall."

"I don't have to come with you; I have rights."

Officer Strictor knelt. He spoke so only Rachel could hear. "Look, you can come with me out into the hall or I can drag you out in front of your friends. Your choice."

Rachel's jaw clenched tightly in an attempt to hide her fear. Rachel had talked to Officer Strictor a couple of times already during the school year, but he had called her to his office. He had never come to find her.

Officer Strictor was always assuming she was being mean to somebody. He didn't understand her at all. Officer Strictor wrote Rachel a citation once and made her join the school counselor's anger management group. Mrs. Burns, the counselor, made the group talk about feelings, ways to manage anger, how to set goals and stuff. It was all too mushy for Rachel.

The DMP flashed into Rachel's mind, but she immediately dismissed it. They had no evidence. Rachel stood up slowly. Then she threw her pencil onto her desktop. It bounced upward and then fell to the floor. Nobody picked it up.

Mr. Leslie shut the door to the classroom behind Officer Strictor and Rachel. "Let's go to my office."

Rachel followed Mr. Leslie. She could hear the high-pitched squeaks of Officer Strictor's leather gun belt behind her. Once behind a closed door in Mr. Leslie's office, Officer Strictor removed handcuffs from the belt.

"What in the hell did I do? You can't keep me here! I won't stay. Where's my mom? My mom is going to be pissed! She's going to sue you, you…"

Officer Strictor read Rachel her rights calmly as Rachel spat profanities. He pulled her arms behind her back one at a time and then tightened the cold metal cuffs against her skin. By the time he finished, Rachel's rant had turned to heaving sobs.

"I…don't…have…the…DMP."

"We know you don't," Mr. Leslie answered. "We called home and your mom said it was in your bedroom. Stealing is a crime."

Rachel tried to be steady. "It was only a joke! I was going to give it back. My mom will tell you!"

"Your mom told us to do whatever we needed to." Mr. Leslie opened the door so that Officer Strictor could guide Rachel out.

"What about school? I can't miss any more school." Rachel was grasping at anything to stop what was happening.

"Rachel, I'm not sure you'll be coming back to this school."

"You can't do that! I want to go to college. You…" Rachel didn't finish. Her throat had become too tight to speak. Mr. Leslie shut his office door.

Rachel felt the stares as she was led through the front office and out of the school's main entrance. Officer Strictor's police car was waiting at the curb for her. Rachel was no longer sobbing, but tears ran in a steady stream down her face. They were a flash of warmth that turned quickly cold.

Officer Strictor opened the back door, placed his hand on top of Rachel's head and guided her into the back seat. She was going to jail. As the car pulled away, Rachel glanced at the school. Standing in the entrance was a disappointed Mrs. Burns. The final words Mrs. Burns had said to Rachel at their last group meeting had been, "Your aggressive behavior won't be tolerated forever, Rachel."

Rachel had laughed in her face and said, "Whatever." Rachel wasn't laughing anymore.

Officer Strictor pulled Rachel from the car in front of the Juvenile Detention Center. Keeping a firm grip on her arm, he led her inside. Rachel was truly scared.

Rachel tried not to make eye contact with anyone as she was taken to the back of the building. "Here you go," Officer Strictor said as he unlocked and removed the handcuffs. "I don't think she'll give you any trouble."

When a huge hand rested on her shoulder, Rachel glanced from the enormous shoes beside her up to the tallest muscle-bound bald man she'd ever seen. Rachel shifted her gaze back down to normal human level. Officer Strictor was gone.

Rachel was numb as she was pushed from place to place for processing by "Hulk." He pressed her fingers onto an inkpad to take her prints. He took her shoulder and stood her in front of a white screen before another officer shoved a sign into her chest. Rachel barely blinked when the camera flashed. Last, the giant placed her in a closet-sized room with no way to see out except a small window in the heavy door that was shut and locked. Rachel wished for that humongous hand on her shoulder.

The metal cot moaned as Rachel sat and placed her head in her hands. Rachel tried to blame someone else for her situation. Kaylee, Amar, Officer Strictor, Mr. Leslie, Mr. Hernandez, her mom all popped into her mind, but she couldn't make the idea of any of them being at fault stick. Sitting alone in a cell made it impossible for Rachel to blame anyone except herself. After all, she was the only one who was there.

Rachel was smart enough to realize she was at one of those crossroads Mrs. Burns was always talking about. Did she want college and independence or trouble and incarceration? A future filled with cramped windowless spaces and metal cots didn't appeal to her.

Finding herself actually in jail caused Rachel to come to grips with the problems that resulted from her harassing behaviors. By the time Rachel's mom came to pick her up, Rachel had decided she had to change and began to set some new goals for herself. She would write them down, call Mrs. Burns for an appointment and see what she thought. The school counselor would probably be shocked that Rachel had been paying attention to the lessons of the anger management group and was now thinking seriously about her future.

TEEN CONNECTIONS

- In what ways does Rachel fit the definition of an aggressive personality?
- Why do you think Rachel is aggressive?
- Why does Rachel begin to change her aggressive behaviors?

PARENT CONNECTIONS

- How is Rachel's mom an aggressive parent?
- How does Rachel's mom contribute to Rachel's aggressive behavior and anger?
- Should Rachel or any other teen have to work around his or her parent to achieve SMART goals?

Teen Section 5

The Bully

Aggressive behavior is indicated by *C* answers on the quiz in section 3. If these made up ten or more of your answers, you need to stop being a bully! Aggressive personalities are abusers, harassers and bullies. They create win-lose situations. They have to win and the costs are great for their victims as well as for themselves. Aggressive personalities are insecure on the inside yet egotistical on the outside and their inability to control people and situations makes them angry.

Aggressive people show their anger by bullying others and participating in risky behaviors like smoking, drinking, taking drugs and doing other things that show a lack of self-esteem. The toughest thing for aggressive people is to see themselves as aggressive. If they can do this, they can become assertive and stop being harassers. Then aggressive personalities can experience success and happiness.

What if you just had a few *C* answers on your quiz? Does that mean you're off the hook for this section? No! Even if you have only a few aggressive answers, you have things to work on. Maybe you enjoy sarcasm and can't always judge if others are hurt by it. Maybe you can't stand to lose an argument and won't let anything go until you've had the last word. Do your control issues cause you stress? Even though you are mostly assertive, you need to rid yourself of the mean-spirited aggressive part of your personality, for yourself and those around you.

As you read, keep in mind that allowing bullies to menace you or others is an aggressive behavior too. Bullying can also mean being a spectator. If there was nobody cheering the bully on, no one who thought the bully's behavior was funny or clever, then the bully wouldn't do it.

This section will cover everything from the extremely aggressive person to those who have a few aggressive tendencies. We will tell you what it means to be aggressive, why people are aggressive and how aggressive people can become assertive.

What Does Being Aggressive Mean?

We know harassers have aggressive personalities, but being aggressive is about more than being a bully. As you read through what it means to be aggressive, ask yourself if these descriptions fit you or if you're encouraging someone else to be aggressive. Think about situations and people that prompt you to act aggressively. Look back to your *C* list in teen section 3 for guidance. We'll say it again: nobody is perfect. Here are qualities found in aggressive personalities.

Verbally Abusive by Being Loud, Bossy, Sarcastic, Gossiping and Teasing

Aggressive people not only love to hear themselves talk, but also use speech to gain control over others. Harassing others verbally is the most common aggressive behavior. This is probably because it is the most widely accepted aggressive behavior. The intent is clear: to make someone else feel threatened or bad about themselves. When bullies can do that, they gain the control they crave.

Many teens don't realize sarcasm and gossiping are aggressive behaviors. Sarcasm can be fun, but you have to be sure it isn't hurting or offending anyone. It's very difficult to know that, so to be on the safe side you may want to tone it down. Gossip is an attempt to control someone's reputation. When you spread a rumor, you are attempting to control the subject of the rumor. If you think about it that way, gossip is a powerful, aggressive act. Monica showed aggressive behavior when she spread a rumor meant to ruin Jessica's reputation.

> Jessica arrived at school on Monday to stares and snickers from students in the hallway. Jessica thought she even heard someone whisper *slut* at her. She was very confused. It got worse.
>
> Jessica's boyfriend Graydon was waiting for her by her locker. He looked furious. "Jessica, how could you? I knew there was something going on."
>
> "What did I do?"
>
> "Monica told me how you hooked up with Mike this weekend. Everybody knows; it's on the Internet."
>
> "I didn't! I..." Jessica didn't get to explain, because her boyfriend walked away. Jessica didn't realize how jealous Monica was. How was she going to convince Graydon nothing had happened between her and Mike? And how could she get her reputation back?

Physically Abusive and Violent

Aggressive personalities use physical abuse in an attempt to gain control over others and to deal with their stress and anger. Physical abuse can come in the form of hitting, poking, shoving and invading the personal space of others. The goal with physical abuse is to make sure others are intimidated by the aggressive person. If they can make others fear them, then in their minds they have control over those people.

Hitting, poking and shoving are fairly obvious types of physical abuse, but one you may not think about is the violation of personal space. Personal space, also known as a person's bubble, is something that is decided by each individual and varies from person to person. Some of us like people to stay at least an arm's length away when communicating and some of us don't mind more up-close communication with others. Aggressive people always want to cross bubble boundaries, because it makes their victims uncomfortable. They will stand too close, use large hand gestures and touch others a lot, which intimidates the target and makes the aggressive person feel powerful.

Physical abuse is a form of violence, but there is a kind of violence that goes beyond hitting, poking, shoving and invading personal space. This type of violence involves weapons. Aggressive personalities may become obsessed with violence and, if pushed, will act out what they see in movies, TV shows and video games. Aggressive people believe that violence will solve their problems and prove their dominance. In reality, they end up in serious trouble and lose control over their lives. No one respects them because of what they have done.

Need to Win

The need to win is a great thing if you are a member of a sports team. Coaches are constantly telling their teams to "be aggressive." The need to win, however, doesn't work very well in life. For aggressive personalities, life is one big competition and everyone is an adversary. Think about what an awful way to live this is. It creates paranoia and makes good relationships an impossibility. Gina's need to win affected her relationship with her family members.

Gina loved basketball. Her family believed she loved it too much. When Gina's team won she was the fun, laid-back daughter and sister they adored. But when they lost, Gina became a person to be avoided. In a small house with one bathroom, that wasn't an easy thing to do.

One night, after her team had lost, Gina's brother made the mistake of spending a few moments too long in the shower. Gina pounded on the door. Her brother was about to unlock it when Gina's fist came crashing through.

Gina's week was spent ordering and paying for a new bathroom door, holding up a blanket for privacy for whoever needed to be in the bathroom and realizing that losing a basketball game didn't give her the right to be a violent jerk.

Need to Control Others

Aggressive people believe that if they can control others then they will feel in control of themselves. The more out of control their lives become, the more they lash out at others in an attempt to regain control. They use verbal and physical abuse and even acts of violence in an attempt to gain control. This really makes no sense, because as any assertive person knows, the only way to feel in control of your life is to take care of yourself. Success and happiness don't come from other people. They can only come from within.

Personal Needs Come First

Unlike the passive person, aggressive people never think of anybody but themselves. They are always first and they're not out to please anyone but themselves, no matter how badly that may hurt others. Aggressive people make scary parents, because they don't know how to take care of another person. Real relationships are defined by caring. Aggressive people only really care about themselves. Aggressiveness is a lonely way to go. An aggressive parent can create an aggressive child, as seen in Craig's example.

> While aggressive personalities were being discussed in class, Craig, a student who was often aggressive, raised his hand. Mr. Vernal called on him, fully expecting him to say something sarcastic.
>
> "When I was about eight," Craig said, "my dad took me down the freeway on his motorcycle, no helmets, no nothin', going a hundred miles an hour. Was that aggressive?"
>
> Mr. Vernal wasn't sure whether Craig was trying to ask a serious question, but he answered it as if it was. "Yes. He was not thinking of you, his child, whom he is supposed to love, protect and take care of. It was an extremely aggressive act, one an assertive person would never think of doing."
>
> "Oh."
>
> Mr. Vernal knew then why this young person had a tendency to be aggressive.

Don't Know What Respect Is

According to *Merriam-Webster's Collegiate Dictionary, respect* means "to consider worthy of high regard" and "to refrain from interfering with." Respect is a concept easily understood by those who are not aggressive. Aggressive people don't know what respect is and they don't understand that you have to give respect before you get it.

Aggressive personalities don't have respect for themselves either. Aggressive people are more likely to smoke, drink alcohol, take drugs, get into fights and do other things that can cause physical harm or death. They look for things that can calm their anger, give them a sense of control and make them appear tough. Rules and laws were created to provide consequences for those who do not respect other human beings or themselves. In order to be truly successful in the world, you have to know and live the meaning of respect.

Those are the character traits of aggressive people. Even if you are not the classic aggressive case, there are probably people or situations that bring out aggression in you. The key is to know when that's happening and work to stop it. If you are aggressive a lot, please open your mind and read the rest of this section carefully. We hope you make a commitment to become assertive.

- **MYTH:** If I don't fit into all the definitions, then I must not be aggressive.
- **TRUTH:** Any aggressive behavior will hurt your chances at success and happiness. Change even those you don't think are a big deal and you will notice a difference.

Why Be Aggressive?

Aggressive behavior isn't only self-destructive, it is damaging for others as well. So why do it? Because aggressive people are addicted to negative attention, control and anger. If you are an aggressive person, this section might anger you. You will want to deny that it describes you.

Not all of the things we discuss apply to all aggressive people. Please keep in mind that we are not giving you this information to make you angry. We're giving it to you in the hopes that you get past the wall of anger, open your heart and mind and decide to become assertive.

They Fear Appearing Weak or Losing Control

Aggressive people are every bit as afraid as passive people. An aggressive person's biggest fear is looking scared. That is why aggressive people try to make others believe they are in control of everything and everyone. The more they try to gain control, the more they lose it. This causes fear and anger, which they take out on others through bullying. Aggressive personalities cannot figure out that the only person they can really control is themselves.

They Are Egotistical

An aggressive person's ego prevents him or her from appreciating diversity or compromising. Compromising is meeting people in the middle when dealing with issues instead of a "my way or the highway" approach. Understanding differences and compromising both take respect. As we said earlier, aggressive people don't know how to respect others. Our society is built on our ability to work together, compromise and be a team. Aggressive people do not make good team members, because they don't see the value of differences. Until they can see that difference as a good thing and work with others, they cannot contribute to society. Andy's aggressive ego resulted in severe consequences for him.

> In high school, Andy ruled the campus. He was popular and the star of the track team. What he didn't realize was that people were his friends only because they were afraid not to be.
>
> Andy received a track scholarship to college. He assumed that college was going to be just like high school and he would get friends easily. During the first week of track practice, Andy made some racial comments about some of his teammates. They asked him to stop, but Andy kept after the group, because they were different from him. Along the way he tried to recruit others. After all, that was how he had gotten other students to follow his lead in high school.
>
> One night a few weeks later, Andy was jumped on campus and beaten severely. When he had recovered and went back to school, his coach asked him to come to his office. "Andy," the coach said, "you are a talented athlete, but you don't know how to be part of a team. You've been behaving like a bigot and a bully. I want my team to be winners on and off the track, which is why I'm cutting you."

They View Aggressiveness as Manly

Statistically, there are more males who are aggressive than females. Many males who are aggressive were taught that it is not manly to show emotion, to have weaknesses or to lose control. In other words, they have to be macho. It is a sad belief. It is never manly to be a jerk. Assertive men are caring and are able to respect anyone, regardless of differences.

They Don't Know How to be Responsible

Even though aggressive people make bad decisions not only for themselves, but for passive followers as well, they will not take responsibility. They are very good at what we call the blame game. Everything is someone else's fault. It's ironic, because if everything is always somebody else's fault that means somebody else is in control. However, as we pointed out before, control is what the aggressive person wants the most. In Dave's example, he refused to acknowledge that it was his behavior that put him in detention.

> Mr. Hansen was in charge of after-school detention for students who had too many tardy notices. One particular student, Dave, was very hostile toward Mr. Hansen. Mr. Hansen asked Dave, "Why are you angry with me?"
> "Because I have to be in detention."
> "Why is that my fault? I'm just the one who gets paid to sit here with you."
> "Yeah, you're right. It's Mrs. Wild's fault for giving me all those tardies."
> Mr. Hansen smiled. "Then why is Mrs. Wild not in detention?"

It's What They Know

Aggressive people have a problem accepting their weaknesses. Aggressiveness can be a personality learned from someone close. Where do you learn aggressive behavior? From parents or others you're around a lot. Aggressive people pattern their behaviors on what they've seen and heard. Remember, abuse is often a cycle that is passed down from one generation to the next.

Sadly, this pattern can also mean that aggressive people may be victims of abuse at home, so they are determined not to be victims anywhere else. They do the same things that are done to them so they can feel in control of their lives.

It takes a lot of courage and a lot of help to stop doing what you know, to cease the cycle. Accepting help is something that aggressive people resist, so changing will not be easy, but we can promise you it will be worth it.

They Like the Rewards for Being Aggressive

Like passive people who become addicted to the role of victim, aggressive personalities become addicted to negative attention. Creating fear in others and getting in trouble all the time are their rewards. Aggressive people who read this might get angry and deny these traits. Calm down and consider: Would you feel normal if there wasn't someone afraid of you? Would it feel right if there wasn't a parent, teacher or peer angry with you? If you're aggressive, you need to rethink your definition of normal.

We all know aggressive individuals. People try to avoid them. They are in the principal's office often, get bad grades, do unhealthy things and may even be in trouble with the legal system. Aggressive people are addicted to the kind of attention they get. Unfortunately, our prisons are full of aggressive personalities who couldn't break the habit of negative attention. Aggressive personalities who have no regard for others' rights and break the law are punished by our society.

When you stomp on other people, take no responsibility and desire negative attention, life is going to be without freedom and control. Acting aggressively can become a habit. If this habit isn't broken, the aggressive person is in for a difficult life. In Shane's case, grief caused him to turn to a cycle of aggression he couldn't break.

Shane's sister was killed in a car accident his junior year of high school. Shane dealt with his grief aggressively. He dropped out of school and started using drugs to make the pain go away.

Then Shane began stealing to support his drug habit. When he turned eighteen, he escalated to armed robbery. He was caught, convicted and sentenced to two years in the state penitentiary. As soon as he was released he committed another crime. Shane had become addicted to negative behaviors that helped him forget his sister's tragic death.

There is one last point we want to make about why someone is aggressive. Reading some of this may give an aggressive person the idea that being aggressive isn't his or her fault. Understand that your actions are always your responsibility. Also your responsibility: making changes to become a better person.

- **MYTH:** Being aggressive is okay, because I get what I want.
- **TRUTH:** You may get what you want, but at what cost to yourself and others? Assertive people get what they want without the negative consequences that aggressive people experience. They are successful without stomping on others' rights.

Changing the Aggressive to Assertive

Aggressive people can change, but their bad habits must be broken. Aggressive people first have to admit they are aggressive, which also means they have to take responsibility for themselves. It usually takes something big to get them to think responsibly and see they need to change.

"I don't care" is a popular saying among aggressive people. If you're aggressive, you don't care that you aren't liked but only feared, you aren't in control of your life and your anger and stress levels are off the charts?

You don't care that you are not respected? You don't care that your future is bleak, at best? We don't think that's true.

Like passive people, aggressive people believe things will get better when they are finished with school. After all, many aggressive personalities see school as a prison where everyone tells them what to do. They don't view school as an opportunity to learn and prepare for a successful future. What aggressive personalities need to realize is that there will always be people telling them what to do: the government, a boss, the list goes on. The only thing that will change for aggressive people once they are out of school are the consequences. Life after age eighteen means a person doesn't get the number of chances he or she did at school or through the Juvenile Justice System. Statistically, students who harass at school go on to have trouble keeping jobs and staying in relationships and are more likely to commit crimes. The point is, become assertive now.

If you have major issues with aggression, are not open to learning and have a hard time admitting you have a problem, then you need to seek professional help. If you are ready to be confident, happy, successful and calm, you need to be SMART about going forward. You can't change all at once. Aggressive personalities should accept the same goal-setting advice we gave to passive personalities. You have to get past trying to control everything all at once. Choose one or two things that you can realistically control enough to create new habits. That's the SMART way to do it.

SMART Goals[2]

S = Specific. What are you going to do? How are you going to do it? Why is it important to do it?

M = Measurable. How are you going to measure your progress? When will you know the goal is accomplished?

A = Attainable. Is the goal challenging but reachable? Does it require a commitment, but won't stretch you too thin?

R = Realistic. Do you have a reasonable plan to reach the goal? Will the achievement be satisfying?

T = Timely. When are you going to start working toward your goal? Do you have a time frame for achieving this goal?

Vince's ability to reflect and admit to his aggression helped him learn ways to control and change his behaviors.

> Vince made the same promise to himself every year: *I am going to stay out of trouble and get good grades.* He often did very well for a couple of weeks, but such good behavior became too much for him. Then Vince fell into his old pattern of getting into trouble, his grades fell and he gave up on his goal.
>
> Because of his grades and behavior, Vince was enrolled in the alternative high school where his education was structured differently. It was there that he learned how to set small SMART goals.
>
> After he changed a few smaller behaviors, things started going well for Vince. He took on more and set more complicated goals as the year went on. Vince didn't feel overwhelmed, so there was no need to give up or get into trouble. For the first time in a long time, Vince experienced success.

Admit You Are Aggressive

Aggressive people resist seeing that there is anything wrong with them and the way they act. We know some of you will deny what we've discussed about aggression in this section. We invite you to list your aggressive behaviors in your journal. Writing down your aggressive behaviors is an important step toward admitting you have them.

Change the Way You Look

What do others see when they look at you? Are you thinking this is a really stupid question, because you don't care what anybody else sees or thinks about you? Put your ego aside and consider this for a moment. If aggressive personalities answer honestly, they do not look like people with whom others want to have a conversation, spend time or be friends. Changing the way you look can make a big difference in how people react to you.

Watch assertive people. Be open to learning from them. They are the ones who have real relationships with people who genuinely like them. They smile, laugh and have an air of relaxed confidence. Copy what they do: facial expressions, posture, tone of voice, eye contact and the way they carry themselves. Practice in front of a mirror, speak into a recorder or videotape yourself to gain confidence in your ability to be approachable.

- **Eye contact:** When you speak to someone, do you stare instead of using real eye contact? Aggressive people stare to make the other person feel intimidated. Good eye contact is not staring. If this is a problem for you, make eye contact for three seconds during a conversation, then look to the forehead for a second before returning to the eyes.

- **Voice:** Aggressive people tend to fall into two ways of speaking. Many aggressive people are loud. If you've been asked to be quiet a lot, then this is something you should work on. Try to watch your volume level and the number of times you interrupt others. Aggressive people interrupt often, which is one of the reasons they feel the need to be loud.

   The second type of tone used by aggressive people is quiet, steely and threatening. Do you talk through gritted teeth, squint or never smile when you speak? If the answer is yes, concentrate on relaxing your jaw and facial muscles when you speak.

- **Posture:** Do you try to make yourself as big and tough looking as possible? An easy test of whether you do or not is to stand up from a seated position. When you stand, what do you look like? Aggressive people spread their feet apart, fold their arms tightly or place their hands on their hips. They stand rigidly and appear stiff. They strut instead of walking. If this is you, relax! Walking around like that all the time is tiring. Check your posture throughout the day. Shake out your muscles. If you adjust enough, your body will get the point and the tough stance will be a thing of the past. In Garret's case, a class lesson opened his eyes to his aggressive posture.

   Garret, nicknamed GT, stood up when Mrs. Hunt asked the class to stand. GT's stance, like a bodybuilder's, was so imposing he touched the girls on either side of him.

   Mrs. Hunt said, "If you try to be as large as possible when you stand, that's a sign of an aggressive person."

   Several of the students laughed. GT smiled at the thought of his classmates thinking his posture was funny. GT's smile disappeared when Mrs. Hunt duplicated his aggressive strut at the front of the room as an example for the class. The students started to make fun of GT. They laughed, pointed to GT and shouted, "That's you, GT!"

   GT's face turned red; his nostrils flared. "I have to walk that way! I have big pectoral muscles!"

   The class roared with laughter. Mrs. Hunt did her best to quiet them down, but it was no use. After a few seconds, GT scowled and then stomped out of the room.

Physicality

Do you point, poke, hit, slap or gesture close to another's face? Aggressive people have no regard for others' personal space. Whether they realize it or not, they use this invasion of personal space to keep others off balance and make them feel threatened. Keep all body parts at a distance of two feet (about an arm's length) between yourself and another person.

Violence Obsession

If you are obsessed with violent movies, TV shows, video games or weapons and often fantasize about doing something violent, you may need professional help. Please talk with your parent, school counselor or spiritual advisor.

Be Proactive

Proactive people think before they act (speaking is acting) and they take responsibility for their actions. Assertive people are in the habit of having an internal dialogue (also called a conscience), but you may need to be more conscious of your speech and behavior. Ask yourself these proactive questions before acting.

Questions to Answer Before Acting

- Will this help me be successful?
- Will it hurt others?
- Will it hurt me?
- How will it make me feel?
- Have I thought about the consequences?

Aggressive personalities react impulsively and are therefore termed reactive. They do things without forethought and try to control everything without taking responsibility for their bad choices. Thinking before acting means you are more likely to take responsibility for your actions. Taking responsibility means taking control. Control is the one thing aggressive people want the most. If aggressive personalities changed their reactive behaviors they would know what real control is. After learning the difference between proactive and reactive behavior, Alex brainstormed an activity to teach proactive thought to his friends.

Alex set a two-liter bottle on the picnic table in front of him. He said, "This bottle is full of water. It represents a proactive person." Alex set another bottle next to it. "This bottle is full of soda pop and represents a reactive person. And these," Alex removed a package of mints from his pocket, "are problems or difficult situations."

Alex removed several mints from the package and put them into the bottle of water. Nothing happened. "This is how proactive people deal with problems. They take them in, think about them and work out solutions to make them dissolve away."

Then Alex put the mints into the reactive bottle. It immediately became a five-foot geyser of bubbling soda. "This is how reactive people deal with problems. They don't think; they only react and it ends up making a huge mess."

Respect Others

Respect means to have regard for others and avoid hurting them. Because you need to give respect before you hope to get it, here are some ways to show respect so you can get it in return.

A major part of being respectful is learning how to listen effectively. Aggressive people are horrible listeners. It's largely the reason that aggressive people are so often in trouble. They do not listen to the things that others are trying to teach them. They do whatever they wish, no matter the cost to others or themselves. Listening is key to gaining respect. Nobody is going to respect someone who doesn't listen. Here are some ways to become a better listener:

- **Stop talking.** Don't interrupt, don't finish others' thoughts, don't give advice and don't tell other people what to do or think.

- **Find something interesting about the other person.** Not everything is going to be entertaining. If you decide a person or subject is boring, you will probably not want to listen. Find something that will help you focus. If you are struggling to pay attention in class, taking notes is a great idea.

- **Look like you're listening.** Body language is the majority of our communication, therefore it is the number one way we determine whether someone has respect for us. Look like you're listening: unfold your arms, sit forward in your chair or stand up tall, and make eye contact. Looking like you're listening will also help you focus on listening.

Aside from listening, how else can you show respect? How about having regard for others? If aggressive personalities thought of someone besides themselves, they wouldn't be such bullies and they would be respected.

Ask yourself one or more of these questions before you behave aggressively. If the answer is no, then it is not a respectful thing to say or do.

It's All About Respect

- Would I want my comments or behavior to appear in the newspaper or on TV?
- Is this something I would say or do if my _____ (fill in the blank with mom, dad, guardian, boss, girlfriend/boyfriend or anyone you admire) was present?
- Is this something I would want someone else to say or do to my _____ (fill in the blank with mom, dad, guardian, boss, girlfriend/boyfriend or anyone you admire)?
- Is this something I would say or do if the other person's parents or significant other was present?

Respect Yourself

Aggressive personalities not only are disrespectful to others, but also don't have much regard for themselves either. This lack of self-respect is the saddest part of being aggressive. In order to change this, set goals that work toward positive, productive results:

- Getting an education
- Building positive relationships
- Being safe
- Staying out of trouble
- Being physically healthy

It may be hard to pay attention in class, stop bullying or quit a bad habit like smoking, but it will be worth it. You will discover what it's like to be good to yourself and there's no better or more powerful feeling than that. It took a tragic accident for Scott to recognize his aggressive behaviors, but fortunately he chose to change them for the better.

Scott had just signed his letter of intent to play football at the college level. Scott's way of celebrating was binge drinking at a party outside of town. He didn't think twice about getting into his car after the party. He was on his way home when things became tragic.

Scott remembered sirens and a pool of blood. He awoke from that nightmare into a worse one. The lawyer his parents had hired told him he'd killed a twenty-two-year-old woman with his car. Scott had to explain to the lawyer what happened.

Scott was convicted of vehicular manslaughter. So instead of football camp and college, he went to prison.

Scott couldn't take that night back or make it right, but he could learn from his experience. He quit drinking and when he was released from jail, he spoke to area teens about his mistakes and the importance of making respectful decisions. Scott became assertive.

Adjust Your Attitude

Aggressive people need to realize that all people, regardless of age or anything else, make choices every day. The most important of those have to do with attitude. Think about how powerful it would be to choose to have a good attitude. Aggressive people, whether they want to admit it or not, choose to have bad attitudes. When you choose a bad attitude, bad decisions often follow.

My Choices[3]

- My character
- My values
- How I treat others
- How I handle adversity
- How much I learn
- What I accomplish
- My belief system
- My purpose in life
- My attitude

A tumultuous childhood is often a reason a person feels he or she has the right to be unhappy, but in Rex's case he chose to turn his experience into a positive one.

One day when Rex was five years old, social services found him locked in the closet of a crack house. For the next twelve years Rex bounced from foster home to foster home. By the time he reached his senior year of high school, he'd lived with ten different families.

Rex could have used his unfortunate circumstances as an excuse to behave aggressively. After all, he had a right to be angry. Rex chose differently. He chose to have a positive attitude every day. He wrote in his senior essay, "I am not the valedictorian, I am not a jock, I am not going to win any popularity contests, but I am a winner. I beat my life. I chose to have the attitude that nothing or no one would take happiness from me. I have won."

Manage Your Anger

Learning to manage your anger will go a long way toward becoming assertive. So much of an aggressive person's anger comes from being out of control. Anger is one more thing that, if managed, will give you control.

There is a lot of information available on how to manage anger. Here are eight ways to keep your cool:

- **Take a break**. Get away from the person you are angry with until you calm down.

- **Chill out**. Count to ten, take a deep breath, listen to music, imagine you are somewhere else, talk yourself down, write in a journal, strum a guitar—anything to keep you from reacting in the moment without thinking.

- **Exercise**. Doing something physically active is part of chilling out, but it deserves a heading of its own, because it is the one thing guaranteed to help with anger. When we exercise, calming substances called endorphins are released in our brains. They make us feel calm, awake and healthy.

- **Be proactive**. There's that word again. Think before you act! When you're angry is not the time to be reactive.

- **Tell the person you're angry**. Notice that this is after you have calmed down. You're being proactive. It is healthy to express anger in a *positive* way.

- **Use "I" statements**. When you discuss your feelings, begin with the word "I". This will keep you from playing the blame game. However, you must follow the "I" statement with helpful, calm words. Saying, "I want to beat you up" isn't helpful, but saying, "I want you to stop calling me names" is helpful.

> **"I" Statements**
> - I want…
> - I need…
> - I like/love…
> - I dislike…
> - I don't like it when you…
> - I feel like…
> - I'm not going to…
> - I agree/disagree because…
> - I can/can't …

- **Come up with solutions**. Coming up with appropriate answers and solutions takes work. Keeping your anger levels in check is worth the effort. Instead of focusing on who or what made you angry, focus on resolving the issue.

- **Don't hold a grudge**. Holding a grudge is like picking up a hot rock to throw at someone: you're the one who gets burned. People hold grudges against those who aren't acting the way they want them to act. However, people will never act the way you want them to, so a grudge is a major waste of energy.

It's probably not a good idea to start working on the assertive you with the person or situation that makes you angriest. Try starting with the smaller things: not speaking out in class, not approaching the person you usually pick on or not looking so tough all the time. You may find that when you work on the smaller things, the larger issues like self-control and real relationships will follow.

- **MYTH:** I don't need to change my aggressive behavior, because I'm just joking around and having fun.

- **TRUTH:** That statement is an aggressive and egotistical one. Great, you're having fun, but how many people aren't having fun because of you? Please think, have empathy and care.

 FILL OUT AT LEAST ONE GOAL SETTING SHEET AT THE END OF THIS SECTION. STICK TO YOUR GOAL. USE THE OTHER SHEETS AS GUIDANCE UNTIL YOU GET USED TO SETTING AND ACHIEVING GOALS. DON'T FORGET TO BE SMART!

TEEN CONNECTIONS

- In what ways does Rachel fit the definition of an aggressive personality?

  She was loud, verbally abusive, sarcastic, competitive, controlling, egotistical, selfish and disrespectful. This makes her a good example of an extremely aggressive person.

- Why do you think Rachel is aggressive?

  Rachel didn't want to appear weak in any situation or relationship. In her actions she showed no respect for her teachers, her classmates or their possessions. Rachel didn't know how to be responsible and even convinced herself that Amar didn't deserve his DMP, because it was so easy to steal. Rachel possibly learned her aggressive personality traits from her mother. Rachel's mom's behavior was unpredictable but always aggressive. She only chose who was going to be the target in any given situation and Rachel seemed to mimic this behavior in her relationships with peers.

- Why does Rachel begin to change her aggressive behaviors?

  Rachel began to think about change when she realized she was at a crossroad. Rachel wanted to go to college and have freedom. She didn't want to keep experiencing consequences that limited what she could do with her life.

SMART Goal:

Today's date: _____   Completion date: _____

Why do I need to reach this goal?	How and when will I work toward this goal?	# of times (per day, week, month)	Status (how's it going)

Possible Difficulties:

SMART Goal:

Today's date: _____   Completion date: _____

Why do I need to reach this goal?	How and when will I work toward this goal?	# of times (per day, week, month)	Status (how's it going)

Possible Difficulties:

SMART Goal:

Today's date: Completion date:

Why do I need to reach this goal?	How and when will I work toward this goal?	# of times (per day, week, month)	Status (how's it going)

Possible Difficulties:

SMART Goal:

Today's date: Completion date:

Why do I need to reach this goal?	How and when will I work toward this goal?	# of times (per day, week, month)	Status (how's it going)

Possible Difficulties:

Parent Section 5

The Aggressive Parent

Aggressive behaviors are indicated by *A* answers on your quiz. The parent quiz involves questions about individual behaviors as well as parenting behaviors. In teen section 5 you learned what it means to have an aggressive personality, why people are aggressive and how to become assertive. The information applies to all individuals, not just teens. Like your teen, you have things to work on if you have any aggressive answers in the quiz. Parents with aggressive personality traits are probably parenting aggressively as well. This means their teens may behave aggressively like their parents or their children may act passively, because being a victim is the role to which they are accustomed.

This parent section focuses on the aggressive parenting skills that may be contributing to your child's aggression or to his or her victimization. It is important for you to be open and honest with yourself as you consider this information. Parts are going to be difficult for an aggressive parent to admit, but again, remember there are no perfect parents and parents' purpose is to help their sons and daughters through difficult situations like harassment.

What Is an Aggressive Parent?

Teen section 5 explores what an aggressive person is and how he or she behaves. Now we will discuss aggressive parenting styles. Like passive parents, aggressive parents may be contributing to teen behavior that is aggressive or passive; aggressive parents teach their sons or daughters to be either the intimidator or the intimidated. Also, similar to the changes needed in passive parents, aggressive parents have to become assertive if they want to help their teens deal with harassment. As you read, be aware that no one is perfect and you may need to change. This is particularly tough for an aggressive parent, but a paradigm shift will benefit your teen as much as it will you.

Verbally Abusive Through Being Loud, Bossy, Sarcastic, Gossiping and Teasing

Aggressive people often use speech to gain control over others. Aggressive parents use yelling, sarcasm, teasing and being bossy in order to prove to their teens as well as to others who is in control. This can create a teen who believes the way to get what he or she wants is through the verbal abuse of others. The aggressive teen may even begin to use these learned tactics on his or her parent. The result is a noisy, chaotic home full of conflict. Verbal abuse will never achieve control over your teen or anyone else. It will teach your teen how to be a harasser. Becoming an assertive parent means modeling good communication skills when you talk to your teen and others. Positive communication and conflict resolution is the best way to solve problems.

An aggressive parent who is verbally abusive may also influence his or her teen to be passive. These passive teens avoid conflict at all costs, which makes them easy targets for harassers. Unfortunately, aggressive parents count among these teens' harassers. While aggressive people are loud and harassing, passive teens are quiet and want to disappear. They hand harassers complete control of their lives. If aggressive parents gave their passive teens a chance to speak safely and be heard at home, it would go a long way toward encouraging them to stand up to harassers.

Aggressive parents are usually not good listeners. If you are yelling or trying to think of your next comment, you cannot listen effectively. You should know your teen better than anyone, so answer these questions honestly:

- Is yelling at my son or daughter effective?
- Am I teaching my teen responsibility when I try to gain control of situations and people through verbal abuse?
- Is my sarcasm and teasing perceived as funny or hurtful?

Participating in verbally abusive behaviors doesn't make a situation better, but for a teen who is trying to figure out the world and how it works, it is particularly damaging. Not only is the teen inviting harassment problems, but he or she needs to understand that yelling and sarcasm will not gain the desired control or domination. It can be difficult for aggressive people to break their habits, because it means relinquishing control, even though that control is false. Aggressive parents have to stop bullying their teens and listen to them before their teens can stop harassing or being harassed by their peers. Jake's father modeled aggressive behaviors that Jake translated into poor attendance and work ethic in school.

Jake failed his English class. If he wanted to graduate on time, he needed to take a night school class. Jake's dad sent him to night school with a check for his tuition. Jake signed a behavior contract and began the course.

Within the first few weeks, Jake violated attendance rules as well as behavior guidelines. The night school contacted Jake's dad and informed him that his son was going to be suspended. Jake's dad was furious with Jake, the school and the teacher. After verbally and physically attacking his son at home, he stormed into the school office and demanded a meeting with the principal and the night school teacher. The principal agreed.

Once everyone arrived, Jake's dad began to yell. "You people are wasting my damn money. I paid for this class and so Jake will be in it. I've heard how hard this teacher," Jake's dad pointed to the night school teacher, "is to get along with. She probably just doesn't like Jake. I'm sick of the teachers around here playing favorites. I will tell you what's going to happen. You will take my son into that class and he will graduate on time."

"Mr. Sanders," the teacher said, "Jake was present in class for the entire period only once out of the four times we've met. He was given warnings about his behavior many times. Night school is an optional program."

"You're a liar!" Jake's dad pounded the table with his fist.

"No," the principal replied. "She's telling you the truth."

The night school teacher calmly slid Jake's dad his check across the table, got up and left the room, taking Jake's chances of graduating on time with her.

Physically Abusive and Violent

Aggressive people do not handle stress and anger in healthy ways. Neither do aggressive parents. Aggressive people may take their emotions out on others through physical abuse and violence. For aggressive parents, their children make readily available targets. Teens can become physical abusers and be prone to violent acts when their parents are constantly modeling abusive behavior. Because teens are maturing physically, they may turn on their aggressive parents and create households where violence prevails. It is up to parents to model and guide their children toward positive conflict resolution and dealing with emotions. Abuse or violence is only going to exacerbate harassment, because it is a vicious cycle; those who are abused abuse others and so on. The cycle has to be broken.

Teens who are physically abused may be beaten into submission. When teens succumb to the violence at home, they will be passive in situations outside their homes. They are targets for harassers. Being beat up and humiliated strips a teen's sense of self-worth and security. Aggressive parents need to remember that raising children is about building them up, not tearing them down, emotionally or physically.

Parents whose idea of providing consequences or attempting to control their teens includes physical abuse are creating environments of fear. Honestly answer these questions:

- Do I discipline my teen through shoving, poking, violating personal space or hitting?

- Am I teaching my teen responsibility when I try to gain control of situations and people through physical abuse?

- Do I encourage my teenage son or daughter to solve his or her problems through physical violence?

Assertive parents foster strong individuals. A strong person does not have to use physical strength to deal with emotions or gain control over situations. A parent's responsibility is to show his or her teen that anger should be dealt with by utilizing firm words and actions that are never abusive. If your teen is experiencing violence at home, he or she will probably experience it elsewhere. Please learn to be an assertive rather than aggressive parent and find a more positive way to express emotions and resolve conflicts.

Need to Win

Aggressive parents manifest their need to win when they strive to be seen as perfect parents, regardless of what is happening behind closed doors at home. They push and pressure their children to excel at things like school, sports or other social activities. Aggressive parents aren't thinking about their teens but about themselves and how they will appear to others. Teens react to these expectations in different ways. Aggressive teens adhere to the attitude that it is okay to do anything as long as they win. For example, they will cheat to get good grades, take steroids to enhance athletic ability or bully others in order to gain popularity. Victories gained in an aggressive manner do not reflect well on the parents or the teens. Aggressive parents need to realize they are actually sending their teens down a failing path when all of life is seen as a competition.

The other way in which teens react to this type of pressure is to cave in and become passive. They develop poor self-esteem, because they feel they can never be good enough. This low opinion of themselves causes the teens to become targets for harassers. Teens want to please their parents, but for teens with aggressive parents, this may be impossible. Aggressive parents need to challenge their teens without crushing them. In order to do this, they have to change their own behaviors.

Assertive parents realize their teens aren't perfect and neither are they. They are supportive of their teens and they are cognizant of their teens' strengths and weaknesses, likes and dislikes. Knowing their sons and daughters well, they can help them set challenging yet achievable goals, also known as SMART goals. Aggressive parents cannot help their teens out of harassing situations until they get to know their teens and put their sons' and daughters' needs before their own. Be aware that your life and your teen's life are not in competition.

Need to Control Others

Aggressive people are obsessed with control. So are aggressive parents. For aggressive parents, raising children is all about controlling them, their spouses, the school, the administrators, the teachers and others associated with their families. The teenage years are a rite of passage when adolescents seek independence and autonomy. A parent controlling everything is in complete opposition to this cultural imperative and there are consequences. Controlling parents often have out-of-control teens. Teens become harassers, because they crave the control that they aren't allowed to have over their own lives. Fighting for control is an abusive cycle that is difficult to break, but if a parent wants his or her teen to be successful, happy and free from harassment, it has to be stopped.

It is a sure sign of defeat and passivity if teens allow their parents to completely control their lives. They become victims, because it's the easy way out. Becoming passive with aggressive parents means that teens don't have to take responsibility, make decisions or stand up for themselves. If they give up with their parents, they will surely acquiesce to peer harassers too.

Parents cannot actually control their children. Aggressive parents, like aggressive people, need to realize that they can only really control themselves. An aggressive parent is a frustrated, exhausted person. Parents can be responsible for their children, guide them, listen to them, teach them, keep them safe and secure, support them and love them. That is what creates an assertive teen, not control. Attempting to control your teen will only result in chaos for your teen as well as your family unit. When you become assertive instead of aggressive, assertive parenting will follow and you will have the control you crave.

Their Own Needs Come First

Aggressive people don't parent well, because they don't know how to take care of others. Aggressive people are verbally and physically abusive, competitive, controlling, disrespectful and irresponsible. None of these personality traits produce a parent who is willing to put his or her teen first. Parents have to put their teens' needs before their own sometimes. When the parents come first all the time, the teens may adopt the same ego and attitude. They will take care of their own wants and needs without a thought of others' desires, needs, rights or safety. The father we spoke about in teen section 5 who took his young son out on a high-speed motorcycle ride on the freeway exemplifies aggressive parenting. The son's style became patterned on his dad's aggressive behavior. The aggressive parent perpetuates a dangerous cycle.

When the parents consistently put themselves first, it sends a message to their teens that they aren't worth enough to be cared for by their parents. Passive teens don't believe they deserve to be loved and, because of this perceived lack of self-worth, they adopt the passive behavior of always being last. Therefore, they are the prime targets for harassers. Aggressive parenting is neglectful. Parents cannot meet a teen's emotional needs if they are self-absorbed.

Teens who feel cared for and who know that they come first once in a while are those who stand up for themselves and aren't likely to violate the rights of others. Aggressive parenting is selfish parenting. Parenting should not be used as an opportunity to boost egos or project power. Assertive parents take care of the ones they love and still find the time and effort necessary to take care of themselves as well.

Don't Know What Respect Is

You have to give respect in order to get it. This applies to your children too. If you don't demonstrate respect for your teen, he or she won't respect you in return. Parents who do not model assertiveness for their teens can expect sons and daughters who believe as they do: that respect equals fear. Aggressive teens may not only be bullies at school. If they believe fear is respect, then they may try to elicit fear from their parents as well. In this case, the aggressive teens and their aggressive parents will surely clash and create family disorder.

Aggressive parents think they are being good parents when their children behave out of fear. What they are actually doing is forcing their teens to be passive, because the teens are afraid to be anything else. This lack of respect from parents serves to create victims who don't think they deserve respect from anyone. Every human being, no matter his or her age, deserves to be respected. The aggressive parent needs to learn what respect really means.

Your teen can know and live respectfully if you do. Parents need to model respect, which includes having regard for their teenagers and avoiding violating their sons and daughters through aggressive behaviors.

Refuse to Take Responsibility for Their Teens

Aggressive parents don't know how to be responsible for other human beings. They don't understand that being in control of their families is not the same as being responsible for them. Taking responsibility is not verbally or physically attacking sons, daughters or others when a mistake is made. Teens cannot learn responsibility or how to be assertive if they are being controlled and abused by aggressive parents.

Aggressive parents also need to let their teens be independent and experience consequences for their mistakes. They cannot adopt the attitude that "my child never does anything wrong," "it was just a joke" or "kids will be kids." If your teen is a target or is in trouble for harassment, there is a reason, and an aggressive parent has to put his or her ego and need for control aside and work assertively with those involved to resolve the issue. That is a parent's responsibility.

Aggressive parenting behaviors, including a lack of responsibility, may produce teen harassers. These teens may simply be emulating their aggressive parents' styles. Teens act out what is done to them in the home. If your teen is a harasser, you need to ask yourself these questions:

- Is my aggressive parenting style contributing to my teen's aggression?

- What personality changes do I need to make in order to model assertive behavior?

- Does my teen need me to back off and let him or her experience negative consequences for his or her behavior?

Aggressive parenting is loud, abusive and seeks conflict. Therefore, aggressive parents are irresponsible. This could be why your teen is a harasser. It is the parents' job to discover why their teens are bullies, including examining their own negative personality traits and discussing these shortcomings with their families. When parents become responsible, their teens can too.

If you want to be an assertive parent, take responsibility and stop being controlling and abusive. If your teen is currently a victim, you need to ask yourself these questions:

- Is my aggressive parenting style contributing to the victimization of my teen?
- What personality changes do I need to make in order to model assertive behavior?
- Do I make my teen a victim at home?
- Does my teen need me to back off and let him or her handle some things on his or her own?

Taking responsibility for the teen you have raised is necessary if you are to stop an aggressive cycle which usually includes harassment. If you are honest in your answers to the questions, the next step is to make these admissions to your spouse and to your teen. Your willingness to be open and honest is key to changing negative behavior and taking responsibility.

Assertive parents excel at taking responsibility and they teach their children, through modeling and guidance, how to be responsible for themselves and for others as well. Assertive teens have reasonable responsibilities for their ages and are able to make decisions on their own regarding those responsibilities. Because the consequences when they mess up are not physically or psychologically harmful, they feel safe in taking responsibility for their actions. We will discuss in more depth how assertive parenting works in parent section 6.

Be aware that it will be an uphill struggle for teens to stop being harassers or victims if there is an aggressive parent at home. They need parents to be responsible, not angry and controlling. They need parents who respect them and love them selflessly. You cannot help your teen out of harassing situations if you are an aggressive parent.

Change can happen. Helping your teen can happen. Becoming an assertive person and parent is the key.

Aggressive versus Assertive Thought Processes

We've examined what being an aggressive person and an aggressive parent means as well as how to become assertive instead. Realize that becoming an assertive person is necessary before you can become an assertive parent. Now we'll contrast the thought processes of an aggressive parent versus an assertive one. If you recognize any of these aggressive thoughts as similar to your own, you have work to do to become an assertive parent.

Aggressive Parent Thinking	Assertive Parent Knowing
I don't understand why my children are always yelling at one another, fighting and teasing. Things are always chaotic at our house.	I can't expect my teen to show respect for anyone if I don't model respect. When there is respect in the home, there is no chaos.
My son or daughter and I will do whatever it takes to get what we want and be winners.	Winning isn't everything. Spending time with my teen and not making winning the number one priority is more important.
I will get my teen to do what I want him or her to do through intimidation.	Intimidation is not an effective way for my teen to learn self-control. Intimidation will teach my son or daughter to be a harasser or a victim.
I don't understand why my child expects me to go to all of his or her boring school activities.	Being a parent involves supporting my child in the activities that are important to him or her. Supporting my son or daughter is giving him or her the respect he or she deserves.
I know that I should stop smoking, but it's my life.	When I choose to participate in risky behaviors I should expect my teen to follow my example.
I always know what's best for my teen. After all, I am the parent.	I know that my teen will never make good decisions on his or her own if I don't model good decision making and then allow my child to practice and reap the rewards or consequences.

Aggressive Parent Thinking	Assertive Parent Knowing
My child's discipline problems are caused by the fact that he or she is so much more intelligent than any of the teachers. He or she is bored!	My teen's bad behavior should not be blamed on others. My teen needs to understand that he or she is responsible for his or her behavior and attitudes.
I feel that it is my right as a parent to let referees, teachers, coaches, etc., know what I expect for my child.	I do have a right to express my concerns about my teen, but I realize that other people have rights as well and that my violating their rights will not benefit my child or me.
It's important that my child knows who is boss!	My teenage son or daughter should obey me because he or she respects me, not because he or she fears me.

As we stated in parent section 4, it is never too late to become an assertive parent. But part of becoming an assertive parent is realizing your teen has to meet you halfway. Your son or daughter has some responsibility in the harassing situations he or she is in. If your teen doesn't make the needed changes to become assertive, he or she needs to experience the consequences.

You can stop being an aggressive parent. When you do, you will find that not only will you help your teen stop and prevent harassment, but also you will be a much calmer, happier person, because you are a respected part of a family that is raising successful children through modeling and guiding them to learn positive, assertive behavior.

- **MYTH:** If I parent assertively, my child will turn out to be a wimp.
- **TRUTH:** If you parent assertively, your child will turn out to be independent, happy and successful. Parenting aggressively creates wimps, otherwise known as victims. It also creates harassers. Neither a victim nor a harasser can be truly successful or happy.

USING THE GOAL SETTING SHEETS AT THE END OF THE SECTION, FILL OUT AT LEAST ONE FOR AN AGGRESSIVE BEHAVIOR YOU HAVE AND ONE FOR AN AGGRESSIVE PARENTING SKILL YOU HAVE. USE THE OTHER SHEETS AS GUIDANCE UNTIL YOU GET USED TO SETTING AND ACHIEVING GOALS. DON'T FORGET TO BE A SMART PARENT!

PARENT CONNECTIONS

- How is Rachel's mom an aggressive parent?

  Rachel's mom was verbally and physically abusive with Rachel and others. Rachel never knew where she stood with her mom and she feared her. It also didn't bother Rachel's mom to let the school and law enforcement take care of Rachel. She obviously felt that she had no responsibility in the situation.

- How does Rachel's mom contribute to Rachel's aggressive behavior and anger?

  At the very least, she did little to stop it. Only once in the story did Rachel's mom provide consequences for Rachel's behavior and these consequences were aggressive and ineffective. She got her out of minor trouble with teachers and told Mr. Leslie to do whatever he wanted to when she found out about the DMP theft. It is probably safe to assume that Rachel learned much of her aggressive behavior from her mother.

- Should Rachel or any other teen have to work around his or her parent to achieve SMART goals?

  Absolutely not, but we can guess Rachel will have to. The strongest evidence for this is with whom Rachel decided to share her positive goals. Rachel wanted to tell Mrs. Burns, a teacher. Teens are going to share with other people instead of parents, but the reason should never be because they are afraid of what their parents might say or do if they confide in them.

SMART Goal:

Today's date: Completion date:

Why do I need to reach this goal?	How and when will I work toward this goal?	# of times (per day, week, month)	Status (how's it going)

Possible Difficulties:

SMART Goal:

Today's date: Completion date:

Why do I need to reach this goal?	How and when will I work toward this goal?	# of times (per day, week, month)	Status (how's it going)

Possible Difficulties:

SMART Goal:

Today's date: Completion date:

Why do I need to reach this goal?	How and when will I work toward this goal?	# of times (per day, week, month)	Status (how's it going)

Possible Difficulties:

SMART Goal:

Today's date: Completion date:

Why do I need to reach this goal?	How and when will I work toward this goal?	# of times (per day, week, month)	Status (how's it going)

Possible Difficulties:

Chapter Six

Winners and Positive Parents

I Survived My Passive and Aggressive Parents: Jeanne's Story

Jeanne told us a disturbing tale about her abusive father and passive mother, which shows the influence of these types of parenting figures on sons and daughters. In Jeanne's case she finally was able to rise above the cruelty she suffered by asserting herself, choosing good friends and finding positive role models.

My dad is a bully and my mom is a doormat. At thirty-eight years old, I still have trouble admitting that without feeling guilty and disloyal. The bond between parent and child is the most complex type of relationship and I battled with it every day in my effort to become who I am, rather than who I was brought up to be.

I was raised in a conservative religious household where both parents subscribed to the "traditional" roles of male and female in the marriage: my dad was dominant and my mom was compliant and sub-servient. I was fourth in a family of nine children and we were expected to do, feel and believe as we were told, no questions asked.

Disobedience in any form was dealt with swiftly and harshly, with Mom usually reporting the offender to Dad, who carried out the punishment. Punishment could be in the form of beatings, lectures, removing privileges (such as using the phone, television or car), adding extra chores or grounding. None of this was that unusual;

many of the families in the town where I grew up belonged to the same religion and managed family affairs in a similar fashion.

In public and often at home my dad could be a great guy. But he also had a mean streak that caused him to enjoy controlling and hurting others. My siblings and I were the usual targets. My mom's role on these occasions was to keep her mouth shut and clean up the damage afterward.

The first incident I can recall that was aimed at me personally occurred when I was seven years old. I was crazy about animals and was always campaigning for a pet of my own. My parents weren't big on pets, because pets meant extra work and expense. In a moment of weakness, my dad allowed me to bring home a kitten that I named Shadow. I loved that cat and had him for over a year when we moved to another town. Because the house was new, my dad made a rule that no pets were allowed inside. I was sad, because Shadow had always slept on my bed, but I didn't dare disobey.

One day while my parents were gone, my older brother brought Shadow inside to torment me. I managed to get the cat away from him and back outside before my parents returned. My younger sister, not realizing the consequences of her tattling, immediately ratted me out.

"Dad, Jeanne had the cat in the house while you were gone!"

My dad turned to me and said, "I told you not to bring that cat in the house. Go get him and bring him to me right now."

"But, Dad, I didn't bring him in! Tom did it to tease me. Shadow didn't make any messes."

"I don't care. The rule was broken. Bring me your cat."

I went outside and called Shadow to me. I cuddled him and told myself it was okay, that Dad would probably just lock him in the garage for a few days to teach me a lesson. I knew it was more likely that Dad would take him to the pound or drop him off somewhere, but those were possibilities I would not consider.

I delayed as long as I could, but finally I took my cat inside and handed him over to my dad. He took him from me without a word and went down to the basement. My sisters and I huddled upstairs, speculating about what Dad was going to do. Even though Shadow was my cat, we all loved him. Suddenly, one of them looked out the window and screeched. We saw Dad and my older brother walking toward the back of our property. My dad was carrying Shadow and, to my horror, my brother was carrying one of my dad's rifles.

Once they reached the trees we could not see them very clearly. I wasn't really scared, because I didn't believe Dad would actually shoot my cat. I thought he was just trying to teach me a lesson. I watched as Dad raised the rifle and fired two shots. I couldn't see my brother or Shadow. A few minutes later, Dad and Tom came walking back to the house, Tom looking shaken and very contrite. My conviction that they wouldn't hurt my cat was starting to waver.

I stayed upstairs with my sisters for over an hour, all of us afraid to show our faces. Finally one of them had the courage to venture out and soon came back, reporting that Dad was asleep in front of the TV and Mom was busy in the kitchen. I sneaked out of the house and ran to the trees. It took awhile, but I finally found Shadow. My precious cat, two holes blown through him, had been left under a light covering of leaves where he could easily be found.

I stared at the body for a long time before covering it back up and going back to the house. I was too scared of my father's response to give Shadow a proper burial.

None of us discussed the Shadow incident after that day. A few days later, my dad came home from work and gave me a stuffed white cat with a red ribbon around its neck. No explanation was given and I knew I was expected to act thrilled with the gift, so I did. I named the toy Shadow and I still have it to this day.

Dad loved to water ski and wanted each of us to learn. He bought a boat and we went out most weekends to the river or a nearby reservoir. Dad's idea of teaching a person to ski was to give basic instructions, get the person up as quickly as possible and then whip the boat around as fast as he could until the person crashed. Crashing was always considered good fun and even if you were exhausted you had better fall at least three times before you were allowed back in the boat. Mom refused to go out on the boat with us.

One day after I had crashed at high speed several times and was bruised, tired and frustrated, I found myself physically unable to get back up on the skis. After I made several failed attempts to get up successfully, Dad circled the boat close by and started shouting instructions.

"Lean back and keep your tips together! You're letting go the minute you get out of the water."

"Dad, I'm tired. I don't want to go again. Let someone else try."

"Stop your bellyachin' and get back up there. You'll never learn if you can't stay up for more than five minutes!"

So I sucked it up and tried again. This time he jerked me out of the water so fast one of my skis came off and I plowed into the water head first.

Dad circled back around, laughing. "You gotta keep your skis on! Do it again."

"Dad, I can't. I'm too tired to hold on to the rope and I hurt my neck on that last crash. Let me back into the boat."

"Stop being a boob. Aren't we having fun?"

"No! I'm done. Come pick me up!" At this point I had started to cry which angered him.

"Jeanne, if you don't get back up and stay up on this next try, I'm going to sell your horse!"

Although I believed he would make good on his threat, I was too upset and crying too hard at this point to do anything but blubber. Finally, in disgust, he came back and picked me up. Once I was in the boat he said, "You're grounded, you big baby. Now stop bawling before I give you something to cry about!"

Luckily he didn't sell my horse after that incident, although I was grounded for a week. I never did gain much skill or appreciation for waterskiing.

I was a good student but somewhat indifferent; it was easy for me to get good grades without a lot of effort. I was more interested in socializing with friends and spending my time riding my horse or playing basketball and volleyball. One of my older sisters constantly pushed herself to be perfect: straight As, leader in school and church activities, never "acting out." She developed stomach ulcers and migraine headaches in the sixth grade. She and I were close but not without competition. She thought I should try harder and I thought she should loosen up.

One semester, after our report cards arrived, Dad sat the older siblings down to talk about our grades. To my older sister he said, "Great job on earning straight As again! The rest of you kids need to be more like her."

"Jeanne, you had six As and two Bs. Not bad. But, you know, you are ten times smarter than your sister. If you weren't so lazy, you could run circles around her."

I couldn't have cared less about getting better grades than my sister and I felt terrible about the effect his callous remark must have had on her. My dad often tried to play us against each other like this, for what purpose I never could understand. If anything, it drove us closer together and strengthened my resolve to be my own person.

Most evenings, we gathered together before bed for family prayers. With so many people to gather, it usually took awhile from the first announcement to the time we were all assembled. Dad passed the time that we were waiting by picking one of the children and teasing him or her. The teasing was supposed to be in good fun, but the subjects he selected were usually hurtful.

"Hey, Jeanne! With those long legs of yours and no body, you look just like a frog. I think we'll call you Froggy. What do you think about that, Froggy?"

If my younger sister laughed, he turned on her. "What are you laughing at? Your cheeks are so chubby, when you laugh your eyes disappear. I think we'll call you Chipmunk Cheeks. What are you storing in those fat cheeks, acorns?"

Then he attacked one of my brothers: "Oh and look who doesn't have a sense of humor tonight. Ol' Dumbo Ears. With goofy ears like that I would think you'd *have* to have a sense of humor! What do you think, kids? Doesn't he look like Dumbo?"

And on it went. If you didn't join in the "fun," you were likely to be the next person targeted. Sitting quietly and not saying anything was interpreted as not joining in. So whoever the victim was for the evening had to tolerate the entire family poking fun at him or her and had to keep a smile on his or her face; any show of hurt, anger or tears earned a harsh lecture, being sent to your room or even a swat. Mom usually looked on with a bland smile on her face and said nothing.

My parents held the belief that during the teen years children forget their religion and fall victim to the evils of public school and the social temptations that present themselves. I was in ninth grade when their attention turned to me. I had learned some lessons from watching my older siblings make mistakes. I knew to avoid dropping out of school and getting married because of pregnancy and to avoid the horrors of drug and alcohol use. In spite of "keeping my nose clean" and adhering to all the rules, Dad constantly accused me of drinking, having sex and every other thing defined as "bad" by our religion.

By the time I was a high school sophomore, I was weary of all the unfounded accusations and started to stand up to my dad rather than meekly take his abuse. I am not sure why I was the first child in our family to have the courage to do this. Perhaps it was because I had more time to develop my personality and self-confidence while Dad was focused on my older siblings. Whatever the reason, things got ugly fast: the more he tried to tighten his control, the more I fought it.

The conflict between my dad and I continued to escalate. He took my younger siblings out of public school and forced my mom to homeschool them. I was a junior in high school at the time and somehow convinced him that it was too late to take me out; it would hurt my chances of getting into college.

College was another point of contention between us. Dad wanted me to attend a college associated with our religion but I refused, preferring to attend the state university, because it had a good business program. During one of our debates, my dad said to me, "Why do you think you need to go to college anyway? You don't need a degree to raise babies."

Things reached the boiling point one day when Dad and I had a particularly nasty discussion before school regarding my talking on the phone to a friend of whom he did not approve. Dad went off to work, where he must have thought about our conversation all morning.

After my lunch period, the office aide came into my chemistry class and informed the teacher I needed to go to the office to answer a phone call from my father. All my classmates turned to look at me in wonder. Pulling someone out of class to take a call—even from a parent—was simply *not* done.

I went to the office, picked up the telephone and stood in silence while Dad yelled at me over the phone line. Although everyone in the office tried to pretend they weren't listening, I knew they could hear him shouting. I finally mustered the courage to interrupt his tirade. "Dad, can we continue this conversation at home? I really need to get back to class."

"Fine," he said and hung up.

Twenty minutes later, the office aide returned to my class. My father wanted to speak to me again. This time the class stared at me in open disbelief and I tried not to think about what my dad said to the office staff to get them to break the rules *twice*.

I took the call and listened to another ten minutes of infuriated lecturing but did not respond, because everyone in the office would overhear my side of the conversation. I was starting to get angry too but tried to keep my voice calm. "Dad, I really can't talk about this now. Can we *please* discuss it at home tonight?"

"No. We need to get this resolved right now. If you can't live by my rules, then you can't live under my roof. In fact, that's it. I want you out of my house!"

After I got home from school that day, my best friend helped me pack my things and I left. As I walked through the house with my final box of belongings, I tried to catch my mom's eye as she sat working with her Cub Scout troop on a project. She never said a word nor did she look up as I walked by.

I would love to report that everything got better once I got away from my father, but the truth is, that was just the beginning for me. I moved away and lived with a friend who was in college, working part-time jobs after school to help pay the rent. After I finished high school I started speaking to my parents again, but they considered me a lost cause and warned my siblings who were still at home against having any association with me.

I went on to college, paying my own way by working several jobs. It was during this time that I really struggled with who I wanted to be. I went through friends and boyfriends like they were disposable. I could never figure out which role I was supposed to play: in some relationships I was a doormat, in others I was a tyrant. My moods came and went like my friends and were generally controlled by whatever was happening around me.

When I was twenty-two, I realized I was in imminent danger of becoming just like my parents or living my life blaming them for the mess that I felt myself to be. I made a conscious effort to break this up and down cycle and take charge of my life. I focused more effort on deepening and strengthening the bonds I had with people who had proven themselves to be my true friends. I approached dating relationships from a much more rational perspective and began to look for someone with whom I could have a true partnership rather than a power struggle. I started to seek out mentoring relationships with older men and women through work, school and volunteering. I employed simple tricks to humor myself out of a bad mood: listening to music when I was feeling weak, watching comedy movies when I was depressed or sprinting through the park when I was angry. I spent a lot of time volunteering at the local hospital and Special

Olympics. By the time I was twenty-four, I had formed my ideal image of the kind of person I wanted to be: honest, compassionate and strong.

I have often been asked how I turned out as well as I did given my family situation and also how I became so resilient. Even after a lot of soul-searching, I am not certain how to answer those questions, but I think a number of factors influenced me.

I learned at a young age to watch and learn from other people's mistakes. I also made it a point to learn from my own mistakes and not repeat them. It took me a while to figure out the kind of person I wanted to be when I grew up, but I knew from a very young age what I did *not* want to be—and that included becoming either my father or my mother.

I was a voracious reader. I used to read the dictionary, find words that sounded impressive and try to work them into my vocabulary. I read everything I could get my hands on, including a full set of encyclopedias (we didn't have the Internet when I was a child) and boxes of condensed books that my mother rescued from someone's trash. I think all that reading was a way for me to escape my reality and at the same time help expand my worldview.

I surrounded myself with friends and mentors whom I admired or looked up to in some way and then tried to live up to their examples. I continue to have an extensive network of friends who make up my support system and I spend a considerable amount of time and effort cultivating and maintaining those relationships.

I am a success by most people's definitions: I put myself through college, have had a series of rewarding professional positions, have been happily married to the same man for thirteen years, am healthy, have a wide network of good friends and recreational interests, am active in my community and generally have an optimistic outlook on life. Even so, I will never escape the reality that my parents continue to see me as a disappointment, because I did not choose the life they expected for me. Depressing as that may sound, I consider it one of my proudest accomplishments.

I have one message for young people who find themselves in a similar situation: No matter your circumstances, *you* have the right, the capability and the responsibility to choose the type of person you will be.

TEEN CONNECTIONS

- How did Jeanne become assertive?
- What are the ways she demonstrated assertiveness?
- How did Jeanne maintain her assertive personality?

PARENT CONNECTIONS

- What incidents in the story demonstrate that Jeanne's mom had a passive personality?
- What incidents in the story demonstrate that Jeanne's dad had an aggressive personality?
- How did Jeanne become assertive despite her parents' passive and aggressive personalities?

Teen Section 6

How to be a Winner

Assertive behavior is indicated by *B* answers on your quiz. If these make up fifteen or more of your answers, we have one thing to say to you: Way to go! Assertive personalities are successful, confident and happy people. We believe that if the world was full of assertive people, we would have no bullies or victims. Harassment wouldn't exist.

Assertive personalities are admired, because they know what respect is. They give it and they get it in return. They are able to give and receive respect, because they first gained respect for themselves. It takes hard work to become assertive and it takes work to maintain an assertive personality. But, as we've said many times already, it is well worth it.

If you have fourteen or fewer *B* answers on your quiz you should still congratulate yourself. After all, you are doing some things right. Because we have already looked at the things you might not be doing so well, in this section we'll focus on the good stuff. Pay attention to how you feel when you're assertive. It feels great when we are good to others and ourselves. Let's discuss what it means to be assertive, the benefits of being assertive and how to maintain assertiveness.

What Being Assertive Means

Knowing exactly what it means to be assertive is crucial in order to understand why learning to be assertive is so important in relation to harassment. Truly assertive people don't let harassment or bullying happen to them or to others. We firmly believe that assertive personalities are the types of leaders needed to create a society where people will be nice to and assist one another. However, before we can change the world, we need to discover how to be assertive and make these qualities and behaviors central to our personalities.

Acting in Your Own Best Interest Without Hurting Others

Assertive personalities go after what they want and what is good for them. How is that different from how aggressive personalities act? Assertive people achieve their goals without hurting themselves or others along the way. They do not violate the rights we outlined in chapter 1. Because of this, assertive personalities create win-win situations. Everybody wins, because assertive people get what they want and others are not belittled, stepped on or made to feel used. Instead they feel important, secure and equal. All involved are victorious. After Cody decided he wanted to go to college and realized he would have to do it on his own, he was able gain the needed independence and achieve his goal.

Cody was legally blind. He could see shadows and movement, but that was it. Cody had supportive parents, teachers and an outreach person to provide the assistance he needed and even some he didn't. Cody leaned heavily on those around him. If something was difficult for him, he passively let others take care of it.

In his junior year of high school, Cody became interested in college. He realized that if he wanted to attend college he would have to act on his own. After all, he couldn't take his mom and the rest of his support team to college. Cody would have to go after what he wanted and stop depending on others.

When Cody graduated from college, it was a real achievement, because he'd done it by himself. He'd asked for support only when he really needed it. Cody acted in his own best interest, made it through college and started the career of his choice.

Standing Up for Yourself

Assertive personalities not only know their rights, but also are not afraid to stand up for their principles. Aggressive personalities still try to bully assertive personalities, but the difference is that assertive people stand up for themselves. We will go into specifics about how to stand up to bullies later, but the end result of standing up for yourself is that harassers don't mess with assertive people. Harassers are defeated by an assertive individual's confidence.

Being Proactive

As we discussed in teen section 5, proactive people think before they act and they take responsibility for their actions. Being proactive provides control. Because assertive people make good choices, they have the control that passive and aggressive personalities do not. This leads to control, which leads to security and independence. Learning from her past mistakes, Sue took a proactive approach to achieve different results.

Sue was ready in September when the counselors started registering students for classes. She had made up her mind that she would not make the same mistakes she did the previous year. At that time Sue didn't pay attention when the counselors gave instructions on which classes to take and how to register for them. It had taken hours of standing in lines to straighten out the mess of a schedule she ended up with.

Now Sue listened carefully and took notes on what the counselor said. She discussed her options with her parents and made a list of required classes and electives she would like, including a couple of alternatives in case a class signup list was closed.

Because of her proactive thinking, Sue didn't have to stand in any lines to straighten out her schedule. Everything went smoothly and she was able to take the classes that benefited her future plans.

Being Honest

Assertive personalities act with integrity. They don't lie, cheat or steal. They know that doing anything dishonest takes away from their integrity and that integrity is the most important thing any of us possesses.

Honesty also has to do with expression; that is, the way you look on the outside. When you aren't trying to gain an advantage or inspire pity with your words or body language, that is honest expression. An assertive person makes normal eye contact and his or her tone of voice is natural, not loud or menacing, quiet or whiny. Posture is upright and body language is relaxed and non-threatening. Assertive people are generally those with whom we like to talk. They are approachable and friendly.

Becoming a Respected Leader and Team Member

Assertive personalities know that being a leader doesn't mean being bossy. People willingly follow a leader, because they admire the leader's ability to work within the team. The best leaders are those who are also excellent team members. Here are five leadership skills which are not just applicable to leaders; they are also effective traits of assertive people.

- **Strong communication skills:** listening and speaking
- **Appreciating differences:** seeing others as equals, with everyone having something unique to contribute
- **Leading by example:** working hard and earning respect
- **Problem solving skills:** defining the challenge, developing alternative solutions, then selecting and implementing the best one
- **Striving to be better:** constantly setting goals to reach higher

Do you fit the definition of assertive? Do you act in your own best interest without hurting others? Do you stand up for yourself? Are you proactive? Are you honest? Are you a respected leader and team member? No one is all those things all the time, but imagine how great it would be if everyone strove to fit the definition of assertive.

- **MYTH:** I only have a few answers on the personality quiz that aren't assertive so I don't have anything to work on.
- **TRUTH:** Nobody is perfect. We all have things to work on. If you had any answers that weren't assertive, those are areas to work on, because they could be stumbling blocks to success and happiness.

Why Be Assertive?

Teen sections 4 and 5 explore why people are passive or aggressive. Now let's focus on why you want to be assertive and how this assertiveness will assist you in achieving your life goals.

If you have parents who are assertive, be thankful for them. Assertive parents make it much easier for their children to see why they want to be assertive. If your parents are passive or aggressive, we hope you realize that happiness and success won't happen unless you break away from the cycle your parents created. We saw in Jeanne's story how she came to this realization. Although it may have been harder for her than for those with assertive parents, she grew to understand the reasons why someone would want to be assertive. We hope this part of the section gives you, like Jeanne, an understanding of why being an assertive person is so important.

Having Self-Confidence and Self-Respect

Self-confidence and self-respect are not traits that bullies or victims have. Self-confidence and self-respect lead naturally to kindness toward others and a willingness to stand up for oneself. Assertive personalities are secure about who they are and they like themselves. When this happens, it is easy to be nice to other people as well as yourself.

Because they have self-confidence and self-respect, assertive people don't participate in activities that are emotionally or physically harmful. Assertive persons would never smoke, take drugs, participate in sexually risky behaviors or do anything else that would harm their bodies or brains and therefore their futures. When Megan sacrificed her self-respect in a moment of passiveness, she took action to gain it back despite knowing the consequences.

Megan was at a party with a couple of her basketball teammates celebrating a win over their rivals. The party was going great until a marijuana joint was passed Megan's way. Her teammates each took a hit. Megan passively decided to try it too. As she inhaled, she felt her self-respect leave to make room for the drug.

The following Monday, the coach called Megan and her teammates into her office. "I heard about a party Saturday night where some of my players were doing drugs. Is this true?"

Megan's friends denied their involvement right away, but Megan couldn't say anything.

"Megan, is it true?" The coach looked at Megan intently, as did the other girls.

"I did it," Megan said.

"Do you other girls want to change your story?" Megan's teammates shook their heads. "Then you can go." Once the other girls had left, the coach said to Megan, "I am going to have to suspend you from the team, but I appreciate your honesty and I respect you for it. You didn't have to come clean, you know."

"Yes, I did. For me."

Gaining Respect From Others

There are two things assertive people do that earn admiration: They respect themselves and they respect others. You cannot begin to gain respect if you have none for yourself. As far as showing others respect, we discussed in teen section 5 that listening to others, appreciating differences, thinking of others, being proactive, avoiding violations of others' rights and having a genuine regard for others earns their respect. Assertive people give and get respect. Aggressive and passive personalities will never gain respect. An honest comment from a friend caused John to try a new approach to his problems and discover a relationship of respect.

John called his mom every time something didn't go right at school. She always came to the school and took care of the situation for him.

One day, John's history teacher, Mr. Jackson, criticized him for rarely participating in class.

After the period ended, John dug through his backpack to find his phone. He needed to tell his mom what Mr. Jackson said. John's classmate Brenton approached him as he dialed. Brenton was one of the few people who was nice to John. "What are you doing?" Brenton asked.

"Calling my mom to tell her what Mr. Jackson said to me today."

"John, I gotta be honest with you. Did you know people make

fun of you, because your mom fights your battles for you? Everybody would respect you a lot more if you dealt with things on your own. Why don't you start by talking with Mr. Jackson yourself?"

John took Brenton's advice and talked to his teacher about being shy in class and promised to try to speak up more often. Mr. Jackson told John that he respected John for coming to him first. John liked the way being respected felt. Not only did Mr. Jackson respect him, but so did his classmates when he stopped depending on his mom to come to his rescue.

Having Better Friendships and Relationships

Assertive personalities have good relationships, because they are built on respect. When someone doesn't think he or she is better than or less than but equal to another person, it creates a positive relationship. The foundation of a strong relationship, whether it is a working relationship, a friendship or a romantic partnership, is mutual respect and admiration.

Without respect, which we know assertive people possess for themselves as well as others, there will be abuse in the relationship. Having healthy, abuse-free relationships with other human beings is necessary for us, because we are social animals and need companionship. In order for a relationship to be healthy and truly work, the people in that relationship have to act assertively.

Experiencing a Sense of Belonging

Assertive people have the sense that they belong to a family, a school, a community, a state, a country, a culture, a society, a world. When you feel like you belong, it not only gives you a sense of security but also gives you a sense of responsibility. When you are a part of something larger than yourself you won't do anything to harm that to which you belong, nor will you allow others to hurt it. There is a great sense of pride if you are a positive contributor to something beyond yourself. Hector discovered the sense of belonging through required service work and chose to turn the experience into a positive one.

Hector didn't choose to work at the food bank. It was something the judge told him he had to do.

Hector showed up at the food bank angry. He was put right to work sorting and boxing food for holiday meals. It wasn't until he saw the results of his work that Hector began to feel good about what he was doing. When a little girl threw her arms around him and said thank you, when all he had done was carry a box of food to her parents' car, Hector was hooked.

Hector could choose to contribute to his community or to harm it and himself in the process. He chose to belong, to remain a volunteer at the food bank after his mandated service was completed and never to do anything that would result in his going before a judge again.

Enjoying Less Anxiety and Stress

One of the greatest advantages assertive people have over passive and aggressive personalities is they experience less anxiety and stress. When you like yourself enough to create healthy habits, others respect you, your relationships are based on respect and equality and you feel like you're a part of something larger than yourself.

This is not to say that assertive people never become anxious or stressed, because they do. The difference is that assertive people don't create these emotional states for themselves and they know how to deal with them in positive ways. We'll discuss methods of dealing with stressful and anxious situations later in this section.

Reaping Rewards for Being Assertive

Assertive people love the feeling of being good to themselves and others, being appreciated by their friends, family and those who come in contact with them and experiencing happiness and success.

Why doesn't everyone choose to be assertive? We think they want to, but passive and aggressive personalities have to be willing to break habits and work to get there. People are not always willing to do that. The results of being assertive are great, but getting there can be tough. Many times it's easier to be passive or aggressive. The key is to remember the whys of being assertive. Remember that self-confidence, self-respect, respect from others, a sense of belonging, less anxiety and stress and countless rewards are worth the effort.

- **MYTH:** I do volunteer work, so that makes me assertive.
- **TRUTH:** Assertive people are well-rounded, which means that although doing volunteer work is great, by itself it doesn't necessarily mean you are assertive. The same goes for getting good grades, having a lot of friends, etc. If you are passive or aggressive in other parts of your life, doing one thing assertively isn't going to cancel out negative behaviors.

Maintaining an Assertive Personality

Once you've worked hard at becoming assertive, this doesn't mean you'll be able to manifest that quality in every situation you face. A personality, particularly an assertive one, has to be maintained. It can be tempting even for the most assertive people to fall into passive or aggressive patterns of behavior, particularly with people or situations they don't like or think are stressful. Laura had several issues causing her stress, so she mapped out a plan to manage everything and remain balanced.

Laura's younger sister had been diagnosed with a rare form of cancer. This condition meant the family had to keep someone with her at all times and they had to travel to see doctors who specialized in the illness. Laura's parents couldn't do it on their own, because somebody had to work in order to carry insurance and pay the medical bills. Laura would have to help.

At sixteen, Laura was already an assertive person, but missing so much school and being unable to spend time with friends on top of constantly worrying about her sister's health took its toll. Nevertheless, Laura was conscious of what she had to do to maintain her assertive personality, keep herself balanced and support her sister.

Laura made time to do things to relax to avoid becoming stressed out or angry. When she had to miss school, she kept in touch with her teachers and got assignments so she wouldn't fall behind. Laura talked with friends on the phone or through e-mail so they could support her emotionally or simply distract her with their everyday stories. She remained positive, because if she didn't she felt she would become buried in the problems. Bad attitudes are catching and Laura certainly didn't want her attitude to influence her sister's recovery. Laura also wanted to continue to work toward her goal of becoming a nurse.

After months of fighting the disease, Laura's sister died. Laura's greatest consolation was that she was there for her sister until the end. Going back to school wasn't stressful, because she had remained in touch with her friends and let them support her and because Laura found a way to keep up-to-date with her schoolwork. Laura remained assertive under the most difficult circumstances.

Here is some advice to help you maintain the key to your success and happiness: an assertive personality.

Dealing with Stress

Stress has both positive and negative attributes. We all need some stress in our lives. If we had none, we wouldn't accomplish much. In order for us to perform at our highest levels we have to have some stress.

However, when there's too much stress and we feel symptoms like stomach problems, aches and pains and being overly tired, we have to find a way to reduce the stress to a manageable level. If stress gets to be overpowering and we don't deal with it assertively, we will react passively or aggressively. The result of that is never good. You can keep an assertive outlook by dealing effectively with stress. Here are some tips:

- **Figure out what causes you stress**. If you know what it is, you can avoid it or plan how to deal with it.

- **Manage your time**. Feeling like there isn't enough time is the number one cause of stress. Do you use an agenda? Planning will help free up time for things like relaxation. Maybe it's time to work on your time management skills.

- **Find a friend**. Talking with someone you care about and who cares about you can be a big help when dealing with stress.

- **Take a break**. Get away, even it if it's only for a few minutes, and de-stress through exercise, meditation or simply relaxing.

- **Just say no**. This is a time management issue as well. Saying no to things is important so you don't get overbooked, overloaded and stressed out.

- **Gain control of your temper**. Anger is not helpful to stress levels. We discuss anger management and tips on how to deal with your temper in this section.

- **Find a way to release stress**. Exercise is the best, but reading, making or listening to music, meditating or doing anything else you enjoy can help you relax.

- **Get some help**. If you find that you've tried everything you can think of and stress is still getting the better of you, seek help from a counselor.

Dealing with Anger

It is easier for assertive personalities to deal with anger because of the good habits they've created. However, even assertive people sometimes have to deal with anger. Everyone gets angry at times and this is normal, but in order to keep being assertive you cannot let anger control you. The assertive person learns to deal with anger in a healthy way. The tips we discussed in teen section 5 apply here as well:

- **Take a break**. Get away from the person you are angry with until you can calm down.

- **Chill out.** Count to ten, take a deep breath, listen to music, imagine you are somewhere else, talk yourself down, write in a journal, strum a guitar—anything to keep you from reacting in the moment without thinking.

- **Exercise.** Doing something physically active is part of chilling out but it deserves a heading of its own, because it is the one thing guaranteed to help with anger. When we exercise, calming substances called endorphins are released in our brains. They make us feel calm, awake and healthy.

- **Be proactive.** There's that word again. Think before you act! When you're angry is not a time to be reactive.

- **Tell the person you're angry.** Notice that this is after you have calmed down. You're being proactive. It is healthy to express anger in a *positive* way.

- **Use "I" statements.** When you discuss your feelings, begin with the word "I". This will keep you from playing the blame game. However, you must follow the "I" statement with helpful, calm words. Saying "I want to beat you up" isn't helpful, but saying "I want you to stop calling me names" is helpful. (Refer to teen sections 4 and 5 for lists of "I" statements.)

- **Come up with solutions.** Coming up with appropriate answers and solutions takes work. Keeping your anger levels in check is worth the effort. Instead of focusing on who or what made you angry, focus on resolving the issue.

- **Don't hold a grudge.** Holding a grudge is like picking up a hot rock to throw at someone: you're the one who gets burned. People hold grudges against those who aren't acting the way they want them to act. However, people will never act the way you want them to, so the grudge is a major waste of energy.

Checking Your Attitudes

One of the most important things assertive people do is choose to have a good attitude each and every day. If you find yourself wanting to behave in a way that isn't assertive, ask yourself what your attitude is. If it isn't good, use the stress tips or the anger management tips to turn it around. Once we deal with our anger or stress it becomes easier to have a positive outlook.

Keeping Friends and Family Close

Assertive personalities create positive relationships, but sometimes even assertive people don't use them. It may feel passive or aggressive to lean on someone else, but it's not. We all need help from time to time, including assertive personalities. Find out whom you can count on to support and assist you when you're overwhelmed. If life's problems seem to be overpowering you, part of being assertive is letting others help you when you need it. Scott and Becca developed a friendship where they could lean on each other in tough and stressful times.

Scott and Becca were assertive teens. They had a standing date to meet for coffee every Saturday morning. They called their mornings together "the venting". It was a time when they discussed what went right and wrong with their weeks and explained problems to each other to discuss potential solutions.

Without their Saturday meetings, they knew that life's stresses could become overwhelming. Simply talking things through and discussing problems with a trusted friend was a great way to relieve stress and maintain their positive outlooks.

Being Aware That Others Are Watching

In the passive and aggressive chapters, our advice was to watch and copy the actions of assertive people. Those aren't the only people who are going to watch assertive personalities. It is human nature to measure ourselves against others. It's how we gain our role models. If you are assertive, know that people admire you and want to be like you. You are a role model. Remember this when you feel like you want to be reactive instead of proactive and are tempted to behave passively or aggressively. Keeping in mind that actions speak louder than words will help also.

Remembering How Great Win-Win Feels

Behaving passively or aggressively doesn't create win-win situations. It takes away self-respect, self-confidence and respect from others. It is easier to lose respect than it is to gain it. Everybody slips up from time to time. Learn from those mistakes and work toward getting back that great feeling of respect from yourself and from others. Remember the satisfaction that comes from being in win-win situations. Remind yourself how it feels and repeat it as much as you can.

Challenging Yourself to be Better

The moment you stop setting challenging goals is the same moment you become passive or aggressive. Working toward and reaching our goals gives us a sense of accomplishment and success, which is important for our self-confidence. Review the SMART method of goal-setting often. Understand that even the most assertive people should take time to review their goals periodically. Assertive personalities are not immune to becoming over-confident and taking on more than they can realistically achieve when it comes to goals. Maintain your assertiveness by playing it SMART.

Maintaining assertiveness is all about keeping yourself in check. Know what it means, why you want to be assertive and how it feels when you are assertive. Then ask yourself, "What are the consequences of these actions?" Are you treating others the way you would like to be treated? Are you standing up for yourself without hurting others in the process? Most importantly, reflect on how you feel about you.

- **MYTH:** If I am assertive then I should be able to solve any problem on my own.
- **TRUTH:** One of the things assertive people do well is knowing when they need help and asking for it.

 LIST SOME OF THE THINGS YOU CAN DO TO MAINTAIN ASSERTIVENESS USING THE QUESTIONNAIRE AT THE END OF THIS SECTION. BE AWARE OF YOUR GREATEST RESOURCES.

TEEN CONNECTIONS

- How did Jeanne become assertive?

  Jeanne had to learn self-respect or else her dad would have defined her as he did her mom. When her dad kicked her out of the house, she could have given up and become passive or aggressive, but she consciously chose to have respect for herself. She wouldn't let herself become her parents. When Jeanne gained self-respect she became her own person, which led to success. Jeanne also befriended assertive people and used them as examples and for support.

- What are the ways she demonstrated assertiveness?

  Jeanne was forced to leave her home, but she didn't give up on her life. She finished high school, worked hard and put herself through college. She then worked on her relationships until she knew they were healthy, strong and assertive situations where she was an equal, not a doormat or a tyrant. Because of her hard work, Jeanne became confident, successful and happy.

- How did Jeanne maintain her assertive personality?

She worked on keeping assertive relationships with her friends, family and husband. She exercised on a regular basis and was conscious about her health. She was involved in charity work and always made time for fun.

How Do I Maintain Assertiveness?

List some of the things you can do to maintain your assertiveness. Be aware of your greatest resources.

Three things I do to manage my stress:

1. _____

2. _____

3. _____

Three things I do to manage my anger:

1. _____

2. _____

3. _____

Three situations where I struggle with my attitude:

1. _____

2. _____

3. _____

Three people who can help me:

1. _____

2. _____

3. _____

Three people who are observing me:

1. _____

2. _____

3. _____

Three times I felt great because of my assertiveness:

1. _____

2. _____

3. _____

Three goals toward which I need to work:

1. _____

2. _____

3. _____

Parent Section 6

The Positive Parent

The parent quiz involved questions about individual behaviors as well as parenting behaviors. Assertive behavior is indicated by *B* answers on your quiz. In teen section 6 we focused on what it means to become an assertive person and how to maintain an assertive personality. Being assertive is important for parents, because teens look to them first and foremost for ways to navigate through their lives. They watch you, learn from you and need your guidance. Parents are a teen's most powerful instructors, because they have been involved from the beginning and should know their teen better than anyone. Like Jeanne, whose story we told earlier, some teens may be able to get out of an abusive cycle like harassment on their own, but success rates increase immensely when an assertive parent is involved. Now we will discuss some general techniques that assertive parents should employ to ensure their teens are not victims or the perpetrators of harassment.

Being an Assertive Parent

The information in teen section 6 absolutely applies to adults as well as teens. It is just as important for an adult to have the ability to maintain an assertive personality, including handling stress and anger, because there is a lot at stake: jobs, physical and mental health, relationships and family members who watch and learn from you. You need to work on your own behaviors first if you are going to parent effectively and help your teen face harassment. Teens can become assertive and therefore prevent harassment on their own, but they are still children and therefore shouldn't have to and may need help. The support of a parent makes it a lot easier for teens to escape adolescence unscathed. There are some general things that assertive parents can practice in order to help their children avoid harassment and the damage it can do.

Walk the Walk and Talk the Talk

Assertive parents raise assertive children. Your teen observes you and learns from you and has been doing so since he or she was born. What you are teaching your son or daughter has everything to do with how he or she handles life, including harassment. You can be the role model your teen needs. Assertive parents do many things, but here are some examples that your teen needs to see and hear from you that can prevent harassment.

- Stand up for yourself.
- Be proactive.
- Cultivate relationships that are based on respect.
- Act in control, but don't be obsessed with it or willing to give it away.
- Make mistakes, confess to them and learn from them.
- Live the laws of integrity.
- Take pride in your family.
- Show an interest in getting to know your teens and what they are doing.
- Work to maintain an assertive personality: manage stress, deal with anger and other emotions positively, check your attitude, keep your allies, friends and family close.
- Remember that your behavior will be studied and emulated, so put yourself first once in a while.
- Accept help when the going gets tough.
- Deal with adversity in an assertive way.
- Constantly challenge yourself to be a better person and parent.

Teens are struggling to become abstract thinkers and independent in thought and action, but this doesn't mean they don't need role models. In fact, they need them more than ever. They will never admit it, but the first place they look for a role model is their parents. Parents have to realize that despite the eye rolling, shoulder shrugging, yelling, ignoring and the "You don't get me" and "I hate you" comments, teens are listening and watching. When they are with their peers, it is often their parents' behaviors they emulate, not anyone else's. Their brains are still developing and their hormones are raging, so they may not see how to create win-win situations, but they can remember how their parents did. Model assertive behavior and make the world a safe, secure and successful place for your teen. Britney's mother modeled and explained her assertive behavior to Britney, enabling Britney to use this behavior in the future.

Britney often accompanied her mom, Peggy, to library board meetings. Britney was in the audience when a woman named Andrea made her case for taking a young adult novel off the shelf. She ended the argument by saying, "If we let children read smut like this, teen pregnancy will skyrocket."

Peggy countered for the board, "My daughter has read the book and I previewed it. I believe the material was relevant for teens and did not promote promiscuity. But regardless of my opinion, censorship is a slippery slope. If we take that book off the shelf, we may have reason to remove them all. Libraries are not—"

"If you are in charge of buying books for the library," Andrea interrupted, "then I'm sure there are more that should be gone. We have a responsibility to protect the innocence of our children and that means that parents should be the ones to talk about certain subjects like sex with their children. Our society is going to hell in a handbasket because of liberal parents like you who are letting books and TV raise their children."

Britney wanted this Andrea person to know that her mom was a great parent and that she was mistaken if she believed Britney was going to be a slut because she read a book. Britney waited for her mom to put this crazy woman in her place.

Britney was shocked when her mom said, "Thank you, Andrea. We will take your request under advisement. Next item of business?"

After the meeting, Britney asked her mom why she didn't tell the woman how wrong she was. Peggy said, "She was obviously looking for a fight and I refused to give her one. If I had engaged with her, we would have been there all night and we had more important library business to address."

Her mom's strategy made sense to Britney and she tucked the memory away for later use.

Act as Your Teen's Guide and Mentor

Teens do not need parents who take care of everything for them, commonly known as the helicopter parent. What teens must have in order to develop into assertive, independent young adults are parents who offer choices, consequences, rewards, an ear to listen, a shoulder to cry on, opportunity, encouragement and the guidance of a mentor. Here are the types of guidance that modern teens need from parents in order to become assertive and therefore harassment-free.

Teens need parents to:

- Be role models.

- Help them to be proactive through posing open-ended questions: What can you do? What can you say? Who can you go to for help? Will your actions hurt you or others? What are the possible consequences? Are you being assertive? What would you like me to do?

- Set limits and enforceable consequences.

Tips for Rules and Consequences

Setting Rules:

- Pick your battles. You shouldn't have too many rules for teens to keep track of. Create rules that focus on their safety and keeping your stress level low.

- Include your teens. It's not being passive to discuss what the rules are, why you're setting them and what the consequences will be when they break them.

- Focus on fairness. Can they realistically stick to your rules?

Setting Consequences:

- The consequence should fit the crime. It should make sense to a teen.

- Consequences are enforced by both parents. If the teen has two involved parents or guardians, then parenting should be a team activity. If one of you is always doing the enforcing then one parent is set up to be the bad guy (aggressive parent) and the other is the pushover (passive parent).

- Consequences should never be physical. When you punish your teens physically you are victimizing them, which may contribute to their aggressive or passive behaviors. Withholding cherished activities or material possessions can be effective with teens.

- There should be rewards. If a teen makes the right decisions, rewards—more verbal than material—are effective.

- Offer choices, but let them make the decisions.
- Let teens experience life, both the good and the bad.
- Listen, *then* talk.
- Offer support, advice and advocacy, but only when they ask.

Teens need to grow, learn and mature. Whether we like it or not, this is largely an independent process. This doesn't mean that teens no longer require parents or that they aren't paying attention to you. They simply need you in a different way than they did when they were younger. In Ian's case, his parents outlined the consequences of his low grade and his options.

Ian was normally an A/B student, but when his parents received his progress report there was a D in Spanish. Ian's parents discussed what to do about Ian's grade and then they sat down to discuss it with him.

"Ian, we are disappointed with your grade in Spanish," Ian's dad said. "We know you are capable of better. You want to get your driver's license soon, but we can't afford your insurance unless you have a B average and qualify for the good student discount."

"That's not fair! That class is stupid and I hate the teacher. I can't get it up to a B."

Ian's mom said, "Well, your choices are to improve your grade and get your license or to continue doing poorly, because you don't like a class that you chose to take. I've had a few Spanish classes and I'd be willing to help you."

Within a month Ian raised his Spanish grade and was on his way to getting his driver's license.

Know Your Teen

Parents may believe that getting to know their teenage sons and daughters is extremely difficult, maybe even impossible. Teens are moody, rebellious and not at all shy about letting parents know they don't need them. Parents have to ignore teen rants and be parents. Before parents can be guides, mentors, supporters and advocates, they have to try to know their teens. Teens who believe their parents care enough to want to know them will trust their parents and see them as allies.

Getting to know your teen may not be easy, but there are some universal truths about teens that may give you some assistance. Every person on this planet is unique, but there are still some norms to which the majority adheres. The same holds true for teens. In general, teens:

- Want the freedom to get to know themselves.
- Need to be validated.
- Consider trust extremely important.
- Value time with those closest to them, including their parents.
- Need to be heard.
- Desire safety and security.
- Can see through dishonesty.
- Respond well to being treated like the young adults they are.
- Want to be assertive, respected and successful.

Teens have most of the same needs and desires that adults do. Try the ideas on this list in order to explore the feelings, opinions and wishes of your teenage son or daughter.

Being aware of psychological norms is only a small part of knowing your teen. The larger question is who is your teen as an individual? This is also the tougher question to answer, because your teen may not know quite yet. The answer may also be in constant flux. The important thing is that you make the attempt to know your teen and do your best to keep up with his or her personality changes. If you know your teen most of the time and recognize his or her personality experiments, you are ahead of the game. When dealing with harassment issues, you should be aware of these personality components. Here are some things you should learn about your teen:

- His or her opinions.
- What he or she is passionate about.
- Whom he or she trusts.
- How to challenge him or her to be better.
- What he or she is doing and with whom he or she is doing it.
- His or her limitations, strengths and weaknesses.

Do I Know...?

- My teen's hot buttons?
- When something is bothering my teen?
- If my teen's behavior or routine changes?
- When my teen needs guidance?
- What my teen's breaking point is?
- If my teen will ask for help?
- When my teen needs me to advocate for him or her and when he or she needs me to back off?
- If my teen has friends who are supportive of him or her?
- What my teen does well that may help him or her?

You need to know your teen as an individual before you can know how to help him or her through difficult situations such as harassment. Teens can be rebellious, sarcastic, moody and judgmental. Despite their assertions to the contrary, they want their parents to recognize who they are and who they want to be. Knowing a teen well is particularly important when dealing with harassment. No one is better equipped than parents to realize when something is bothering their sons and daughters and how to handle the situation in ways that keep their teens safe and empower them at the same time. Assertive parents can maintain this balance, because they know their teens. May's knowledge of how her daughter responded to situations helped her to start a dialogue with her daughter about a harassment issue at school.

May could tell there was something wrong with her daughter, Liz. She knew her daughter would not respond to direct questioning, so May got Liz in the car with the promise of one of Liz's favorite activities: shopping. The nearest shopping mall was two hours from their rural home. May knew there would be plenty of time to talk about "nothing," which she hoped would lead to the something that was on Liz's mind.

May's plan worked. After talking about plans for Christmas and the latest gossip, Liz said, "There's this guy in my gym class who keeps saying gross things to me. I guess it's not a big deal."

"Does it bother you?" May asked.

"Well, yeah."

"Then it's a big deal. What are you going to do about it?"

"I don't know. I've told him to quit being a pervert, but that hasn't stopped him. I don't know if I should tell my teacher or not. I don't want to be a snitch. My friend Kyle said he'd beat the guy up for me, but I don't want Kyle to get in trouble."

"What's your PE teacher like?"

"He's pretty cool."

"Cool enough to want to help you?"

"Probably."

By the time May and Liz reached the mall, Liz had made the decision to let her PE teacher help her deal with her harasser.

Parents have an integral role in influencing their teens to become assertive. We say *influencing* because, unlike when children are younger, parents can no longer tell teens what to think or do. They have to be much more subtle and teach through modeling, acting as mentors and taking an interest in their teens. Teens must decide to be assertive on their own, but making the right decisions is much clearer if they have successful examples.

- **MYTH:** My teen doesn't know what he or she wants out of life.
- **TRUTH:** Yes, he or she does. Teens might not be able to express it to their parents, because they aren't able to verbalize it yet, or they may not want to express their desires, because their parents haven't shown an interest. They may not trust their parents to listen to and validate them, but they do know the kind of people they want to be and the lives they want to lead.

 LIST SOME OF THE THINGS YOU CAN DO TO MAINTAIN ASSERTIVENESS AS AN INDIVIDUAL AND A PARENT USING THE QUESTIONNAIRE AT THE END OF THIS SECTION. SHARE YOUR ANSWERS WITH YOUR TEEN.

PARENT CONNECTIONS

- What incidents in the story demonstrate that Jeanne's mom had a passive personality?

  Jeanne's mom's role was cleanup after her husband's destructive behaviors. She did nothing to stand up for herself and even less to help her children. Perhaps most shocking was that she let Jeanne walk out of their house at age sixteen, leaving her to navigate alone in a world for which she wasn't prepared.

- What incidents in the story demonstrate that Jeanne's dad had an aggressive personality?

  He had to be in complete control. He used manipulation, violence, verbal and physical abuse, sarcasm and teasing to ensure that everyone around him knew who was in charge. He put his needs and desires before anyone else's. As long as he was in control and getting his way, he believed life was good.

- How did Jeanne become assertive despite her parents' passive and aggressive personalities?

  Jeanne is proof that teens can overcome. But she shouldn't have had to do so. Home is the last place where teens should have to experience harassment. Jeanne prevailed over her childhood, but that is not the same thing as making it through unscathed. She would be the first to tell you that there are scars and she lives with them every day.

How Do I Maintain Assertiveness?

List some of the things you can do to maintain your assertiveness. Be aware of your greatest resources.

Three things I do to manage my stress:

1. _____

2. _____

3. _____

Three things I do to manage my anger:

1. _____

2. _____

3. _____

Three situations where I struggle with my attitude:

1. _____

2. _____

3. _____

Three people who can help me:

1. _____

2. _____

3. _____

Three people who are observing me:

1. _____

2. _____

3. _____

Three times I felt great because of my assertiveness:

1. _____

2. _____

3. _____

Three goals toward which I need to work:

1. _____

2. _____

3. _____

Dealing with Harassment Issues

An Interview with Allison and Quinn

Allison's husband, Jim, is in the United States military, so their family relocates every few years. One year, Jim received orders for Hawaii. Allison and their children, Quinn, age ten, and her brothers, ages nine and five, prepared for what they thought would be an exciting adventure. They would probably tell you it was an adventure, but we feel that it was one of the hardest kinds of experiences. The entire family had to deal with harassment. Quinn, however, had a more difficult time than anyone else.

Quinn and Allison wanted to tell about it, because they are eager to help others through their own harassment experiences, so Jennie interviewed them for this book.

> ### When your husband got his orders to go to Hawaii, what did you learn about the social environment there?

Allison: When Jim got the order, many military people asked if we were sure we wanted to take our family to Hawaii. They told us that the schools in the area around the base could be really rough. There was harassment and a lot of drugs. But every time we've received orders to deploy to another location there were always people who had negative things to say about where we were going. So I didn't really believe it could be so bad.

In the military you get orders, not choices. We are a close family and we didn't want to be separated. Jim and I knew our children were used to adjusting to tough conditions. We moved into a rented house in a neighborhood with public schools nearby. Private school wasn't an option for us. Cost was the biggest factor, but I was also told by other parents that the problems didn't go away with high tuition rates.

Did the harassment start right away?

Allison: At the elementary school, I helped out whenever I could, for instance in the library, and bullying didn't exist there. But as soon as the children reached middle school, something huge happened. It was kind of weird. Quinn was the only one in middle school right from the beginning, so the problems started immediately for her.

Why was Quinn a target?

Allison: Quinn is a great kid. She is outgoing, bubbly. She just has a great personality. She makes friends easily. Quinn is also very smart and gets great grades. It wasn't anything about her that she could control that made her a target. It seemed that in order to fit in at that school you had to trash on people who were different, especially those who were military. Some people just didn't like the military there.

So Quinn had a strike against her because of the military thing, but the bigger reason the other students harassed her was that Quinn is white, has blonde hair and blue eyes. She really stuck out in a school population that was mostly native Hawaiian and Japanese.

I was talking to Quinn on the phone once when she was at the school and I could hear girls in the background laughing and saying things like, "You white bitch. You scared of us, white bitch? What's the matter?" Of course I became angry and wanted Quinn to give me their names, but she wouldn't. She said that telling me would make things worse. Later that evening, Quinn told me stories of students whose parents got involved and how they got beat up. So it was mostly racial.

Quinn: Being white and having blonde hair, I was so completely different from everyone else. The kids didn't look at what was on the inside; they focused on the outside. If you were a person of color you automatically fit in. If you were white, you were an outsider.

What were some of the other ways Quinn was harassed, besides the name calling?

Allison: Initially Quinn started school and began making friends with some local children. Two of the girls who befriended her insisted on coming to our house. Quinn didn't hesitate to invite them over. They spent all weekend swimming, eating snacks, having a great time. However, when Quinn went back to school on Monday the girls turned on her. They said horrible things about her and about us. These so-called friends said our house was so filthy they came home with bugs. They said we didn't feed them. And they said Quinn's parents were awful and mean. All the other students heard these nasty things about her and our family. That was really hard for her, because she went from being accepted to being tortured by the girls in her class. After that, none of the girls would be Quinn's friend. She came home crying.

Later, Quinn started getting physically abused too. She came home with bruises, because she got pushed on the stairs and she fell down. One time somebody grabbed her backpack so hard that it bruised her shoulder. The girls also tripped Quinn frequently, so she would come home limping. The harassment was mostly verbal but there was some physical battering as well.

Quinn: Another hard part is when everyone is hating you and looking at you like you're horrible and you are nothing. It made it really difficult to look in the mirror and like what I saw. My confidence was reduced to nothing and it was really hard to feel good about myself when everyone was telling me how stupid and ugly I was.

Did Quinn ever feel like there were any adults she could trust at the school? Someone to whom she could talk? Someone who tried to help her?

Allison: Quinn never talked to her teachers about her problems, because most of the time they were part of the problem. How do you tell a teacher that you're being harassed when the teacher is either doing it too or encouraging it by little comments to the class?

They taught Hawaiian history at Quinn's school, which I didn't have a problem with. I did have a problem with the way they taught it. The problems on the island are attributed to the United States and the white people running everything. It creates a lot of anger, so when they are sitting in class talking about what the United States has done to their island, ruining it and taking away their way of life, the focus tends to shift to the only white kid in class. Quinn often came home crying. She felt like not only the children but also the teachers picked her out and accused her: "You did this!" Quinn protested, "I didn't do it."

One time a teacher did stop Quinn from being harassed. She even took the students who were involved to the principal's office. I think they were making sexual comments. I was glad that a teacher stopped them.

But it was only once. There were so many times that Quinn was harassed and I asked her where the teacher was and she replied, "The teacher was standing right there."

Quinn: Having kids constantly tell you that you are not good enough is awful, but when you hear it from your teachers and counselors it really starts to hurt.

Allison: I went in several times and talked to the school administration, but nothing was ever done. Finally, Quinn told me that if I talked to anyone at the school she wouldn't tell me anything any more. Because of that and the fact that going to the school administration wasn't getting me anywhere, I quit trying. I mean, it really put me in a bad position. I asked myself, "Should I go in and keep trying to speak to adults at the school or keep talking to Quinn and giving her as much positive advice as I can?" The fact that I had to make that choice was infuriating.

So you chose to talk with Quinn. How did you try to help her make it through these bad experiences?

Allison: I kept trying to tell her and her brothers that they should make it into a positive experience for them. Now they would know what it was like to be discriminated against and I hoped they would never do that to anyone else. I kept telling them we only had a certain amount of time left to be stationed there, so they should suck it up and try to find someone with whom to be friends. But there were days I just had to drag Quinn to the middle school and make her go to class.

Our family unit is very strong. We do a lot together, which I think helped. When we first arrived in Hawaii there was an earthquake that knocked the power out. The children were initially really bored without the TV and their video games, but we rode skateboards, played ball and board games, went for walks and had barbecues outside. The children had such a good time that every weekend we flipped the breaker, spent a day without power and played as a family. We called it Power Out Day. Things like that really helped.

Nevertheless, sometimes I didn't feel like I was doing a very good parenting job. When Quinn came home and vented about her terrible day and what had happened, it was hard. I was so angry and I just wanted to go to the school and shake those girls, but I had to keep calm and just listen, because that was what Quinn needed. Her coming home to cry and complain about being bullied became a regular thing and she still tells me a lot about her unpleasant experiences at school. Quite often I felt like I wasn't getting support from the school, so what could I say to my children?

Those were times that Quinn was the strong one and I always tried to communicate how much we appreciated her strength, how we believed in and loved her. At one point I felt that we should pull her out of public school and I would homeschool her. I didn't see any other option. I also thought about moving back to the mainland with the children and leaving Jim there. Quinn told me she didn't want that. She said she'd handle it. Moving really wasn't an option anyway. We couldn't afford to do that and we weren't willing to split up the family.

Quinn, how did your mom's and your family's support help?

Quinn: My family was my main encouragement, especially my mom. After a day of being treated like I was nothing, I came home and Mom reassured me how great I was and told me good things about myself. Sometimes one word of praise can go a long way. She helped me keep what little confidence I had and when I was at school I just repeated her words in my mind: "I can do it; I can pull through this."

Allison, what negative changes did you see in Quinn?

Allison: Quinn's grades dropped. She had been a straight A student and she was almost straight Cs when we left. She even got some Ds and Fs, which isn't like her. But the social situation took up so much of her energy, she couldn't focus. Now I know that's what it was, because as soon as we moved back to the mainland her grades went back up.

At one point Quinn wanted to dye her hair black so she wouldn't have to deal with being harassed by her classmates for being blonde. I wouldn't let her. I told her to be strong and that dying her hair wasn't the answer. It was just changing herself to make those nasty girls like her. If it wasn't her hair it would be something else they would find to pick on her for anyway. For example, there were a lot of students who wore expensive clothes, you know, the name brand stuff. We couldn't afford that so they picked on Quinn about how she dressed. It was really never-ending.

All this stuff was going on at school while she was dealing with puberty. That's difficult enough, but then add to that having her dad gone all the time, deployed. I continue to admire her for dealing with all that animosity as well as she did.

What did Quinn do to try to change her situation?

Allison: In the beginning, it devastated her. She ate lunch by herself. She saw new students or outcasts being picked on, but she was afraid to help them. She was concerned that it would make things worse for her. But

Quinn has always been able to make friends easily and she began to befriend other outcasts, students who had been picked on like her. Quinn tried to get more involved. She also joined the school band, which helped a lot.

When she started liking boys, that was pretty intense. The girls who had picked on her liked the boys too. However, these boys really liked Quinn, because she was different. I kept telling her that the boys liked her because she had blonde hair, so she should be proud of that. I advised her to make friends with the boys. That worked so much better. It actually got some of the girls to be friends with her too, because Quinn was so well connected with the boys.

So, I think I helped Quinn with my support, but I also think she came up with a lot of coping skills on her own. The last year we were there, things mellowed out. It was all about jealousy and what those children had been taught.

Quinn, when do you think it got better for you and why do you think it did?

Quinn: It started to get better near the end of seventh grade and the beginning of eighth. I had been in that school long enough that everyone knew me, so picking on me became boring. There was always a steady stream of new white military kids cycling in and out of the school. I also refused to let their words get to me and react the way they wanted. I was able to break out of my shell a little bit and make friends with some kids who happened not to be white. Because of this I was able to see life from their perspective a little bit and could see that all the hate and mean words didn't come directly from them. They had been living their lives constantly being told how white people were nothing but bad and had ruined their way of life. When you're told something like this by your parents and community, why would you treat a white kid any differently than they did?

Now that you are back on the mainland, what would you say the lasting effects of the experience have been?

Allison: It's awful to watch your children go through something like that! We had many discussions about their experiences and even though it was very hard for them and for me, I did feel that they ended up better off for the experience. One of the lessons is that you can take any situation and make it positive or you can just focus on the negative and stay angry. The children experienced harassment and bullying firsthand and even though it was horrible, we always knew that it was temporary. They learned how to make an ugly situation as good as possible.

The hardest part of my job in helping my children get through that experience was explaining how the other children could be so mean, especially since I was having some of the same experiences my children were. Mine weren't anywhere near as bad, of course, but there were little things like sitting in a diner waiting to be served for forty-five minutes before we finally gave up and left. If a prank, graffiti or other vandalism occurred in our neighborhood, my children were automatically blamed. It's really hard to explain to your children why people act that way. Now that it's over, I can say they learned a great deal from their experiences, because they will never treat someone like we were treated.

It definitely made Quinn more assertive. She was nervous about starting high school, but after a short while she decided it was okay. She came home and said, "Mom, these kids are so nice."

Because of what happened to her in Hawaii, Quinn knows what it's like to be a teen who doesn't fit in. She now draws those students into her group. She identifies the misfits and makes them her friends. So now her friends are a very diverse group.

Overall, it's made Quinn stronger and that's a good thing.

Quinn: First, I believe it made me a much stronger person. I can now do things that I would never have done before. Such as if I see someone else getting bullied, instead of walking by and ignoring the situation like other kids did to me, now I go and help. That's something that I never thought that I would have the courage to do.

I also now have a much broader perspective about what goes on in the world. I have a larger view of racism and how it can't be taken lightly. I think that everyone should be treated the same and you can't make distinctions among people by putting them into categories. You can't learn anything about a person by what color his or her skin is. I think that people who only look at the color of people's skins reveal a lot about themselves.

I also don't let myself get pushed around anymore. The traits that made me different and that people made fun of I have managed to see as positives instead of negatives. Those things make me who I am and I will never again be ashamed of who I am. I won't try so hard to be like everyone else. I will be myself no matter what people say.

And lastly, I now know that no matter what life throws at me, I will always have my family right behind me to catch me if I fall.

TEEN CONNECTIONS

- What did Quinn do to try to make the harassment stop that didn't work?
- What did Quinn do that made the harassment stop?
- Why does Quinn help those who are being harassed now?

PARENT CONNECTIONS

- What would you do if you knew your teen was being harassed and your teen begged you not to get involved?
- At what point do parents need to intercede in a harassment situation?
- How would you determine whether the adults in a harassment case are condoning the harassment or are the harassers themselves?

Teen Section 7

Deal With It

Like most things in life, the answers to problems like harassment are complicated. In order for this last chapter to be meaningful, we needed to give you the background knowledge and the right vocabulary. To teach you how to deal with sexual harassment you need to know what it is. To stand up for your rights you need to be aware of the laws that protect you from being harassed. Most importantly, gaining the key to dealing with harassers means learning to be assertive. The earlier parts of this book have led to this. Now we will tie it all together, as well as show you how to take the right steps to deal with harassment.

This section is for the victims and for those who have to share their environments with harassers. The first part will hopefully help convince you that even if you are not a target, stopping harassment is everyone's problem and you need to step forward to help end harassment situations and environments. Finally, we'll reveal how to deal with harassment. Here are proven things to do and say in order to prevent harassment.

Be a Change Maker

The most effective strategy for preventing or stopping harassment is to change the environment where it's found. If harassment is happening at a school, then the learning and social environment is affected for everyone. Therefore, it is not just the victims and the harassers who are responsible for making harassment go away. It is everybody's responsibility. There has to be a fundamental shift in what people believe is acceptable behavior. "Staying out of it" is saying it's okay to harass or be harassed. People who stay out of it are part of the problem. Assertive personalities have to step up and be a part of the solution.

Staying out of it can have devastating consequences. In extreme cases, school violence occurs. At the very least, the school is full of distrust, fear and insecurity. It's not enough to stand up only for yourself. Be willing to stand up for others and stand up for a healthy, safe, secure and fun school. We'll tell you how.

Don't Be a Bystander

Doing nothing, staying out of it, is the same as encouraging the harasser. Harassers aren't going to stop what they're doing, because it's succeeding. And victims need allies, positive influences and someone to show them how to be assertive. This is why you need to be a leader and a team player.

You lose the right to call yourself assertive if you ignore bullying happening around you. Remember that assertive personalities become a part of something larger (like a school or community) and they take responsibility for their environments. That means assertive personalities stand up for their rights to be safe and secure and to get educations. It also means they stand up for others' rights to have those things too.

What's to stop the harasser from targeting you next? If you were picked on, who would stand up for you? Staying out of it is being passive. When you're a bystander you are revealing yourself as a possible victim.

We will give you some ideas on how to help victims. There are also more details for dealing with harassers, whether you are a victim or someone who is helping, throughout the entire section.

- **Do not confront the bully,** particularly if you think he or she is dangerous. If you think physical harm is a possibility, find an adult who can help you. If it's a minor bullying situation then ask the harasser to stop in a non-confrontational, assertive way and get the victim away from him or her.

- **Tell the victim what you know about harassing behaviors, the law and your school policy.** Many victims don't know they're being harassed or they might think they deserve to be bullied. You could recommend that they read this book.

- **Encourage the victim to talk to a trusted adult.** Explain to him or her that everybody deserves to be treated with respect. It may help if you offer to accompany the victim. If he or she doesn't make a report and the harassment persists or becomes severe, then you need to be the one who goes to a responsible adult.

- **Listen to the victim's experiences.** Listening doesn't mean you tell the victim what he or she should do. It means you let the victim talk and come to conclusions on his or her own. You can also suggest some things for him or her to say to the harassers, help him or her talk to an adult and plan ways for him or her to stay safe.

- **Don't give advice.** This is closely related to listening, because good listeners don't give advice. If you tell the victim what to do and it doesn't work, he or she may see it as your fault. Your job is simply supporting the victim. Allow the person his or her own conclusions. Ask questions like, "What are you going to do?" and "What do you think will happen if you do that?" Share your knowledge of harassment, ask questions, give compliments and listen, but don't give advice.

- **Focus on the victim, not the harasser.** Harassers aren't going to listen to you and will only see your attempts to talk to them as personal slams that make them angry. Mediation only works when the people involved see each other as equals. Harassers already see themselves as better than their victims and chances are they see themselves as better than you too. The victim, on the other hand, could use a friend and an ally.

- **Don't badmouth the harasser to the victim.** It is tempting to put down the harasser: "Man, that guy is stupid!" But this is not helpful to the victim. You may even create a situation where the victim won't trust you, because you are showing that you can be a bully too.

- **Help the victim come up with a plan to be safe.** Many victims need tips on where they can be safe, people they can be safe with and ways to get help if they feel threatened. This should also include a password to let friends and family members know they are in trouble. Using a password will help victims without tipping off the abuser that reinforcements are on the way.

Trevor was able to empower a harassment victim by helping her to come up with solutions and giving her the courage to follow through.

Trevor was sitting just a few rows up in the gym when the meanest clique of girls in school approached the quietest girl in school. The head mean girl looked angry. Trevor imagined that it was probably because she was wearing the school's pants. They were plain, tan, shapeless slacks given to students when their pants from home didn't meet the dress code. Trevor was right.

"Hey, Chloe, you're going to do something for me," the nasty clique leader said. "During your aide hour today, you're going to get the pants that Ms. Tuller took from me. They're in the back room of the office."

Chloe didn't say anything.

"Didn't you hear her?" Another one of the mean girls was in Chloe's face. "You do this or we'll make your life a living hell."

Trevor heard Chloe agree to steal the pants. The mean clique strode away like a pack of satisfied wolves.

Trevor moved to sit next to Chloe. "Hey, I'm Trevor."

"Hi."

"So, you look too smart to do what those girls want you to do. You've probably already figured out there's something in those pants that they don't want anybody to find."

"What am I supposed to do? You know who they are, right?"

"I know who they are and I also know that they shouldn't treat people the way they do. Somebody needs to stand up to them. It could be you."

"How?"

"I don't know, but why should you get into trouble for them? Have they ever done anything for you? What do you think you should do?"

"I guess I could talk to Ms. Tuller."

"That's a good idea. I'll go with you if you want."

It Only Takes One Person to Break Away from Conformity and Stand Up

One person can make a difference. It has been proven time and time again and yet many still doubt this truth. Make a difference. If you don't, maybe you doubt your own power. Thinking that you can't be a leader, that you can't make a difference, is a passive belief. And it is one you need to get over. If you want our world to be safe, secure and fun, you need to have the courage to make a difference.

Teens will talk to other teens about tough issues before they will talk to an adult. Harassment is a tough issue. But victims aren't going to turn to other victims for advice. They will turn to those who can help: the assertive people. Assertive personalities are the leaders and role models and they want to be in these roles. They want their schools and communities to be safe places to learn and grow. Here is a list showing how you can be a source of strength for victims:

- **Make acceptance cool**. Go out of your way to be a nice person. Pay attention to those who are left out and include them. Send the message with your words and actions that bullying is not funny.

- **Create a social environment where there is no fear.** Pledge not to bully. Be a leader in creating or implementing anti-harassment campaigns and education programs at your school. Be a mentor for younger children and always be a role model.

- **Make yourself available to others.** Realize that what you have to say is important. Give compliments to boost self-esteem and reinforce that harassment isn't the victim's fault. Encourage others to speak up and speak out about harassment. Keep in contact with those who need help the most.

- **Help out.** Offer to mentor younger children or your peers at school, start or join support groups for your peers or find ways to raise awareness about harassment at your school. Speak to your counselor about ways you can help. Be the person whom victims can trust.

If you want your school to be a place where successful futures are built, you need to have a role in that. There is no sitting on the sidelines when it comes to harassment.

- **MYTH:** I shouldn't report my friend's abuse, because she told me not to. I don't want her to be angry with me.
- **TRUTH:** Would you rather have an angry friend or a scared friend? An angry friend or an injured friend? An angry friend or a dead friend? Your friend will get over being angry, particularly if you help her overcome the harassment. Eventually she will realize you went against her wishes because you love her, but your friend may never get over the effects of being harassed or abused.

What Not to Do

As well as giving teen readers good advice in *Hey, Back Off!*, we have also explored why some of the things victims do in reaction to harassment won't work. Our goal is to stop harassment without experiencing any additional negative consequences in the process. Here are some things you may be tempted to try or you've been told to try that will *not* work.

Don't Adopt a Passive-Aggressive or Aggressive Personality

Many victims have been harassed so long and/or so severely that they decide they've had enough. This can be a positive thing if a victim decides to become assertive, but if he or she lacks the courage or the knowledge to become assertive, the victim may resort to being passive-aggressive or aggressive.

Passive-aggressiveness is being aggressive in a sneaky, underhanded, manipulative way. This often happens when passive people want to get back at attackers but don't want to stand up for themselves. They may do this by provoking the bullies to get them into trouble or by using sneaky means to embarrass or harm the harassers.

Often, passive-aggressive behavior is glorified in movies and books. The victim hatches a wonderful plan to give the harasser a taste of his or her own medicine and thereby gains revenge. What the movies don't show is the negative effect on victims when they realize they are no better than their harassers, because what they did was every bit as mean and cowardly. These stories also conveniently forget the part where the victim-turned-harasser inevitably faces legal and social consequences. Just because it's undercover doesn't mean it's okay. The only good way to deal with harassment is through assertive behavior. Kade tried an under-handed method of dealing with his harasser, but it did not work for him.

> In the ninth grade, Kade decided he'd had enough of being harassed all the time. Kade sought revenge by getting his harassers in trouble. He knew the right buttons to push, the names he could call them or the insults he could repeat in order to make them instantly angry.
>
> During lunch Kade whispered in Jesse's ear, "Hey, you big pussy, come and get me."
>
> When Jesse leapt from his seat and began the chase, Kade ran to a teacher. "Mrs. Horton, Jesse is trying to hurt me again."
>
> Mrs. Horton knew Jesse's reputation for being a bully and she immediately reported Jesse to the school administration. Jesse got into trouble and Kade got his sweet revenge.
>
> This underhanded scheme worked for Kade until it became apparent to teachers and administrators what he was doing. It was a complete shock to Kade when he was suspended for harassment.

Victims should also know that becoming aggressive isn't a way to regain power. Many passive personalities become aggressive by choosing their own victims. They seek those who are weaker than they are to bully. They are victims in one setting but aggressors in another. They are attempting to feel strong and powerful, but instead of standing up for themselves, they believe the way to get power is to pick on someone else. This is one example of passive personalities becoming aggressive to deal with harassment.

The other instance of passive turning to aggressive occurs when victims turn on their harassers. All too often these are violent situations. The victim wants the bully to feel his or her pain. This approach to dealing with harassment is often glorified in our culture. It's the "victim who finally snaps and beats the hell out of the bully" story. As with passive-aggressive behavior, these stories rarely show the psychological effects on the victim once he or she becomes the harasser. Fights, cyberbullying and school shootings are just a few of the examples of what can happen when a victim turns and becomes aggressive.

Becoming passive-aggressive or aggressive isn't healthy and it definitely won't make your situation any better, nor will it make you feel powerful or give you self-esteem. What it will do is bring you a different kind of negative attention: consequences for your harassing behavior. Becoming passive-aggressive or aggressive may seem like the easy way to deal with harassment and a great way to stand up for yourself. The truth, however, is that it makes you become the kind of person who made you feel threatened and alone. Perhaps the worst part is you will continue to feel this way. Take responsibility for your life and think about what you want that life to look like. Becoming the bully is not the answer. Harassing others will never bring you confidence, success or happiness.

Don't Ignore Repeated Incidents of Harassment

If ignoring a harasser is going to work, you must become an assertive personality. It doesn't work for passive personalities. With a passive personality, the harasser is only prompted to try harder to get a reaction. Try to ignore the harasser and walk away once, maybe twice. If the harassment continues, you will know that ignoring him or her isn't going to work, so you might as well try something else. If you try another tactic and the harasser still won't stop, it's time to find a trusted adult and report.

Don't Use Humor or Laugh It Off

We think it's difficult to be funny when someone is hurting your feelings or you feel threatened. However, victims sometimes attempt to use humor in one of two ways. As you will see, neither is positive when dealing with a harasser.

- **The victim makes fun of him or herself**. The harasser says, "How can anyone be that stupid?" The victim answers, "Yeah, guess what else I did. This is really funny!" The bully isn't going to stop picking on the victim with humor like this. In fact, he or she will probably be encouraged to harass the victim even more. It is a very self-defeating way for the victim to act and it won't make him or her feel any better.

- **The victim makes a joke about the harasser**. The harasser says, "How can anyone be that stupid?" The victim answers, "Speaking of stupid, how about the time you... Now *that's* funny!" The result is that the victim has just made the harasser angry and unpredictable. It's not very smart to provoke a bully.

We suppose that there are those who have figured out how to use humor positively, but we've never witnessed it. We think there are far less damaging and threatening responses to try when dealing with harassers.

Don't Believe That You Deserve to be Harassed or That It's Your Fault

Nobody deserves to be picked on and being harassed is never the victim's fault. Harassers try to convince victims that they "asked for it" or that "you just can't take a joke." Don't make harassment easier on the perpetrator by buying into this line of thought.

It also doesn't mean that victims deserve to be harassed if they try to stand up to the bullies and it doesn't work. In fact, these victims should be proud, because at least they tried. They realized they were being harassed and they let their harassers know that they wanted it to stop. That took a lot of courage! If it didn't work, that just means the victims need more help. We all do on occasion. Asking for that help also takes courage. Don't stop working toward a harassment-free life.

Don't Check Out of Life

Too many times victims can't endure their situations anymore and either don't know how to deal with their harassers or are unwilling to try. This overwhelming feeling makes the victims vulnerable to many things that prevent them from really living.

Skipping or dropping out of school may seem like an option to overwhelmed victims, because they lose their vision of the future. They just want to be unafraid in the here and now. Staying away from school allows them to escape. Personal safety becomes more important than an education or a social life.

Victims who've reached a crisis point may look for things to numb the pain, depression and feeling of failure that harassment causes. Drugs and alcohol become ways to do that. Not only are rehabilitation centers and prisons filled with aggressive people who can't deal with anger, they are also full of passive people who don't know how to deal with their lives. It's ironic that passive and aggressive personality types come from opposite ends of the personality spectrum, but the issues that prohibit them from being confident, successful and happy are quite similar.

Dropping out of school and drug and alcohol abuse are not the only outcomes for victims who don't deal with harassment. Mental illness, depression and suicidal tendencies are also possible results of unresolved harassment issues. Dealing with harassment right away is key for many teens to stay involved in their lives or get back into living. If they deal with the negative feelings and situations, they will enjoy life. Be a fighter! Fight for who you want to be and the kind of life you want to have.

Don't Adopt a "Can't Beat Them, Join Them" Attitude

Trying to become a harasser's friend is agreeing with his or her lowly opinion of you. That doesn't raise self-esteem. It makes harassers safe from consequences, because their new "friends" won't do anything, so they feel safe in escalating their harassment.

If the harasser accepts you into his or her group, he or she will use you. Maybe you will have to do something the bully doesn't want to do because of the consequences involved. Maybe you will have to help him or her find new victims to harass. Maybe you will have to harass someone else. Whatever your use is, there will always be a price for joining a bully and that price is always high. Lin saw joining a gang as the only solution to his problem, but he soon found the consequences to be devastating.

Lin dreamed of the time he could move away and go to college. The largest obstacle standing in his way was the neighborhood where he lived. There was a gang and they wanted him to join. The gang enticed Lin with money and promised his family security if he joined and threatened them if he didn't. Lin refused on many occasions.

Lin was devastated when his mother became ill. Perhaps more crushing was the amount of money the family owed to hospitals and doctors. The family members exhausted their savings, which were originally meant for Lin's college education. The neighborhood gang had a solution for Lin. They would give him all the money he needed for college. Lin thought it was the only way so he said yes.

Lin was numb as he pulled the trigger. He couldn't see anyone inside the house he shot at, which made it easier. He didn't know until the next day he had hit a seventy-year-old man as he slept.

Lin wasn't arrested and he didn't go to jail. His prison was much worse. The gang had him. They would never allow him to go to college, have a normal career, move out of his neighborhood or leave them.

Don't "Kill Them with Kindness"

"Kill them with kindness" is a bad piece of advice that we've heard victims say they've tried to adopt. It won't work. The result of "killing" a harasser with kindness is much like trying to use humor. The victim is indicating to the harasser that he or she is giving up and will not stand up for him or herself. It's self-defeating.

Harassers are angry people and they aren't going to change unless they decide to change. Being nice to them isn't going to make them change and it certainly isn't going to change things for the victims. It will only make victims feel bad about themselves and entice harassers to bully in new and worse ways.

How you choose to react to harassers can have a huge effect on your life. Because of this, knowing what doesn't work is just as important as knowing what does. If you are dealing with harassment, please choose to do it in a way that won't hurt you or others. Read on and we'll show you it can be done.

- **MYTH:** My consequences won't be as bad if I prove he or she harassed me first.
- **TRUTH:** School policies and the law don't have a "They started it!" clause. The only thing considered is what you did.

How to Deal with Harassers

If you are a victim of harassment, we need you to believe three things if this chapter is to help you:

- The harassment is not your fault.
- You have the power to stop it.
- You aren't in this alone.

Assertiveness is the Answer

When you let harassers do their thing, whether you are a victim or a bystander, you give them power and control. In order to take it back, you have to stand up for yourself assertively. Now that you know what it means to be assertive, here are some strategies for dealing effectively with a harasser.

- **Keep it together**. An emotional response is what the harasser wants. This means that reactions like yelling or hitting play into the harasser's need for negative attention. Stand up for your rights without stomping on the bully's. Keeping your composure doesn't mean you aren't hurt or angry, but it does mean you don't show it. When harassers don't get the attention they want, they stop picking on you and move on.

- **Look assertive**. Body language makes up most of our communication. Appearing assertive will dissuade the harasser from thinking you are a good target. If a harasser approaches you, make eye contact, keep your voice in a normal tone and have good, relaxed posture. This will let the bully know you won't put up with being picked on, but you're not looking to fight either. Confident body language is the reason that ignoring the harasser may work. Assertive body language sends an anti-harassment message.

- **Use "I" statements to take the offensive**. Point out to the bully what he or she is doing and why you don't like it. It's not confrontational when you keep the focus on yourself. "I don't like your language" rather than "Come up with some intelligent adjectives." "I want you to stop" rather than "You'd better knock it off." Focusing on what you want and how you feel doesn't give harassers the fight for which they were looking. Therefore they don't feel threatened. When aggressive personalities feel threatened, they become unpredictable.

- **Walk away**. You've stayed in control of your emotions, you've looked confident, you've used "I" statements to express how you feel about what the harasser is doing. Now walk away. One of the things victims often do is stand there and take it, even when they're free to leave. In fact, if the bully is keeping you from getting away, that's a threatening situation and an adult needs to be told about it immediately.

- **Get help**. It is an assertive characteristic to know when you need help and then to ask for that assistance. If the harassment is severe, persistent or pervasive, it's time to tell a trusted adult.

It is difficult to maintain assertiveness in the face of harassment. This is hard for everybody, no matter what their age. Note we said hard, not impossible. Remember that harassment can only be prevented through assertive action. Confident, successful and happy people act assertively no matter the situation.

Make Friends and Get Involved

Harassers seek out loners, because loners have no support. Harassers know people without friends or allies won't try to stop them or report them. The harassers are comfortable, because they believe there will be no consequences. If victims want to stop being targets, they need to make harassers uncomfortable. The best way to do this is to find some friends. Harassers don't approach those who are in a group of supporters. They are cowards at heart, so groups frighten them. It is true that there is safety in numbers. The question becomes: How do you make friends and find allies? Here are some suggestions:

- **Find other victims**. You already have something important in common with these people. Who else gets picked on? Find them and you've found your support system. Depending on the severity of the harassment, you have someone to stand up with you or someone with whom to go and report the harassment to an adult.

- **Be assertive**. Look approachable, make eye contact, smile, stand up straight and speak in a normal tone of voice. It also means you speak when you're spoken to, using complete sentences, not just one-word responses. Start a conversation. Ask questions like, "What are you working on?" or "How do you do that?" Use "I" statements. And most importantly, be yourself.

- **Get involved**. Join a group or club: sports, recreation, dance, art or music groups, academic clubs, service clubs, faith and worship groups, a part time job, scout troops, 4-H, Boys and Girls Clubs and YMCA or YMHA activities are just a few possibilities. If you become part of an activity in which you're interested, you will be around people with whom you have something in common. Person-to-person contact and face-to-face conversations are great ways to communicate and make friends. Becoming a part of a group is a safe, easy way to improve your social skills and fulfill your need to be a social human being. Marta's volunteer and part-time work enabled her to build her confidence and self-esteem.

Marta was a target for bullies at her school. Marta's counselor convinced her to sign up to be a teacher's aide in a first grade classroom. Marta loved working with the students and she came to trust her cooperating teacher. The teacher suggested to Marta that she apply for a position at a child day care center. Marta did and got the job.

Marta quickly became friends with the other teens from her school who worked there. They talked about the children at first, but then, as they got to know one another, they discussed other things. Marta gained confidence in herself.

It occurred to Marta that part of her improved self-esteem was due to the decrease in being bullied at school. The only thing she could conclude was that it must have been because she wasn't alone in the halls. She had friends who stood with her and would stand up for her.

Developing relationships and becoming a part of a group or activity is the surest way to combat fear. Harassers are attracted to fear. Being alone is scary in itself, but when you add being harassed to that condition, it can become unbearable. You deserve happiness. Human connections are required for happiness. Stop being afraid; make some friends!

Have a Vested Interest in School

Feeling like a part of your school goes hand in hand with finding friends and getting involved. Harassment for teens takes place most often at school. The victims are often students nobody knows. Other students don't know them, because they don't talk in the halls or at lunch and they don't say anything during classes. Teachers don't know these students, because they sit in their classes and quietly fail or quietly get As. They aren't participating, but they're not discipline problems either, so teachers often leave them alone. They make perfect targets for harassers at school, because they are anonymous.

School isn't designed to be a torture chamber and there are people who are willing to help you be comfortable and safe. All you have to do is let them know you're there. Attend events, talk to people and participate in your classes. School should prepare you to be a successful adult, both intellectually and socially, but you have to meet the students, teachers and staff halfway to find success.

Plan How to Stay Safe

It is impossible for victims of harassment to feel safe and secure. Combating the fear that victims feel, as well as the harasser, requires getting your sense of safety back. A good way to do this is to have a plan. This plan should include safe places you can go, safe people to be with, what to do when you're in crisis, who you can report to and resources that are available to you. It should also include a password to let your friends and family members know when you are in trouble. Using a password will get you help without tipping off the abuser that reinforcements are on the way. Having these things in place may also convince the harasser you're not an easy target.

CREATE A SAFETY PLAN BY FILLING OUT THE FORM AT THE END OF THIS SECTION. EVEN IF YOUR PARENT OR GUARDIAN IS NOT READING THIS BOOK WITH YOU, HE OR SHE SHOULD BE INVOLVED IN THIS ASSIGNMENT.

Report Harassment to an Adult

You shouldn't think of reporting harassment to an adult as being a tattletale. Nor should you think of it as being a failure. Reporting to an adult may not be the first thing you try when dealing with a harasser but it shouldn't be the last either. So how do you know when you should report? We talked about what the police do in teen section 2. There are three criteria officers use when deciding to get involved in a harassment case. Use these same three criteria to decide if you should involve an adult:

- **Severe harassment.** Harassment that threatens your well-being is severe. If there is physical violence or a threat of physical violence, either spoken or written, that is severe harassment. Severe incidents need to be reported to a trusted adult immediately.

- **Persistent harassment.** Harassment that is repeated despite your attempts to make it stop is persistent. If you've tried the things we've discussed in this section and the harasser is still after you, that is persistent. Report the incidents to a trusted adult, because he or she either has the power to make it stop or knows who does.

- **Pervasive harassment.** Harassment that is spreading should also be reported. This can mean that the harasser is recruiting others to join him or her in harassing you or that the harasser is increasing the number of victims he or she bullies. Either way, it is a situation where a trusted adult should be involved.

One of the biggest worries teens have is that the harassers will retaliate, because the victims told on them. This happens less often than you might think, but it's worth discussing with the adults involved. Use the safety plan you have in place if the harasser does retaliate or if he or she recruits others to retaliate for him or her. You will be safer than you were before reporting the problem.

Another issue may be a lack of trust in adults. Perhaps it is an adult at your school or at your home who is harassing you. Maybe you've seen an adult being bullied and you think of that person as weak and not able to help you. What then? Please know that neither of these scenarios means that all adults are not to be trusted. Think of one adult at your school, from your after-school activities, your religious group or your family who cares and is willing to help you. Find someone you can trust. In order to deal with her harassment issue, Hannah thought of an adult whom she trusted and believed could help her.

> Hannah hated going to Mr. Booker's physical education class. The class ran laps every day. Hannah didn't have an issue with running. It was what Mr. Booker screamed at her while they ran that she didn't like.
>
> It was the same thing each time. Once the first runner finished, Mr. Booker started in on Hannah. "Come on, Hannah! Come on, mashed potatoes! Come on, gravy!" Mr. Booker yelled continuously until Hannah crossed the finish line.
>
> Hannah always finished her run feeling ashamed of her "mashed potatoes and gravy" body. There were friends in the class who thought Hannah should do something about Mr. Booker. Hannah decided to mention it to her math teacher. She liked Ms. Crowley and trusted that she would give good advice.

Reporting harassment doesn't mean you're a tattletale or immature. You didn't cause the problem; you didn't ask to be harassed. Therefore, you can't be expected to solve the problem on your own. You have the right to be protected. That means you have to the right to get help and the right to report harassment.

Concrete Specifics

We have stressed the importance of adopting an assertive personality to deal with and avoid harassment, but we realize changing habits and behaviors can seem like a daunting task. Becoming assertive will take effort, time and courage on your part. To help you on your journey, here are some specific harassment situations with examples of what you can do and say in each instance. Remember, these are just examples; they are not all there is and you may think of other appropriate responses.

When Your Harasser is a Boyfriend/Girlfriend

Dating abuse incorporates all types of harassment. It is prevalent among teens. Dating abuse is a confusing, damaging type of abuse. The person doing the harassing is supposed to care about you. It is easy to get overwhelmed when emotions like love are involved and it may be even more difficult to know what to do.

Here are some statistics which show what an important problem teen dating abuse is today:

The National Youth Violence Prevention Resource Center reports that past estimates of physical and sexual dating violence among high school students typically range from 10 to 25 percent and estimates for college students range from 20 to 30 percent. Not surprisingly, even higher estimates are found when verbal threats and emotional abuse are considered.[1]

The National Teen Dating Violence Prevention Initiative reveals these startling numbers: In a study of gay, lesbian and bisexual adolescents, youths involved in same-sex dating are just as likely to experience dating violence as youths involved in opposite sex dating. Nearly half of adult sex offenders report committing their first sexual offenses prior to the age of eighteen. From their research, 50 percent of the reported date rapes occur among teenagers, 45 percent of girls know a friend or peer who has been pressured into either intercourse or oral sex and 57 percent of teens know someone who has been physically, sexually or verbally abusive in a dating relationship.[2]

What can you do about dating abuse? If you are a witness to an abusive relationship, please use the information in teen section 7 on not being a bystander for ideas on what you can do to help. If you are in an abusive relationship, please know that you need to take action. If you don't, you are at risk for becoming a victim in other relationships and a victim of alcohol and drug use, unhealthy weight issues (obesity, anorexia, bulimia), risky sexual behavior, sexually transmitted diseases, pregnancy, depression and suicidal tendencies. What do you need to do? To say? Where can you turn?

- **Report what is happening to an adult.** It needs to be an adult you can trust and someone who has the experience to help you. Even if the incident was seemingly minor, you should discuss it with a trusted adult. Sometimes you can tell a parent, but if you're not getting support at home, find someone else you can trust to help.

- **Don't try to handle it yourself.** Dating abuse can be an extremely harmful situation, so taking care of it alone is nearly impossible. If you feel safe enough to do so, tell your abuser about the behavior that's bothering you and that you expect it to stop. If the behavior isn't too alarming or serious, this approach may work. If it doesn't succeed or you don't feel safe enough to tell the other person how you feel, you need to report the situation to someone you trust.

- **Break off the relationship.** Don't let your significant other or anyone else guilt you or threaten you into staying in a relationship that doesn't make you feel good. Romance should feel exciting and wonderful. Don't settle for less. If your boyfriend or girlfriend refuses to break up or starts to become a stalker, you need to report this immediately.

- **Create a plan.** Get your sense of safety back. Use the safety plan at the end of this section.

- **Work on your self-esteem.** We spoke about victims and the type of relationships in which they often end up in teen section 4. Aggressive personalities seek passive ones for relationships. Together they become dysfunctional couples. The key to avoiding this cycle or getting out of it is to have a positive sense of self and be assertive.

- **Don't believe that you deserve to be abused.** An abuser attempts to scare and guilt a victim into staying in the relationship: "You'd better not break up with me or else," or "You made me hit you, because you knew I don't like that" or "Please don't break up with me. I'll get better. I won't do it again." Don't buy into that nonsense. Find a person or group to help keep you safe and never believe anyone who says you deserve to be beat up, physically or emotionally. Nobody deserves to be harassed.

- **Find a prevention program or a crisis line.** Dating abuse is a major issue and there are many organizations, resources and telephone hotlines available to you. They will provide you with the information and assistance you need and help ensure your safety. Remember that there is always a place or a person you can turn to for help. Check with the counselor at your school about the resources in your area. There are a lot of great programs available for you.

- **Make a statement.** Making a statement to law enforcement authorities not only will help you become safe and secure and give you strength, but also may ultimately help your abuser. Nearly half of all sex offenders commit their first sexual crimes before the age of eighteen. Abusers don't stop but move on to other abusive relationships unless they get help that makes them rethink and revise their behaviors or they are placed in environments where they can no longer abuse others. These could be the consequences for what they are doing to you. If you make a statement, you may be saving both of you from a miserable cycle of abuse.

Abusive relationships are difficult to handle because of the feelings involved. The harassment that happens within an abusive relationship is confusing and hurtful for the victim. As hard as it may be to admit to yourself, someone who really loves you will never abuse you. Not even once. In Liz's relationship, her controlling boyfriend caused her to seek help from a trusted school counselor.

Liz poked her head into Mrs. Nelson's office. "Can I ask you about a problem I'm having?"

"Sure, come on in," Mrs. Nelson, the high school counselor, answered.

Liz hadn't even sat down before she burst into tears. When she was finally able to speak, Liz said, "I really liked my boyfriend at first. I thought Frank was so cool, because he's older, out of high school and stuff. Not too long after we started dating, he told me he was going to pick me up after school. I thought that was cool. Then he insisted that he come and pick me up for lunch too. Okay, but now he won't let me go to any games or anything. I'm not allowed to see my friends. I hate it!"

"Did you tell him you want to spend time with your high school friends?"

"Yeah. It made him really angry. He didn't hit me or anything, but he yelled and told me to quit being immature."

"What about your parents? Have you told them about the situation?"

"Sort of, but my parents really like Frank, so they didn't seem to understand."

"Liz," Mrs. Nelson asked, "what do you want me to do to help you?"

Liz stood up quickly. "Nothing. I guess I just wanted to talk. I'll take care of it." Liz bolted out the door. Mrs. Nelson made a mental note to keep an eye on Liz.

Two days later, Mrs. Nelson went outside after lunch to get some fresh air. She noticed Liz inside a car in the parking lot, talking with Frank. Mrs. Nelson walked over and stopped to watch. She saw Liz try to move to the car door, but her boyfriend grabbed her arm and pulled her to him. She heard Liz crying and Frank yelling.

Mrs. Nelson ran to the principal's office and told him what was going on. He informed the school resource officer (SRO) and the three of them went out to the car where Liz was being held captive.

The principal and the SRO went to the driver's side to escort

Frank to the office. Mrs. Nelson opened the passenger door. "Liz, come with me."

Liz was thankful for the help and support she received. She ended her relationship with Frank, who was placed on probation after a hearing. Frank agreed never to return to school property or speak to Liz again if charges were not pressed against him. He kept his end of the bargain and Liz returned to being the fun-loving student everyone knew.

Bullying of Gay, Lesbian, Bisexual or Transgender Teens

The harassment of gay, lesbian, bisexual or transgender (GLBT) teens is prevalent in our culture. Anti-gay bullying refers to being harassed because of sexual orientation or gender identity. It is a result of homophobia and can affect not only those who are GLBT, but also those who are perceived to be gay but are not.

Bullying and Gay Youth Facts[3]

- Many gay/lesbian/bisexual/transgender (GLBT) teens have to deal with harassment, threats and violence directed at them on a daily basis. They hear anti-gay slurs such as *gay, homo, faggot* and *sissy* approximately twenty-six times a day or once every fourteen minutes.
- Twenty-eight percent of gay students will drop out of school. This is more than three times the national average for heterosexual students.
- Gay, lesbian and bisexual youths are two to three times more likely to attempt suicide than their heterosexual counterparts.

Teens who are struggling with sexual orientation issues have added vulnerability that harassers seem to target. Homophobia and the harassment that results from it are often due to the harasser being insecure about his or her own sexuality. Bullying, as we've discussed, is the way harassers deal with insecurities in general. Another cause of anti-gay harassment may also be that the harasser is affiliated with an organization that promotes aggressive behavior against homosexuals. A victim with more vulnerability because of sexual orientation plus a harasser who secretly questions his own sexuality and/or joins an aggressive organization that expresses hatred toward alternative lifestyles make for an especially nasty harassment problem.

If you are a witness to or a victim of GLBT bullying you need to stop it. Every human being deserves respect. Do not let your insecurity about sexual orientation or a group mentality turn you into a harasser. If you witness anti-gay bullying, the section entitled "Don't Be a Bystander" in teen section 7 will give you ideas on what you can do to help. Be assertive in aiding the victim and stopping the harassment.

In our school halls there is the common use of phrases such as "That's so gay!" It's derogatory and it's offensive, so that makes it harassment. Flippant anti-gay comments are harassment. Casually saying things like "That's so gay" is an aggressive habit that needs to be broken.

Don't let being abused because of your sexual orientation or perceived sexual orientation make you feel like less of a person and put you at risk for dropping out of school or developing mental health issues including depression and suicide. Here are some ideas for what you can say and do:

- **Don't deny or confirm.** Your sexual orientation is none of anyone's business. Denying that you're gay or confirming that you're gay are both no-wins. These answers will often make the harasser escalate his or her bullying, because either answer lets the harasser know he or she has gotten to you. Stand up to your harasser by focusing on how you feel about his or her behavior.

- **Use "I" statements.** I want you to stop... I don't like it when... I don't understand why… I feel like you're trying to get a reaction out of me. "I" statements focus on your feelings and the harasser's behavior. Remember, while you are using "I" statements you must look and sound assertive.

- **Report what is happening to a trusted adult.** It may not be easy to talk to anyone else about anti-gay harassment, but if the harassment you are experiencing is severe, persistent or pervasive, you must do this. If you're not sure who would be supportive, a school counselor, teacher or trusted adult are a few of the people who often will help you to take the right steps toward stopping harassment. Remember, you are protected by law as a human being and by school district policy as a student. In some states, anti-gay harassment is considered a hate crime, which is a felony.

- **Have a plan.** Get your sense of safety back. Use the safety plan at the end of this section.

- **Work on your self-esteem.** Your sexual orientation is a large part of who you are, but it is far from the complete picture. Refuse to let others define you and tell you there is something wrong with you. Know that the harassment is not your fault. You should have pride in who you are, which includes your personality, talents, the way you treat others and your sexual orientation. You have a lot to offer this world. Find family, friends and other sources of support who will see you, not a label. As a GLBT teen, you may feel you are dealing with more than the average teen. If things seem overwhelming or if you just need to talk, please see your counselor at school or seek professional counseling services.

- **Don't believe you ever deserve to be harassed.** Unfortunately, there will always be those who are homophobic and feel justified in treating GLBT people badly. Those people may even be in your family, which is particularly tough. Whoever it is, don't get wrapped up in their opinions of you and believe that you deserve to be abused. You have the right to be safe and secure. You never deserve to be harassed.

- **Find a support group.** Join or help start a Gay, Lesbian and Straight Education Network (GLSEN) chapter or another diversity group at your high school. You need to find your allies. If you're not comfortable doing something like starting or joining a club, there are community groups or online groups. Enlist others who are struggling with the same kinds of things you are and also straight supporters who will want to aid you. Never feel alone, because you aren't. An estimated 10 percent of the population is GLBT. There is support for you.

Parents should be a part of your support group, but that doesn't always happen. One of the toughest situations GLBT teens face is when or if to tell their parents they're gay. You have to make this decision. If your parents are assertive people and have always been supportive, your instincts will probably tell you to trust them. Keep in mind even the most supportive parents may be shocked by your disclosure at first, so you may need to give them time. But if your parents are assertive, their love for you will conquer all.

If your parents are aggressive or passive or they have demonstrated hate toward homosexuals and you are still dependent on them, wait until you are older, more independent and self-sufficient to tell them about your sexual orientation. You don't want to leave yourself open to harassment at home, nor do you want to be kicked out onto the streets. As a teen, you are a minor and deserve to be supported while you get an education and discover who you are and what your place is in the world.

You are the best judge about how your parents may react to having a child who is gay and it is your decision when or if to tell them. When you do decide it's time to reveal your sexual orientation, we believe it is a good idea to see a counselor for advice before you break the news. Whatever happens, remember you are a good person and there is nothing wrong with you because you are gay or straight.

Whether you are being harassed because you are GLBT or you're being abused because a harasser wants others to think you are, you must do something about it. You deserve respect no matter who you are or what you believe. Harassers often hide behind religious or political beliefs, but that never justifies aggression. Anti-gay harassment is no different from any other type of harassment or abuse. Assertive people don't harass, because they believe every person deserves respect. In John's situation, confidence in a supposed friend resulted in harassment until John sought the advice of a trusted school counselor.

High school was a social dilemma for John. He knew he was expected to date girls. Although he liked his female friends, he was not comfortable with the whole dating thing. John finally admitted to himself that he was attracted to males. The implications of his feelings were overwhelming and he needed to talk to someone.

John and Ted had been best friends since the first grade. John trusted Ted completely and felt that he would be respectful of John's feelings. John asked Ted to find some time so that they could talk in private. When they had their conversation, John felt like he had confided in the right person. Ted listened to him, seemed to accept his sexual orientation and promised that he keep their discussion confidential.

The next Monday, John was met at the school doors by a group of his male friends. A guy named Rick stepped forward. "You faggot, how long have you been checking us out in the locker room? You better stay the hell away from us!" The others added their own homophobic clichés before they let John pass to get to his locker.

At the beginning of first period, a couple of the students who sat next to John made a point of moving across the room from him. In the halls, he heard whispers and taunts as he passed. It was very clear to John that Ted had told people about their conversation.

John didn't see Ted during the school day. However, when the last bell rang, John went to Ted's locker. Ted rounded the corner and stopped. He briefly looked at John before ducking his head, turning and walking away. John was devastated.

Unsure of how to handle his peers' comments, John went to see his school counselor. She guided him in assertively dealing with the harassment that was happening. With the help of his school counselor, John found a real support system. Unfortunately, it didn't include his childhood friend Ted.

Dealing with Bullying

Bullying is a repeated act of aggression for the purpose of harming someone physically or psychologically. It is the term that covers all obnoxious behaviors. Here are some specific strategies that may work against bullying.

What to Say:
- I want you to stop…
- I don't like it when…
- I feel like you're trying to get a reaction out of me.
- I don't understand why…
- I'm going to get help.

What to Do:
- Be assertive—remain calm, but be direct.
- Walk away (calmly, assertively).
- Tell the bully how he or she makes you feel and what you want him or her to do.
- Have a safety plan in place.
- Report severe, persistent or pervasive bullying behavior.

Dealing with Sexual Harassment

Sexual harassment is bullying or harassment that is sexual in nature. It is meant to embarrass, intimidate, scare and confuse. The key when dealing with sexual harassers is to be very direct. If you simply turn red and storm away or tell the harassers they're gross, you are giving them what they want. Tell them exactly what you want them to stop and why. Being direct in the beginning also helps, because if you have to report the harassers later, they can't say that they had no idea they were offending you. If a sexual harasser touches you inappropriately or forces him or herself upon you, that is severe harassment and it needs to be reported immediately.

What to Say:

- I want you to stop…
- I feel very uncomfortable when you…
- I am offended when you…
- I don't think that's funny because…
- I'm going to get help.

What to Do:

- Be assertive—remain calm, but be direct.
- Walk away (calmly, assertively).
- Tell the harasser what you want him or her to stop doing and why.
- Have a safety plan in place.
- Report severe, persistent or pervasive sexual harassment incidents.

Dealing with Stalking

A victim is unable to get away from a stalker. The victim is put under surveillance. The victim's right to privacy has been violated, so he or she fears for his or her safety. Stalking situations are severe and persistent harassment and should be reported. Take stalking seriously, because it often leads to a serious crime. You can try telling the person that he or she is making you uncomfortable. Do not accuse him or her of being a stalker. This will put the person on the defensive and his or her behavior could become more unpredictable. Make sure you talk to him or her in a safe situation like in a public place. If that doesn't work, report the person.

What to Say:

- I feel like you're following me.
- I see or hear from you too often.
- I feel uncomfortable when you say or write…
- I think you pay too much attention to me and it makes me uncomfortable.
- I'm going to get help.

What to Do:

- Be assertive—remain calm, but be direct.
- Report the harasser's actions.
- Make sure your safety plan is in place.
- Change your phone number, get a new e-mail address, block the stalker from your online social networks.
- Change your routines where you can.
- Involve law enforcement.

When you are being stalked, you need your safety plan. Tell your parents or a trusted adult about what's going on, don't be alone and always let a trusted person know where you're going to be. Change your cell phone number if the stalker is using that number to get to you. Most cell phone companies will change your number at no cost. A small number of them charge a fee. Change your e-mail address and lock the stalker out of your social networking sites. Change your routines so your whereabouts are unpredictable and therefore you are harder to stalk.

Many stalkers are cowards and won't pursue you when it becomes difficult to do so. If the stalker doesn't back off, get the law involved. Your right to privacy, safety and security will be protected.

Dealing with Hazing

Hazing is a type of harassment sometimes used by groups to maintain a pecking order. New members are hazed to prove their worthiness. Hazing is often physically and/or psychologically damaging. You need to look into the organization and its admission requirements before you decide to join. Research the organization's history, traditions and prerequisites for membership. If you are hazed at school or for a school activity, let a trusted adult know, because it is illegal. You have dignity and you have rights. Don't become a member of a group that violates those rights. Have the courage to say no.

What to Say:

- What are the requirements for membership?
- Is there an initiation? What does it include?
- What is the purpose of the initiation? What will it prove about me as a potential member?
- I want to join an organization that doesn't require hazing.

What to Do:

- Be assertive—remain calm but be direct.
- Have the courage to stand up for your right to have dignity.
- Report hazing or planned hazing to school officials.

Dealing with Cyberbullying

Cyberbullying is the use of cell phones, the Internet or other digital devices to send messages or images that are intended to embarrass, slander or harm another person. The harassing behaviors take place in cyberspace. Take these threats seriously. Change your e-mail address. It's easy and free. Change your cell phone number—most phone networks will do it for free. Some charge a small amount. Block the harasser from all of your social networking sites.

If you feel safe and have someone with you who will support you, you may want to talk to the harasser face-to-face. If you don't feel safe with a face-to-face interaction, arrange to have an adult authority present. Cyberbullies need to see and hear that there are consequences for their actions. They like to harass through electronic devices, because it is at a distance and they don't have to see the effects of what they do. You can change that by telling them how you feel.

Sexting is sending or receiving messages or photos of yourself or others of a sexual nature using cell phones, computers or other electronic devices. Don't send something you don't want the world to see. Once it's out there, you can't get it back. Don't forward an image or message that you think may be sexting to someone else. You will be subject to the consequences of that too. In some states the consequences are that you must register as a sex offender if the picture is of someone under the age of eighteen. If the image is being passed on, report it. Sending this type of photo is a form of harassment.

What to Say:
- Nothing, unless you can say it in person.

What to Say, Face-to-Face with an Adult Present:
- I want you to stop…
- I don't like it when…
- I feel like you're trying to get a reaction out of me.

What to Do:
- Be assertive—remain calm but be direct.
- Report the incidents of harassment.
- Make sure your safety plan is in place.
- Change your phone number, get a new e-mail address, block the cyberbully from your online social networks.

Do Not:
- Do not post or send anything that you don't want others to see.
- Do not forward anything that could be offensive to or hurt another person.

Ongoing harassment leads to humiliation, insecurity and low self-esteem. If you don't stop it right away, the results will follow you into adulthood. Use what you've learned in this book: pay attention to how you feel, make changes to become a strong person and realize that there are people willing to help you. In return, you can help others.

We hope you have gained both the knowledge and the courage to deal with harassers positively. Remember that this requires one thing: assertive behavior. All the strategies that we've explored to stop harassment depend on assertiveness. It is that important.

Preventing harassment takes assertive work from everybody. When dealing with any form of harassment and any harasser, please make sure you stay safe. Pay attention to how you feel. If you feel threatened, report to an adult. Your "gut" is usually right.

We've given you strategies that will work and the reactions that won't work when dealing with harassment of all kinds. The key, however, is to act on what you've learned in this book. Know when it's harassment. Know that you have rights and you don't have to endure it. Most importantly, in order to deal with a harasser successfully, you must be assertive!

- **MYTH:** I've already tried all of this stuff and it doesn't work.

- **TRUTH:** One or more things are happening here: you didn't try very hard, you weren't assertive or you chose a passive adult to trust to help you. You have power and you can stop harassment, but it takes effort, courage and assertive behavior.

 LIST IN YOUR JOURNAL THINGS YOU THINK WOULD WORK TO HELP SOMEONE ELSE WITH HARASSMENT AND HELP YOU DEAL WITH A HARASSER.

TEEN CONNECTIONS

- What did Quinn do to try to make the harassment stop that didn't work?

    Quinn did a couple of things that didn't work. She became a loner. She ate her lunch alone and she gave up on trying to make friends and/or allies. Quinn wanted to dye her hair black. Luckily, her mom helped her to see that if she dyed her hair her harassers would only move on to something else. Changing her appearance wouldn't have worked.

- What did Quinn do that made the harassment stop?

    Quinn did a lot of things that were great and she did them in a situation that was worse than most, because she didn't have supportive adults at her school. Quinn found an adult she could trust: her mom. Quinn talked to her mom and looked to her for advice. Quinn not only used her mom for support, but also found security in her whole family. They gave her confidence and they gave her the will to continue on. Sometimes she did the same for them. Quinn got involved in her school through joining the band. That helped her to make friends. Also helpful was finding other students in her school who were being picked on. Because Quinn was unique, the boys were attracted to her. On her mom's advice, Quinn used her differences to gain friends and allies among the boys in her school. Not wanting to ruin their own chances for romance, her female harassers toned down their behavior.

- Why does Quinn help those who are being harassed now?

    Quinn knows what it's like and how it feels to be harassed. She realizes the importance of having friends and allies to combat harassment. She wants to help others avoid the situation that she was in and she wants to contribute to an environment that is completely unlike the school where she was harassed. She wants her new school to be a place that helps her be successful.

My Safety Plan

Fill in the answers to these questions. Your responses will provide the information you need to become safe and secure. If you can't answer some of these questions about where and to whom you can go to seek help, you should get assistance from a trusted adult, like a school counselor.

1. Where are the places I can go where I know I will be safe?

_____ _____

_____ _____

_____ _____

2. Who can I be with and feel safe?

_____ _____

_____ _____

_____ _____

3.   Who are some adults who can help me? What are their phone numbers?

_____

_____

_____

_____

_____

_____

4.   What password can I use to let the people I trust know that I am in trouble?

_____

5.   Where are the resources available to me and how do I access them?

_____

_____

_____

_____

Parent Section 7

Assertive Parenting in Action

So far we have discussed harassment categories, harassment law and assertive parenting with regard to harassment. This section gives you specifics when it comes to helping your teen deal with harassment. If you, as a parent, are the victim then we urge you to utilize this chapter, because the information will apply to you as well as teens.

This section for parents is set up very much like the teen section. The first part will hopefully show you how and why your child—victim or harasser—needs your help. Parents cannot leave the serious issue of harassment to a third party to handle for them. Parents need to work with their school administrators, law enforcement officials or other organizations in order to protect their children and ensure they are safe and secure. Next we will describe the things you may be tempted to tell your teen to try when dealing with a harasser that will likely make the situation worse. Finally, we will cover some specific tips, strategies and advice on how to help your teen. We will provide questions you should ask and proven actions you can take to help your teen prevent or handle harassment.

Don't Stay Out of It!

The most effective strategy for preventing or stopping your teen from being harassed is to be there for him or her, whether it's to listen, guide decision making or work with the school or other officials. When you have the attitude that it's solely the responsibility of a third party to stop what is happening to your teen, that's a passive behavior. When you do nothing, your teen may believe you don't care about him or her and that the harassment he or she is experiencing is okay or perhaps even deserved. Staying out of it can be very damaging to your teen. Conversely, jumping in and solving all of your child's problems allows your teen to remain passive or aggressive, as the case may be. Parents need to find a balance between parenting and empowering their teenage sons and daughters. Let's review modified versions of the suggestions found in teen section 7 and add a few more.

- **Do not confront the bully or his or her parents!** As much as you may want to, you cannot stand up for your teen; he or she has to do it for him or herself. That's how your teen will gain respect from peers. If you try to stand up for your child by confronting the bully or the parents of the bully, you will make the situation worse for your teen. Also, it is useful to keep in mind that the bully's parents may be a large reason why he or she is a bully in the first place.

- **Tell your teen what you know about harassing behaviors, the law and the school's harassment policy.** Knowing what constitutes harassment is a way for you to validate what your teen is going through, something that is very important to him or her. Being familiar with the law and the school's policy is imperative if you are going to guide your teen's decision making as he or she stands up against the harasser.

- **Encourage your teen to talk to a parent or another trusted adult.** Teens are often reluctant to come to their parents with harassment issues. They may think they will disappoint or worry them. Therefore, when you recognize there is something bothering your teen, offer to listen. If your son or daughter refuses to confide in you, brainstorm with him or her about others with whom he or she can talk. Parents should realize that harassment issues don't have to be—nor should they be—taken care of completely within the family. There is help available for your teen and for you.

- **Listen to the victim's experience.** Listen to the victim's words but also watch his or her body language and hear the tone of voice. Many times, parents' first instinct is to offer their best advice and lecture their children. Most teens don't respond to this and will usually stop talking. Be a good listener, ask open-ended questions, guide decision making instead of lecturing and ensure that your teen knows you are there for him or her, because you love him or her.

- **Don't become a harasser.** If you express anger with the bully, his or her parents, law enforcement or the school, your teen will perceive that you are playing the blame game and may believe he or she has no personal responsibility in the harassment situation. If you act on your anger, then you are no better than your teen's bully. There is no such thing as a good bully or a time when harassment can work in your favor.

- **Help your teen come up with a plan to be safe.** Later in this parent section you are going to complete the safety plan at the end of teen section 7 with your teen. This not only gives your teen the security of knowing that there are places and people for him or her to turn to, but also gives the assurance that you are concerned with his or her safety and are there for support.

- **Be visible in your teen's life.** Knowing your teen's friends, what your teen does in his or her spare time and showing up to games, concerts, shows and project demonstrations is important for harassment prevention, because it provides your teen with the confidence that you are there to support him or her. Teens who feel supported are less likely to become the victims of a harasser. There is the added bonus that a harasser may see you and know not to pick on a teen whose parents are visibly supportive. The key is to remember to remain an assertive parent, not one who smothers his or her teen as he or she hovers over every aspect of the teen's life. Again, find a balance so your teen feels supported but not suffocated.

- **Become acquainted with the other adults in your teen's life.** Attending activities like back-to-school nights, participating in parent-teacher conferences, chaperoning youth activities, joining parent organizations and other such things creates a network of support for your teen. When your teen is a victim of harassment, there are usually people who want to get involved and make it stop. You need to find out who those people are.

- **Find some support for yourself.** Standing on the sidelines of your teen's life can be very lonely. Finding support goes beyond being acquainted with those who are available to your teen. You need to realize that there are other parents who have similar struggles raising their teens. Once you become involved in your teen's life, get to know his or her friends' parents and the parents of teens involved in the same activities, talk with parents who are members of the same organizations and do anything else you can to get to know those parents who are facing the same raising-an-adolescent challenge you are.

Parents cannot be bystanders. Staying out of your child's harassment situations, whether he or she is the victim or the harasser, can have dire consequences. Your teen may become violent toward him or herself or others. At the very least, your inactivity will cause distrust, fear and insecurity in your relationship with your teen. Your teen needs to know you are there for him or her. Being an assertive parent is taking responsibility not only for yourself, but also for the teen you are raising. If you don't parent assertively, which means that you are sitting on the sidelines and not in the game, chances are you are part of the problem.

- **MYTH:** We are a family who takes care of everything ourselves, including harassment.

- **TRUTH:** Your teen probably feels very safe and secure in your home, but he or she is not there all the time. We all need support from family and from outside people as well. Unless you want your teen to live with you forever, because he or she fears leaving the security of your home, your teen has to know there are other people outside the family to trust.

 HELP YOUR TEEN FILL OUT THE SAFETY PLAN AT THE END OF TEEN SECTION 7.

What Not to Do

As we researched, met with and interviewed teen victims and their families, law enforcement and school authorities, it became increasingly clear that some teens were getting detrimental advice about dealing with harassers. Sometimes they received that advice from well-meaning parents or other authority figures. Parents may be tempted to do things which ultimately will not help their teens deal with harassment. Here are some things parents should *not* do:

- **Don't become a passive-aggressive or aggressive personality.** Seeing their children in pain makes parents angry and sometimes it is very difficult to remain assertive, but parents have to. They have to resist the urge to tell their teens to beat up the harassers or formulate sneaky schemes to get back at them. When you do either of these things, you give your teen permission to become the bully, which is the very thing you want to thwart in the first place.

- **Don't forget that your reaction has everything to do with your teen's.** You are being watched by your teen. When your child comes to you after being harassed, he or she is gauging your reaction. If your teen comes to you in pain, because he or she has been victimized by a harasser, you trivialize his or her victimization if your initial reaction is to tell your child to ignore the harasser, to use humor or laugh it off, to make a friend out of the harasser or to use kindness. In essence, parents who tell their teens to try any of these techniques set them up for more abuse, because their teens' harassers see these as challenges rather than deterrents.

- **Don't play the blame game or become a helicopter parent.** If your teen is being harassed, it is his or her responsibility to stand up for him or herself. This is not the same as saying your son or daughter has to do it alone, however. You child can get help from a number of people, including parents. If you act as the helicopter parent or play the blame game, you are telling your teen he or she has no responsibility and no decision-making ability and you don't have any confidence in him or her.

- **Don't check your teen out of life.** Harassment happens everywhere, to all age groups, regardless of cultural, social or economic status. If your solution to your teen's victimization is to take him or her out of the situation where it occurred, you are teaching your child to run. He or she will be running forever. We all have to learn to deal with negative events in our lives. If we don't, we will never be successful. Success requires going forward; it doesn't include retreating. Instead of switching schools or pulling your teen out of activities, help him or her to become assertive. Teach your teen that checking out is not a positive solution. Running away from problems will make him or her a victim forever.

If these misguided attempts at stopping harassment work at all, it will only be a temporary fix. More than likely, employing these strategies will make the situation worse for your teen. When discussing what to do about harassment with your teen, it is worthwhile to talk about the future. For example, if you beat up your harasser, he or she may stop bullying you, but then what? Hopefully your teen answers that he or she would get into trouble and would become the bully that he or she originally despised. Teens need help seeing the ramifications of their actions and they need parents to guide them toward effective solutions, not the seemingly easy ones that teens or their parents may choose on impulse.

- **MYTH:** Fighting worked to resolve issues when I was young. In fact, it was encouraged.

- **TRUTH:** Maybe fighting worked and maybe it didn't, but modern harassment is not the same as what parents experienced when they were younger. It has become much more insidious and much more dangerous. If harassment is dealt with using violence instead of assertiveness, it can escalate beyond hand-to-hand combat and the injuries suffered will be far worse than a black eye.

How to Help Your Teen Deal with Harassers

Harassment is a complex issue and the responsibility for what is happening does not lie with only one person. You and your teen both have to build your knowledge about harassment, the resources that are available to assist in harassment situations and the difficult personality changes that may have to be made before harassment can become a non-issue in your lives. The teen sections along with the parent sections provide you with the information needed to accomplish all these things. *Hey, Back Off!* provides a comprehensive guide to harassment prevention.

If your teen is a victim of harassment, the next section is designed to help you, but be aware that:

- Your help has to be assertive or it will be no help at all.

- The harassment your teen is experiencing is not your fault, nor is it your teen's fault.

- Your teen has the power to stop harassment, particularly with your guidance.

- You and your teen are not in this struggle alone.

You and your teen need to hold some fundamental beliefs if you are to be successful in stopping your teen's harassment by bullies.

By now you are aware that assertive parenting is the answer. Finding support and getting involved will make your job easier. Having a vested interest in your teen and his or her education and activities will make your teen feel secure and will therefore deter harassers. Making a plan and discussing with your teen how to keep him or her safe is necessary if you and your teen are going to triumph over the harasser.

Parents need to remember the three qualifications for reporting harassment to school or law authorities. The harassment needs to be severe, persistent or pervasive. If any one of these three is occurring, you should encourage your teen to report the situation. Remember, as we've indicated previously, reporting is difficult for teens, but parents can help them understand that harassment is not their fault and they aren't failures because they can't make it stop on their own. This is one of those situations where help is needed, because it involves their physical and psychological safety. Help your teen brainstorm about trusted adults close to the situation to whom he or she can report situations. Reporting severe, persistent or pervasive harassment will be empowering for your teen, because it's a way for the teen to stand up for him or herself.

If your teen absolutely refuses to report the incident, because he or she believes it will make things worse or thinks it will be tattling, you may need to step in. Be up front with your teen about when and to whom you are going to make the report. Explain to your son or daughter the meaning of severe, persistent and pervasive harassment, how retaliation will be less likely if the incidents are reported to authorities and that you are going to report if your teen doesn't, because you love him or her and it's your responsibility to keep him or her safe and secure. You need to put your teen's safety first. If what is happening to your teen is severe, persistent or pervasive, your teen is not safe. Therefore, you have to report if your child won't. After attempts to speak with his daughter about her verbally abusive boyfriend, Ted spoke with the school counselor, despite knowing his daughter would initially be angry with him.

Ted was seriously worried about his daughter, Maddy. She was dating Dave, a high school dropout whom Ted overheard verbally abusing her. Also concerning was that she had been caught skipping classes twice and her grades were dropping. Ted felt that it was due to Dave's behavior. He tried unsuccessfully to discuss the situation with Maddy. After many sleepless nights, Ted decided he had to take action to protect his daughter's safety.

Ted began with Maddy's school. He made an appointment to speak to Mr. Lavinka, the school counselor. Ted explained the situation to Mr. Lavinka and then said, "I know I don't have enough evidence to go to law enforcement, but I want to be proactive. I guess I'm asking if you could help me keep an eye on Maddy or perhaps you could try to talk to her. She might listen to you. She seems to like you."

"Of course I can."

Mr. Lavinka followed up with Maddy. At first she was angry that her father had gotten involved in her love life, but eventually she realized that her dad was worried about her personal safety and her ability to be successful if she continued to date Dave. She made plans to break up with her boyfriend.

Whether your teen reports harassment or you do, you will have to get involved in the processes of school policy and legal proceedings. Most teens, because they are under the age of eighteen, cannot be viewed in the eyes of the law as victims without their parents' consent. For that reason, you cannot stay out of harassment situations. It is empowering for teens to stand up for themselves and report on their own; if they do, parents have to be there to back them up. If they won't report and parents are worried about their safety, parents have the right and responsibility to report in order to protect their children against the damages of harassment.

When dealing with harassment, it is worthwhile for parents and teens to focus on what they can control. You cannot control what the harasser tries to do, but you can control what you do, whether it is to help your teenage son or daughter employ a strategy to make the harassment stop or to report it to an authority. Be assertive. Be aware that fault is not the same as responsibility; we have a responsibility to get ourselves away from or help others out of harassment situations, but we are not at fault for what a harasser does. Know that your teen can take back control of his or her life and you can guide him or her in making the assertive decisions that will make that possible. With the help that is available to you and your teen, you can achieve harassment prevention.

Concrete Specifics

Helping your teen hinges on being an assertive person and parent. However, we are aware that becoming assertive doesn't happen overnight. Aggressive and passive behaviors, like any habits, are hard to break. You and your teen may need help with harassment at this point, so that you can eventually work through your negative personality traits and become assertive. In this section, we focus on the parent's point of view.

We give some concrete, specific things to say and do to help you help your teen deal with various types of harassment, but you need to remember a few things. First, these are only examples. We cannot anticipate every situation or each assertive alternative for dealing with it. Second, you cannot be the only one using these antidotes. Your teen has to do his or her part as well. Otherwise, you are falling into the passive trap where you take care of everything for your teen and he or she remains a victim. Again, the best way to solve harassment issues, no matter what they are, is to be assertive. This means you are a guide, not a dictator.

Many of the questions you can ask and the things you can do are similar across several types of harassment. We believe it is worthwhile to be repetitive in this case. However, there are a few clarifications that need to be made before you read through our suggestions. The question, "Whom can you count on for immediate help?" refers to a friend your teen trusts to help him or her out of tough situations. If your teen doesn't have someone like this in his or her life, that is a concern you may want to address with a counselor. All teens should have friends their own age they can trust. The question, "How can I help you?" means just that: help. It is imperative that you don't let your teenage son or daughter convince you to solve everything for him or her. Depending on the age and maturity level of your teen, you may have to explain or simplify some terminology. Now let's help your teen deal with a variety of harassment situations.

Teen Dating Abuse

By now you realize that dating abuse is a serious issue for teens. The teen years are a time when adolescents often experiment romantically and sexually. Parents should be there to ensure their teens are acting in safe ways, which includes knowing whether their sons and daughters are respected by their boyfriends or girlfriends. It is extremely important that teens' parents are not involved in abusive relationships themselves. If they are, it is likely that their teens will repeat the patterns they learned from their parents. Next, we'll focus on ways to support your teen to get out of an abusive relationship.

What to Say:

- What does your ideal relationship look like? Is your current relationship close to or far from that ideal?
- Do you feel respected in your relationship? Why or why not?
- Does your boyfriend/girlfriend make you feel good about yourself?
- How are you going to get out of this relationship?
- Whom can you count on for immediate help?
- Who are some adults you could go to if your boyfriend/girlfriend treats you badly?
- How can I help you?

What to Do:

- Model assertive relationships.
- Rehearse the breakup with my teen.
- Set age-appropriate dating limits for my teen.
- Create a safety plan with my teen.
- Listen to my teen and guide his or her decision making.
- Assure my teen that he or she doesn't deserve to be abused and real love doesn't involve abuse.
- Encourage my teen to report to or seek help from an adult whom he or she trusts.
- Report the abuse to the authorities if I feel my teen is in physical danger.

You may notice that what you say or do does not include forcing your teen to break up with an abusive boyfriend or girlfriend. Trying to make teens do anything usually has the opposite effect. Attempting to make them break up may cause teens to see themselves as Romeo or Juliet or other star-crossed lovers whom someone is trying to keep apart. A more effective strategy is to deny your teen the drama by discussing the relationship and allowing him or her to come to his or her own conclusion that it isn't healthy. Also let your teen know that you are there for him or her and that you care first and foremost for his or her safety, which may include reporting the harassment in order to protect him or her.

Bullying of Gay, Lesbian, Bisexual or Transgender Teens

Parents need to deal with anti-gay harassment their teens experience just as they would other types of harassment. As a parent, you need to be an assertive role model, a guide, a listener and your teen's number one supporter. Unfortunately, this type of advocacy doesn't always happen and many GLBT teens are living on the streets or committing suicide because of parents' reactions to their sexual orientations. It is not a show of faith or strong principles to reject your child for being gay. He or she needs your support more than ever.

Helping Your Teen Deal with Bullying

Bullying is the catchall term for all types of harassment and all harassers can be called bullies. Teens may use the term bullying to describe all kinds of behavior. It may be up to adults to define it accurately and then guide teens toward the proper line of action. Here are some examples of what you can say or do.

What to Say:

- What happened?
- What have you tried or what can you try to make the bullying stop?
- Whom can you count on for immediate help?
- Do you feel like the bullying is severe, persistent or pervasive?
- Who are some adults you could go to if the bullying becomes severe, persistent or pervasive?
- How can I help you?

What to Do:

- Model assertive behavior.
- Rehearse responses with my teen.
- Create a safety plan with my teen.
- Assure my teen the bullying is not his or her fault.
- Listen to my teen and guide his or her decision making.
- Encourage my teen to report if the bullying is severe, persistent or pervasive.
- Report severe, persistent or pervasive bullying if my teen won't.

Helping Your Teen Deal with Sexual Harassment

In the teen section we urge teens to be direct with sexual harassers and to tell the harassers exactly what they want them to stop doing. This is hard for many adults to do, but it is *extremely* difficult for teens. Adolescents often giggle uncomfortably whenever the word *sex* is used, even if it's in their science class. You can imagine what sexual harassment can do to teens. You need to help your teen be direct and make sure he or she understands that what someone else did or said is no reason for him or her to feel ashamed.

What to Say:

- What happened?
- What have you tried or what can you try to make the harassment stop?
- Is your approach direct and assertive?
- Whom can you count on for immediate help?
- Do you feel like the harassment is severe, persistent or pervasive?
- Who would you go to for help if the harassment becomes severe, persistent or pervasive?
- How can I help you?

What to Do:

- Model assertive, direct behavior.
- Rehearse responses with my teen.
- Create a safety plan with my teen.
- Assure my teen the harassment is not his or her fault and therefore he or she should not be ashamed.
- Listen to my teen and guide his or her decision making.
- Encourage my teen to report if the harassment is severe, persistent or pervasive.
- Report severe, persistent or pervasive sexual harassment if my teen won't.

Helping Your Teen Deal with Stalking

If your teen is being stalked, then in reality your entire family is being stalked. This harasser is keeping tabs on your teen, who is a part of your family. Parents have to be a visible ally for a teen who is being stalked. Because stalking may happen largely outside of a school's jurisdiction, you may need to find help in navigating the legal system. Use your school's resource officer as a guide.

What to Say:

- How is this person's attention making you uncomfortable?
- What might you try to get this person to leave you alone?
- Do you feel you'll be safe if you try and talk to the stalker about his or her behavior?
- Do you think we need to report this to the authorities?
- Whom can you count on for immediate help?
- How can I help you?

What to Do:

- Model assertive behavior—remain calm but be direct about the dangers of stalking.
- Create a safety plan with my teen.
- Change phone numbers, e-mail addresses and make sure the stalker is blocked from my teen's social networks.
- Assure my teen that he or she has a right to privacy.
- Listen to my teen and guide his or her decision making.
- Encourage my teen to report.
- Report if my teen won't—after all, I am a victim too.

Helping Your Teen Deal with Hazing

Before your teen joins a sports team, club, fraternity or sorority, ask whether hazing is involved for initiation. Keep in mind that even a little hazing that may seem innocent has a possibility of escalating quickly. This is why all hazing is illegal. Also remember that the longer hazing activities go on, the worse they become. If your teen wants to join an organization that you were once a part of and you were hazed, those initiations have had a long time to build up to something dangerous. Parents should also be aware that the penalties for hazing are much stiffer now. There are numerous parents who wish they'd asked questions before their teens got into trouble with the law, were injured physically or psychologically or even killed by hazing rituals.

What to Say:

- Why do you want to join this organization?
- What are the requirements for membership?
- Does this organization have a reputation for hazing new members?
- Do you know the damages of hazing?

What to Do:

- Research clubs, teams and other organizations my teen wants to join.
- Listen to my teen and guide his or her decision making.
- Assure my teen that membership is not worth sacrificing his or her dignity or safety.
- Encourage my teen to report if hazing has already happened or he or she thinks it will happen.
- Report hazing incidents if my teen won't.
- Report organizations that I suspect may use hazing if my teen won't.

Helping Your Teen Deal with Cyberbullying

Cyberbullying is the latest and most insidious form of bullying. It is subversive and therefore harder for parents and officials to detect. Parents have to become vigilant monitors (not dictators) of their teens' technology use. Teens should know their parents are monitoring them for their safety and not to intrude on their privacy. Most teens are fully aware of what cyberbullying and sexting are, but many are unaware how damaging they can be. As the parent who pays for these electronic devices, you have a right to keep your teen safe. If you don't know how to use technology, you need to learn. Your teen would probably make an excellent teacher!

What to Say:

- What happened?
- Would you feel comfortable saying something to the cyberbully face-to-face?
- What have you tried or what can you try to make the cyberbullying stop?
- Whom can you count on for immediate help?
- Is the cyberbullying affecting your ability to socialize and enjoy activities?
- Do you feel like the cyberbullying is severe, persistent or pervasive?
- Who would you go to if the cyberbullying becomes severe, persistent or pervasive?
- How can I help you?

What to Do:

- Monitor my teen's technology use—let my teen know I trust him or her but I want to keep him or her safe.
- Create a safety plan with my teen.
- Lock abusive users out of my teen's social networking sites, change my teen's e-mail address and cell phone number.
- Make technology public domain in my house.
- Assure my teen that cyberbullying is not his or her fault.
- Listen to my teen and guide his or her decision making.
- Encourage my teen to report if the cyberbullying is severe, persistent or pervasive.
- Report severe, persistent or pervasive cyberbullying if my teen won't.

- **MYTH:** I shouldn't allow my teen to have a cell phone or a social networking page. It's too dangerous.
- **TRUTH:** You are inviting a rebellion if you ban technology that many teens believe is a necessity. Technology is so pervasive that most teens will find a way to use it. It is much more effective to fight cyberbullying if there are no secrets and you can openly monitor what's happening in cyberspace.

As you can see, helping your teen with harassment prevention is all about getting your teen to think, discuss and make some decisions on what to do about his or her victimization. The level of your involvement should be regulated by your teen unless you believe he or she is in danger. Your primary role is as a mentor who listens, offers support and guides your teen toward an assertive solution. As we've stated many times, it doesn't work to tell teens what to do. If you sit down and have an adult conversation where you ask open-ended questions, you will find it will be effective. Your teen will feel as if he or she has an ally who cares about his or her safety and his or her maturation into an independent, successful adult.

PARENT CONNECTIONS

- What would you do if you knew your teen was being harassed and your teen begged you not to get involved?

  Find out why your teen believes your involvement would do more harm than good. Then ask your son or daughter what he or she plans to do to make the harassment stop. It has to be understood that if you are going to remain quiet, your teen needs to convince you that he or she is going to be proactive. It should be unacceptable to you if your teen's answer is to do nothing. Guide his or her decision making regarding what he or she should do, just as Allison did with Quinn.

- At what point do parents need to intercede in a harassment situation?

  If the teen's solution is to do nothing and/or the harassment becomes severe, persistent or pervasive, a parent needs to act. In a typical harassment situation at school, there are people to turn to for help. Hang in there and become effective allies for one another.

- How would you determine whether the adults in a harassment case are condoning the harassment or are the harassers themselves?

  Harassment does not go away when the teen years are over. Teens have to learn how to stand up for themselves or else there will always be people who are willing to stand by and do nothing and there will always be people who want to take advantage of others. Age doesn't matter. Neither does race, religion, culture, gender, sexual orientation or anything else. It's all about personality. Aggressive personalities harass; assertive personalities prevent or handle harassment.

Conclusion

You've read *Hey, Back Off! Tips for Stopping Teen Harassment,* so what happens now? How do you go forward? Our goal for this book is to educate teens, their parents and other adults in a straightforward, level-appropriate manner about what constitutes harassment, harassment law, personality types in relation to harassment issues and how to deal with harassment effectively. *Hey, Back Off!* provides information and hopefully a call to action in the important fight against harassment. It is now up to you, teens and parents, to supply the other half of the equation for the harassment epidemic. You must act. It is knowledge plus assertive action that will stop and prevent harassment.

HARASSMENT KNOWLEDGE

Harassment	Retaliation
Quid Pro Quo	Severe
Hostile Environment	Persistent
Bullying	Pervasive
Sexual Harassment	Aggressive
Stalking	Passive
Hazing	Assertive
Cyber-bullying	Parenting Strategies
Empathy	Awareness
Rights	Reporting
Support Systems	School Policy
Due Process	State Laws

ASSERTIVE ACTION

Respect	Connect
Decision-making	Change
Stand up	Rehearse
Honesty	Teamwork
Responsibility	Discuss
Deal	Be Proactive
Analyze	Learn
Listen	Express
Report	Belong
Make "I" Statements	Guide
Challenge	Advocate
Make Choices	Manage
Think	Lead
Model	Plan
Work	Support
Set SMART Goals	Reflect
Become Assertive	

STOPPING AND PREVENTING HARASSMENT

Acting Assertively

Any action you take has to be assertive if it is going to be effective. If your actions are not assertive then you are in a passive or an aggressive role and you will make the harassment problem worse instead of being a part of the solution. Therefore, your first actions in preparation for taking on harassment involve becoming assertive. You have to analyze your personality, know your weaknesses and come up with a plan to change. You are trying to be a fighter and before you can step into the battle, you must have mental and emotional toughness, self-confidence and allies. These are all things you cannot obtain without being assertive. Becoming assertive is the preparation needed to be victorious over harassment.

Hey, Back Off! has hopefully given you important information about passive, aggressive and assertive personalities. It has also given you ideas for actions to take to become assertive. If you still feel that becoming assertive is overwhelming, let's look once again at SMART goals. Setting SMART goals is key, because those goals have to be Specific, Measurable, Attainable, Realistic and Timely. SMART goals are challenging but they are not overwhelming. Here are some things you may choose to focus your goals on:

- **Checking physical appearance.** Make good eye contact, but don't stare. Your posture should say you're approachable, not that you want to disappear or beat somebody up.

- **Making decisions.** Don't let others make them for you and don't make decisions for others. That applies to parents too, particularly regarding their teenage children.

- **Gaining real self-confidence.** You cannot believe that you are life's loser and expect that a harasser won't target you. And for those aggressive personalities, your inflated ego is simply an indication of insecurity. Real self-confidence makes you feel good from the inside out.

- **Controlling the only person you can: you.** Allowing others to control you will get you victimized. Attempting to control people and situations will make you frustrated and angry.

- **Respecting yourself and others.** Respect will only happen when you make it a requirement in your relationships. That includes the relationship you have with yourself. You must realize that you will never get respect until you give it. You cannot give respect to others when you have none for yourself.

- **Taking responsibility for yourself. If you are a parent, also taking responsibility for the teen you are raising.** Becoming responsible is the way to gain self-respect and respect from others and it is vital in gaining self-confidence.

Becoming assertive won't happen all at once. Choose a place to start and set a few SMART goals. Once you begin to be assertive, not only will you be effective in stopping harassment, but also your assertive actions could influence a friend, another victim or other people who are being harassed or harassing others.

Remember that you cannot change anyone but yourself. Parents cannot change their teens. Parents can only provide boundaries and consequences, be role models, guide, advocate and offer support. When parents employ the blame game, become helicopter parents or attempt to solve their teen's problems, they are teaching their teens to be aggressive or passive. If you focus on being an assertive person and parent, your teen will have a better chance of following your positive example.

Teens have to understand they cannot change their parents. But teens can break the cycle of abuse in a family. You can choose to be an assertive person who respects him or herself as well as others. This is not easy when the people who are supposed to offer guidance are passive or aggressive. Some suggestions offered in *Hey, Back Off!* are to surround yourself with friends and mentors you admire, learn from others' mistakes as well as your own and expand your world view. Trying to force others to change is a frustrating proposition and you will fail. You can experience success and even influence others when you focus on an assertive you.

Apply what you learned about assertiveness. *Hey, Back Off!* gives you the tools to deal with and stop harassment in your life so that it will become a minor annoyance instead of a crisis. You will also find that you have a desire to help others, which is the most positive outcome possible. Assertive people feel as though they are a part of things around them. When you belong to something larger than you, there is a feeling of responsibility to make it better. We've talked a lot about the need to become involved and be a part of positive change in life. When enough people refuse to be on the sidelines, then we will successfully stop and prevent harassment.

Use Your Words

Often someone older and wiser tells us to "use your own words" to describe our feelings. After speaking to teens about harassment for a number of years, we realized teens didn't really know if what they were experiencing was harassment, because they didn't have the words to label it. Parents often don't have a harassment vocabulary either, because when they were teens nobody talked about harassment except to tell victims they needed to toughen up, because bullying was part of growing up.

Hey, Back Off! gives readers a harassment vocabulary and information on what constitutes harassment. If you completed the "Felt It, Did It" exercises at the end of section 1, you've already begun to use your harassment education. This activity should have helped you realize that some of the things you've experienced were harassment and some of the things you've done were also harassment. The act of making connections like this is helpful in preventing future bullying.

In the past, when we taught harassment vocabulary and explained the behaviors involved in each category to our students, it made a difference. We heard teens in the halls reminding one another they shouldn't do a certain thing, because it's harassment. We also heard the usual victims stand up and say knock it off, because they now had terms that validated what they were feeling. Adults and teens alike have to know what a thing is and be able to describe it before they can begin to fight it.

Connecting behaviors, terms and feelings is not the only application for this harassment information. It should also make for some informed discussions so you and your parents can describe what is happening to you. Shared harassment vocabulary eliminates confusion and therefore frustration. Having words gives you the confidence to know that you have a valid reason for someone to listen, because you've been harassed. Harassment escalates and becomes more dangerous when victims are silenced. Use your words and talk to an adult you trust. You will be heard.

You can also use this harassment vocabulary with your harasser. In the sections on becoming assertive and in teen section 7, we discussed "I" statements, which are powerful to use with harassers, but they can be even more so if you use the very words that are utilized to create anti-harassment law and policy. Here are some examples:

"I" Statements

I want you to stop touching me that way, because it is sexual harassment.

I need to know more about the qualifications for joining your club. I don't want to be hazed.

I know it is the victim's decision whether something is harassment or not and I believe this is.

I dislike your harassing jokes and I don't think they're funny.

I am uncomfortable when you and your girlfriend kiss in front of me.

I'm not going to post that on my Web page, because it is cyberbullying, which is against the law.

I don't have to put up with harassment (or be more specific and use bullying, sexual harassment, stalking, hazing or cyberbullying).

I feel like you're trying to get a reaction out of me by bullying me.

"I" statements are great for expressing yourself, but they can be really effective when coupled with the information you received in section 1. Knowing what is happening to you and telling it to the harasser is empowering for you and frightening for him or her. Harassers don't like their victims to stand up for themselves. Being direct and precise takes away their power.

Help Is On the Way

Harassers violate our rights to be safe and secure. Having rights means there is built-in support for you, because individual rights must be protected by law. Unlike harassment vocabulary, which is straightforward and consistent across the country, harassment laws are instituted by individual states. There will also be some differences in school policies, because they are written from state law. Educate yourself and your family about the laws and policies on harassment in your state and school district. You have to know who your allies are and what kind of support they can bring to your fight against harassment.

State laws as well as school district policies are public information and are typically easily accessible online or can be requested at schools, public libraries or government offices. If you believe the laws or policies in your state or school district are incomplete, become assertively involved in the democratic process. Keep in mind that if you hope to effect meaningful change you have to be assertive.

Finding and accepting support is an extremely important action you should take early and often when working on harassment issues. In fact, in order to truly stop harassment it will take a team effort. Approach others you think you can trust and assertively ask for help, then remain assertive and work with them. Here are some things to focus on in your search for support:

- **Harassment that is severe, persistent or pervasive needs to be reported to a trusted adult.** It is an assertive characteristic to know when you need help and to ask for that help. If the harassment fits your definition of severe, persistent or pervasive, it's time to find an ally quickly. If the harassment is happening at school or is affecting the learning process at school, try to find a trusted adult on the school staff to whom to report. If you don't feel like you know anyone who can be depended upon, go to the counselor. If there is support at home, parents or guardians can help you make contact within the school system too.

- **Parents and family members are important support systems.** Family members who are assertive make good allies. They can guide, mentor and be role models for you. Knowing they care and support you will make you stronger.

- **There is strength in peer groups.** All too often, the people (teens or adults) who are overwhelmed by harassment lack social connections. Teens need to locate other victims, make friends and get involved in school and outside activities. Being alone makes you a visible target. Parents of teens dealing with harassment also need support from other parents. Make friends and get involved in school functions and organizations with other parents.

- **Make a plan with people who care about you.** Whether it's with a parent, other trusted adults or friends, creating a safety plan will make you feel safe and secure, because you know you have places, people, actions you can take and resources available to back you up and help you in emergency situations.

- **Counseling professionals specialize in family and individual counseling.** As we have stated, harassment cannot be stopped or prevented until the individuals involved become assertive. If this seems like an impossible task for you as a teen or as a parent, then it may be time to seek a professional's assistance.

Being independent and assertive does not mean you are alone. Being alone is a passive trait. In the majority of cases gaining media attention, teens did not seek help. We want all teens and parents to know that assertiveness means asking for help and support with a dangerous issue like harassment.

Finding the right kind of support is essential. We've seen teens and parents align themselves with people who work against them and make harassment issues worse. Most often these are so-called friends. Ask yourself if your friend is supportive. Is he or she content to watch you struggle with harassment? Does the friend participate in harassing behaviors against you or others? If you are a parent, is the advice you get from your friends contradictory to what you now know to be helpful to your teen? If the answer is yes to any of these questions, it is time to find someone who is truly helpful. You and your family's safety and security should be supported by real friends.

Parents, school staff and law enforcement are available. Members of your church or clubs may also be good resources. Now is the time to find a trusted adult and tell that person what is happening. It is absolutely a strong move to get help when you need it. This is not only true for teens, but for adults too. Going forward from here means banding together to fight the problem of harassment. It is far too big for any one of us to handle on our own. Stopping or even slowing the spread of harassment takes law enforcement, school personnel, caring professionals, parents and students working together.

Ready, Set, Go!

We applaud you for reading and discussing *Hey, Back Off! Tips for Stopping Teen Harassment*. It is, we believe, a valuable first step, because education is necessary for teens and their parents, but it is just the beginning of your fight against abuse.

Be aware that harassment is a complex problem for which there is no easy fix. All too often we have seen attempts made to solve the problem of harassment among teens through a handout, a poster in the hallway, an assembly or a cliché that is supposed to make the bully go away. These attempts fail. Without education and assertive action the number or severity of harassment issues will not change for the better. Informed individuals who will do what it takes to become assertive, educate themselves, find support and stand up for themselves and others can become part of a movement to stop the harassment epidemic. It is now time to act assertively and stop harassment. You have the power to make a difference in your own life and in the lives of others.

The End and the Beginning for Teen Readers

We hope that this book is your first step toward becoming an assertive person who is free of harassment. Our goal in writing *Hey, Back Off!* was to present a comprehensive guide to harassment prevention for teens and their parents. We know just how difficult it can be to stop teen harassers, because they have graduated from playground bullies to full-fledged, underhanded and hurtful harassers who are intent on making their victims' lives miserable. We believe, and hopefully now you do too, that harassment can be stopped through learning about what harassment is, how behavior originates from personality types and how you can deal assertively with harassers and their actions.

Knowing the meaning of harassment and all its subcategories should help you know when you are the victim of harassment or are participating in harassing behaviors. You now know how to speak with your friends, your parents or other adults if you should need to tell them what is happening to you. Realizing that what you're undergoing or perpetrating is harassment and being able to talk about it is the first step in harassment prevention.

There are laws and policies in place to prevent harassment, because everyone, no matter his or her age, has the right not to be injured or abused. Part of acting effectively against harassment is having the courage to use the laws, policies and people like the police, school staff and your parents that are meant to keep you safe. When harassment is severe, persistent or pervasive, standing up for your rights and keeping a sense of safety and security means reporting the problem to a trusted adult. You have to act in your own best interest, before harassment causes you psychological or physical damage.

Remember that the key to harassment prevention is an assertive personality. Assertive people don't harass others and they are not victims. Assertive people know how to get what they want without hurting others.

They are not afraid to stand up for themselves and they are not afraid to get help from trusted adults when they need it. Because of these abilities, they are respected, confident and successful.

We realize that becoming assertive is a difficult process that may take some time and SMART goals. Therefore, *Hey, Back Off!* has given you tips and strategies on how to deal with your harasser now. It takes courage to ask for help if you are being harassed. Please remember that you are not in this alone. There are a number of trustworthy adults at your school, at your place of worship or in your family who want to help you.

Reading *Hey, Back Off!* is definitely a great sign that you are ready to act to prevent harassment. Thus the end of *Hey, Back Off!* is the beginning of taking charge of your life and becoming an assertive, confident and successful you. Go for it!

The End and the Beginning for Parent Readers

Reading this book with your teen is an important first step in letting your teen know you empathize with him or her, are there to support him or her and are willing to work together to maintain a balance between helping and empowering him or her. The key is to keep working, keep acting your part until harassment is a non-issue in your lives. Your teen-age son or daughter may not thank you today, but at some point in the future your teen will realize what you did for him or her.

Our goal was to present comprehensive information on harassment prevention to teens first and then to their most influential supporters: their parents. Harassment is an extremely difficult problem for families to deal with and, unfortunately, it has become a prevalent issue that, if it is not addressed, can be dangerous. When a parent-teen team deals with harassment assertively, the success rate will increase substantially. We believe, and hopefully now you share our belief, that parents are the best allies a teen can have.

Remember that teens require proof that their parents are really there for them. The first step, as we discussed in parent section 1, is to validate your teen's experience with harassment. This means that you have shared background knowledge in the form of vocabulary, but more important than words is your willingness to express empathy and be open and honest in talking with your teen. An ally listens to you and is trustworthy.

Be aware that solving harassment issues is not solely up to you and your teen. Parents have allies as well. Your teen's school, law enforcement authorities and even other parents are there for you. All you have to do is ask. They will help you, but keep in mind that assertive parents remain involved as guides for their teens. They don't turn the protection of their teens' rights over to a third party, nor do they leave their teens out of the process.

We have made the case for assertive behavior in your personal life as well as your day-to-day parenting. The information we presented for parents shows that a teen's problems with harassment may be influenced by the personality traits demonstrated by his or her parents. If parents are to help their teens stop and prevent harassment, they must parent assertively. Children learn from their parents. Harassment is a dangerous issue and if teens are to deal with it assertively, they need parents who can be role models for them and guide their actions until they are physically and psychologically mature enough to do it on their own.

We have given you practical ideas for handling harassment, but these suggested actions must be taken assertively if they are to be effective. Take pride in your role of guiding your teenage son or daughter toward a harassment-free life.

Now it is up to you to put into practice the advice, tips and strategies provided in *Hey, Back Off!* Act on your desire to be part of the harassment solution through being your teen's assertive advocate and mentor. You are an important part of fostering a teen who is not a victim or a harasser but a confident and successful young man or woman.

Notes

Chapter One
Teen Section 1
[1] Casey, "Principal Says School Officials Tried to Thwart High School Hazing."
[2] National Crime Prevention Council, "Stop Cyberbullying Before it Starts."

Parent Section 1
[1] ACT for Youth: Upstate Center of Excellence, "Research Facts and Findings: Adolescent Brain Development."
[2] Ibid.
[3] *Merriam-Webster's Collegiate Dictionary*, 10th ed., s.v. "empathy."

Chapter Two
Teen Section 2
[1] Roland, "Summary of Constitutional Rights, Powers and Duties"; Wikipedia contributors, "Civil Rights Act of 1964," *Wikipedia, the Free Encyclopedia*, http://en.wikipedia.org/wiki/Civil_Rights_Act_of_1964; Wikipedia contributors, "Title IX," *Wikipedia, the Free Encyclopedia*, http://en.wikipedia.org/wiki/Title_IX; Wikipedia contributors, "Americans with Disabilities Act of 1990," *Wikipedia, the Free Encyclopedia*, http://en.wikipedia.org/wiki/Americans_with_ Disabilities_Act_of_1990; Wikipedia contributors, "State law," *Wikipedia, the Free Encyclopedia*, http://en.wikipedia.org/wiki/State_law.
[2] Spaulding High School Union District #41 Board of School Commissioners, "Policy on Prevention of Harassment of Students."
[3] Elk Grove Unified School District, "Sexual Harassment Policy."
[4] Hendrickson, interview.
[5] Boise School District Board of Trustees, *Policies and Administrative Procedures*.
[6] Clark County School District, "Clark County School District Regulations: Discipline: Harassment."

Parent Section 2
[1] Hinduja and Patchin, "State Cyberbullying Laws."

Chapter Four
Teen Section 4
[1] Loo, "Create SMART Goals."

Chapter Five
Teen Section 5
[1] *Merriam-Webster's Collegiate Dictionary*, 10th ed., s.v. "respect."
[2] Loo, "Create SMART Goals."
[3] Urban, *Life's Greatest Lessons.*

Chapter Seven
Teen Section 7
[1] Safe Youth Organization, "Teen Dating Violence."
[2] Ibid.
[3] Mental Health America, "Bullying and Gay Youth."

Sources

ACT for Youth: Upstate Center of Excellence. "Research Facts and Findings: Adolescent Brain Development." ACT for Youth. May 2002. http://www.actforyouth.net/resources/rf/rf_brain_0502.pdf (accessed 11 Nov. 2010).

Aftab, Parry. "StopCyberbullying Coalition Roundtable." Parry Aftab. 10 Oct. 2009. http://parryaftab.blogspot.com/2009/10/media-alert-media-alert-media-alert_10.html (accessed 14 Dec. 2009).

American Bar Association. "Teen Dating Violence Prevention Recommendations." American Bar Association. 2006. http://www. americanbar.org/content/dam/aba/migrated/unmet/teenabuseguide. authcheckdam.pdf (accessed 7 Aug. 2009).

Americans with Disabilities Act of 1990. Public Law 101-336. *U.S. Statutes at Large* 104 (1990), codified at U.S. Code 42 §§ 12101-12213 (1990).

Arnett, June and Marjorie Walsleben. "Bullying." *Juvenile Justice Bulletin* (April 1998). http://www.ojjdp.gov/jjbulletin/9804/contents.html (6 Aug. 2009).

Boise School District. *West Junior High School Student Handbook*. 2009.

Boise School District Board of Trustees. *Policies and Administrative Procedures*. Boise: Independent School District of Boise City, 2009.

Bureau of Justice Statistics. "Stalking Victimization in the United States." *Bureau of Justice Statistics Special Report* (Jan. 2009). http://www. ovw.usdoj.gov/docs/stalking-victimization.pdf (accessed 7 Aug. 2009).

Casey, Whitney. "Principal says school officials tried to thwart high school hazing." CNN. May 2008. http://articles.cnn.com/2003-05-08/ us/hs.hazing_1_glenbrook-north-high-school-hazing-junior-girls?_ s=PM:US (accessed, 13 Aug. 2009).

Clark County School District. "Clark County School District Regulations: Discipline: Harassment." Clark County School District. 28 June 2001. http://www.ccsd.net/pol-reg/pdf/5141.2_R.pdf (accessed 25 June 2009).

Cline, Foster and Jim Fay. *Parenting With Love and Logic: Teaching Children Responsibility*. Colorado Springs: Pinion Press, 1990.

Committee for Children. "Steps to Respect." Committee for Children, 2009. http://www.cfchildren.org/programs/str/overview/ (accessed 17 Sept. 2009).

Crawford, Nicole. "New ways to stop bullying." *Monitor on Psychology* 33, no. 9 (Oct. 2002), http://www.apa.org/monitor/oct02/bullying.aspx (accessed 6 Aug. 2009).

DeNoon, Daniel. "Bullying of Gay/Lesbian Teens: Expert Q & A." Web MD Health & Parenting. 1 Oct. 2010. http://www.webmd.com/ parenting/guide/20061201/bullying-harassment-of-gay-lesbian-teens-expert-qa (accessed 10 Mar. 2011).

Elk Grove Unified School District. "Sexual Harassment Policy." Elk Grove Unified School District. 10 July 2002. http://www.egusd.net/ employment/pdfs/bp5145_7.pdf (accessed 13 June 2009).

Ellinghouse, Tim. Interview by author. 9 June 2009.

Equal Rights Advocates. "Sexual Harassment at School: Know Your Rights." Equal Rights Advocates, Inc. 2009. http://www.equalrights. org/publications/kyr/shschool.asp (accessed 23 June 2009).

Fost, Gary. Interview by author. 27 June 2009.

Harrell, Elizabeth. "11 Mistakes Parents Make With Teen Discipline." Lifescript. 19 May 2008. http://www.lifescript.com/Life/Family/ Parenting/11_Mistakes_Parents_Make_With_Teen_Discipline.aspx (accessed 9 Nov. 2010).

Hendrickson, Joseph. Interview by author. 8 June 2009.

Hinduja, Sameer and Justin W. Patchin. "State Cyberbullying Laws: A Brief Review of State Cyberbullying Laws and Policies." Cyberbullying Research Center. Mar. 2011. http://www.cyberbullying.us/Bullying_ and_Cyberbullying_Laws.pdf (accessed 26 Dec. 2010).

Human Resources. "Types of Harassment and Bullying." Loughborough University. Mar. 2009. http://www.lboro.ac.uk/admin/personnel/ typesoharassmentandbullying.html (accessed 4 Jan. 2010).

Limber, Susan and Maury Nation. "Bullying Among Children and Youth." *Juvenile Justice Bulletin* (Apr. 1998). http://www.ojjdp.gov/ jjbulletin/9804/bullying2.html (accessed 6 Aug. 2009).

Lipkins, Susan. "Inside Hazing: Understanding Hazardous Hazing." http://www.insidehazing.com/ (accessed 23 May 2009).

Loo, Tristan. "Create SMART Goals." SelfGrowth.com. 7 Sept. 2006. http://www.selfgrowth.com/articles/TristanLoo5.html (accessed 4 Jan. 2010).

Lumsden, Linda. "Preventing Bullying." *ERIC Digest* (Mar. 2002). http://www.ericdigests.org/2003-1/bullying.htm (accessed 6 Aug. 2009).

Mayo Clinic Staff. "Anger management tips: 10 ways to tame your temper." Mayo Foundation For Medical Education and Research. 25 June 2009. http://www.mayoclinic.com/health/anger-management/MH00102 (accessed 6 Oct. 2009).

Mayo Clinic Staff. "Tips for coping with stress at work." Mayo Foundation for Medical Education and Research. 26 June 2008. http://www.mayoclinic.com/health/coping-with-stress/SR00030 (accessed 14 Dec. 2009).

Mental Health America. "Bullying and Gay Youth." Mental Health America. http://www.nmha.org/go/information/get-info/children-s-mental-health/bullying-and-gay-youth (accessed 10 Mar. 2011).

Mountain States Center for Independent Living. "Assertiveness." Mountain States Center for Independent Living. http://www.mtstcil.org/skills/assert-intro.html (accessed 29 May 2009).

National Archives and Records Administration. "Teaching With Documents: The Civil Rights Act of 1964 and the Equal Employment Opportunity Commission." The U.S. National Archives & Records Administration. http://www.archives.gov/education/lessons/civil-rights-act/ (accessed 4 Jan. 2010).

National Crime Prevention Council. "Stop Cyberbullying Before it Starts." National Crime Prevention Council. 2009. http://www.ncpc.org/resources/files/pdf/bullying/cyberbullying.pdf (accessed 23 June 2009).

North Kansas City School District. "Prohibition Against Illegal Discrimination and Harassment." North Kansas City Schools: Policy Online. 24 Aug. 2010. http://policy.msbanet.org/nkansascity/showpolicy.php?file=AC-C.NKC%20 (accessed 13 June 2009).

Olsen, Stefanie. "A rallying cry against cyberbullying." CNET News. 7 June 2008. http://news.cnet.com/8301-10784_3-9962375-7.html (accessed 17 Sept. 2009).

Petty, Harold. Interview by author. 27 June 2009.

Roland, Jon. "Summary of Constitutional Rights, Powers and Duties." Constitution Organization. 12 July 2009. http://www.constitution.org/powright.htm (accessed 6 Aug. 2009).

Safe Youth Organization. "Preventing Gang Violence in School." National Youth Violence Prevention Resource Center. 3 Jan. 2008. Safeyouth.org (accessed 7 Aug. 2009; site discontinued and now owned by STRYVE).

Safe Youth Organization. "School Bullying Prevention." National Youth Violence Prevention Resource Center. 3 Jan. 2008. Safeyouth.org (accessed 7 Aug. 2009; site discontinued and now owned by STRYVE).

Safe Youth Organization. "Teen Dating Violence." National Youth Violence Prevention. Dec. 2007. Safeyouth.org (accessed 7 Aug. 2009; site discontinued and now owned by STRYVE).

Santrock, John W. *Adolescence*. New York: McGraw Hill, 2007.

Spaulding High School Union District #41 Board of School Commissioners. "Policy on Prevention of Harassment of Students." Spaulding High School & Barre Technical Center Campus. 4 Aug. 2008. http://www.shsbtc.org/publ/handbook.pdf (accessed 25 June 2009).

Szoka, Berin and Adam Thierer. "Cyberbullying Legislation: Why Education is Preferable to Regulation." *Progress on Point* 16, no 12 (June 2009). http://www.pff.org/issues-pubs/pops/2009/pop16.12-cyberbullying-education-better-than-regulation.pdf (accessed 17 Sept. 2009).

Title IX of the Education Amendments of 1972. Public Law 92-318. *U.S. Statutes at Large* 86 (1972), codified at U.S. Code 20 §§ 1681-1688.

Urban, Hal. *Life's Greatest Lessons: 20 Things That Matter*. New York: Fireside, 2003.

Index